An American Trilogy

Also by Steven M. Wise

RATTLING THE CAGE
Towards Legal Rights for Animals

DRAWING THE LINE
Science and the Case for Animal Rights

THOUGH THE HEAVENS MAY FALL
The Landmark Trial that Led to the End of Human Slavery

AN AMERICAN TRILOGY

Death, Slavery, and Dominion on the
Banks of the Cape Fear River

STEVEN M. WISE

A MERLOYD LAWRENCE BOOK

Da Capo Press

A Member of the Perseus Books Group

Copyright © 2009 by Steven M. Wise

Set in 11.5 point Adobe Caslon by the Perseus Books Group
Cataloging-in-Publication data for this book is available from the Library of Congress.

First Da Capo Press edition 2009
ISBN 978-0-30681-475-4

A Merloyd Lawrence Book
Published by Da Capo Press
A Member of the Perseus Books Group
www.dacapopress.com

Da Capo Press books are available at special discounts for bulk purchases in the U.S. by corporations, institutions, and other organizations. For more information, please contact the Special Markets Department at the Perseus Books Group, 2300 Chestnut Street, Suite 200, Philadelphia, PA 19103, or call (800) 810-4145, ext. 5000, or e-mail special.markets@perseusbooks.com.

Library of Congress Cataloging-in-Publication Data

Wise, Steven M.
  An American trilogy : death, slavery, and dominion on the banks of the Cape Fear River / Steven M. Wise. — 1st Da Capo Press ed.
     p. cm. — (A Merloyd Lawrence book)
  Includes bibliographical references.
  ISBN 978-0-306-81475-4 (alk. paper)
  1. Swine—North Carolina—Cape Fear River Region. 2. Slaughtering and slaughter-houses—North Carolina—Cape Fear River Region. 3. Slaughtering and slaughter-houses—Moral and ethical aspects—North Carolina—Cape Fear River Region. 4. Animal welfare--North Carolina—Cape Fear River Region. 5. Animal rights—North Carolina—Cape Fear River Region. 6. Indians, Treatment of—North Carolina—Cape Fear River Region—History. 7. Slavery—North Carolina—Cape Fear River Region—History. 8. Cape Fear River Region (N.C.)—Social conditions. 9. Cape Fear River Region (N.C.)—History. I. Title.
  SF395.8.N8W57 2009
  364.1'870975632—dc22
                                        2008054437

10 9 8 7 6 5 4 3 2 1

TO MR. NIKITA,

a modern Thomas Clarkson

CONTENTS

Prologue

In the fall of 2008, I learned that an undercover agent working for People for the Ethical Treatment of Animals (PETA) had been investigating reports of cruelty at a large hog-breeding farm. I asked PETA lawyer Dan Paden to send me some video showing what their agent had seen. I had watched video taken at another hog farm by another PETA undercover operative, whom I called "Mr. Nikita." I had spent months interviewing Mr. Nikita, visiting a North Carolina industrial hog farm, attempting to gain access to the world's largest slaughterhouse, located in Tar Heel, North Carolina, interviewing some of its former workers, as well as a "Pork Visionary," and examining whatever was on display at the 2007 World Pork Expo. This included heavy-steel gestation and farrowing crates so small that a sow could not turn around or lie comfortably within them, the dead sleds and carcass carts that made it convenient to remove the dead sows from their cages, and the incinerators and crematoria required to dispose of their bodies.

I thought that nothing we humans do to pigs could upend me. Then Paden sent me a four-minute highlights clip of what the latest farm investigator had seen. It took me an hour and a half before I was able to finish it. I challenge you to watch with equanimity a man repeatedly smash the heads of tiny piglets onto a cement floor.

In this book, I do not recite the atrocities we perpetuate upon pigs. Instead, I discuss why we think it's okay to inflict them. And that discussion will bring us to the study of history. After I visited the Tar Heel slaughterhouse and Bladen County's industrial pig farms, I discovered that this slaughterhouse, and possibly a factory pig farm or two, rested on what were once the fields of a plantation. On it black slaves had probably raised cotton, for there was enough cotton being raised around it when I was there. I could almost see the old Walnut Grove manor house from the parking lot of the gigantic slaughterhouse complex. Later I understood that both slaughterhouse and plantation occupied ground upon which had strode, and likely lived, Native Americans. These Indians had for centuries admired animals, believed that they were inherently deserving of respect, and given them the respect to which they were entitled. How had we moved, I wondered, from them to us?

North Carolina's settlers were mostly Protestant, mostly Englishmen. They brought their Bibles with them and located varied alleged Divine justifications for exterminating Indians, enslaving Africans, and inflicting hideous cruelties upon mother pigs and their babies, all within a book within that Book, the Book of Genesis. The stories of how the Indian genocide, black chattel slavery, and the war upon pigs were perpetrated, how the first two were overturned by the religious themselves, and how the justification for the last is being vigorously challenged today, again by the religious, is *An American Trilogy*.

CHAPTER ONE

Tar Heel Foundations

[A] lot of common sense has proved, in other times and
places, to be both blind and cruel. In North America,
common sense once included the idea that slavery was a
natural state of affairs, that women should not vote, and
that only heterosexuals were worthy of respect. Good
riddance to all that. Long-standing miseries can't be cured
until the overthrow of the certainties that support them.

—*David Berreby,* Us and Them *(2005)*[1]

The role of the historian is to understand the intellectual
universe which justified slavery, segregation and
imperialism, however much he may deplore these
phenomena; similarly, the historian hopes that his or her
own generation will not be demonised by future
generations for eating meat, say, or despoiling the
environment—or some other offence of which the present
is barely conscious. Indeed, if history shows anything, it is
the failure of past generations to predict which aspects of
their moral life future generations will find intolerable.

—*Colin Kidd*[2]

IN 1990, SMITHFIELD FOODS of Virginia announced its intention to construct a slaughterhouse on 160 acres of rural Bladen County, at Tar Heel, in North Carolina. It was to be the largest abattoir in the world, certainly the largest construction project ever undertaken in Bladen County. Two years later, the gigantic 973,000-square-foot slaughterhouse complex opened for business. In the summer of 2007, I made my first trip to visit it, as well as some of Bladen County's industrial pig farms.

As I approached the intersection of River Road from the south along NC Route 87, I could see Tar Heel's downtown shimmering. Through thick and hazy three-digit-degree August heat, I made out a Subway restaurant, Allen's Tire, Clark's Chapel AME, Zion Church, Minuteman Food Market, Tienda Hispania, the Faith Deliverance Ministries, Tar Heel Middle School, Tar Heel Realty, a U.S. post office, and Tar Heel Treasures and Gifts, which was shuttered. West down River Road stood the Tar Heel Rural Volunteer Fire Department, north was the Smithfield Family Medical Center and Pharmacy, and the Smithfield Employment Center stood on Route 87's northeast side. That was it for Tar Heel. I have returned twice more, and never seen anyone walking.

With a population of 65 and an area of 147 acres, the entire town of Tar Heel is slightly smaller than the slaughterhouse complex; its population is dwarfed by the number of slaughterhouse employees.[3] The high wide boxes of the slaughterhouse stretch half a mile and sit directly across the street from the Smithfield medical and employment centers. Every day 38,000 pigs are trucked into these giant, whitewashed, windowless caskets, where they are killed, then cut to pieces—9 million a year. Bladen County is thinly settled; its entire human population is just 33,000. The quiet parking lots of the slaughterhouse complex are filled with battered, aging, American automobiles. When shifts change, their owners, a couple thousand mostly brown and black faces, pour from the boxes—the knockers, stickers, shacklers, tub dumpers, knuckle droppers, caul pullers, fell cutters, rumpers, splitters, vat dippers, skinners, gutters, and others who spend their days disassembling freshly killed pigs. Cars line the single exit from the slaughterhouse complex to Route 87, ferrying hundreds out, passing identical cars carrying hundreds more in.

Bladen County is also home to one of the heaviest concentrations of industrial pig farms in the world. They feed the slaughterhouse. In 2006, 815,000 pigs were raised on the county's factory farms, 24 pigs for each human resident.[4] Some of the pig farms are so near the slaughterhouse complex that their owners complained to me of the stink. Any stench that would make pig farmers complain will knock you and me over. I wanted to see how these thousands of pigs lived and how the millions died. I wanted to know why pigs were living and dying in such quantities in Bladen County in particular. As a lawyer, I know that the present uncoupled from its past can appear arbitrary and incomprehensible. I needed to probe Bladen County's past to understand its present. And, perhaps, to help determine its future.

Early colonial Bladen County occupied half of present-day North Carolina's 53,000 square miles. For a century and a half, its territory was chipped away so mercilessly that it shrunk to fewer than 900 square miles, yet it remains North Carolina's third-largest county. Today its pieces form portions of 55 present counties, which is why roadside signs proclaim it North Carolina's "Mother County."[5]

The British were the first to try to live in the Carolinas. In 1584, Queen Elizabeth I authorized Sir Walter Raleigh to colonize "such remote heathen and barbarous lands, countries and territories not actually possessed by any christian Prince, not inhabited by christian people." Raleigh dispatched two small shiploads of colonists who were instructed to build a self-sustaining, revenue-producing colony. They touched down on the Outer Banks. Within two years, they had so antagonized the natives that Sir Francis Drake had to haul the survivors away. More British settled nearby on Roanoke Island in 1588. Within two years, they vanished, leaving the letters "CRO" cut on a tree, "Croatoan" carved into a doorpost, and the enduring mystery of what happened. Five voyages were made under Raleigh's authority, each with the end of creating a permanent settlement in what would later be called North Carolina; all came to grief.

The first permanent European Carolinians began walking south from Tidewater Virginia, which had been established upon the founding of Jamestown. That was in 1607. Over the next half-century, colonists continued drifting toward the Albemarle Sound, a large estuary in northern North Carolina, and settling on the banks of the Chowan and Roanoke Rivers in a district they called Albemarle; North Carolina's first named settler, Nathanial Batts, arrived in 1655.[6] The first deed for North Carolina land was recorded in 1662 for a parcel transferred north of Albemarle Sound from Kilcacenen, the Indian "King of the Town of Yeopim," to one George Durant, a future judge of North Carolina's general court.[7]

In 1663, Charles II granted to eight Lords Proprietors title to the enormous tract of land in North America he named "Carolina," after his late father, Charles I, "Carolus" in Latin. Charles the younger intended for Carolina to encompass all land south from Virginia to the Florida-Georgia border; its western boundary was to be the "South Seas," which Balboa had named the Pacific Ocean in 1513.[8] Two years later, Charles II extended Carolina's boundaries both north and south by granting the Proprietors a chunk of southern Virginia along the Albemarle Sound and all northern Florida to present-day Daytona Beach.[9] The Proprietors were permitted to subdivide the massive area as they saw fit, and they did. Carolina they divided into the Albemarle and Bath Precincts, which eventually became counties. In 1712, they cleaved Carolina into north and south; when seven Proprietors sold their interests in North Carolina to the Crown in 1729, it became a royal colony. In 1734, Bladen Precinct, later Bladen County, was created in North Carolina. I saw the portrait of the county's namesake, Martin Bladen, the powerful Lord Commissioner of Trade and Plantations in London, hanging in the county courthouse in Elizabethtown.

I don't know to what depth, exactly, the foundation for the Tar Heel slaughterhouse complex was dug. From conversations with local Bladen County builders, I gather it was probably about twenty-two inches. I was told that some attempt was made to produce an archaeological survey of the land cleared for its foundations. But this wasn't an archaeological dig, consequently not much was reported.[10] The builders would not have had to scrape deeply to strike artifacts of the black chattel slavery that thrived in Tar Heel until the end of the Civil War, or the Indian artifacts that might have lain beneath them, for the soil of Bladen County is more likely to erode than to accrete. Plows often turn up Indian artifacts, a broken glass bottle, a fragment of a spoon, a rusted knife blade, a pottery sherd, a decorated smoking pipe, an ax head, part of a cooking pot, or the remnant of a leather shoe.[11]

The largest artifact of Tar Heel's slave history can easily be seen from Route 87. Just past the sign marking the town's southeastern boundary and the Beth Car Presbyterian Church stands a historical road marker dedicated to Thomas Robeson. That would be Colonel Thomas Robeson Jr., born in Bladen County on January 11, 1740, the eldest of three. His father, Thomas Robeson Sr., was the seventh child of eleven produced by the 1685 marriage of Andrew Robeson Jr., from Scotland via New Jersey around 1676, to Mary Spencer.[12] One of the area's earliest settlers, Thomas Sr. moved to the northwest branch of the Cape Fear River around 1720. In 1735, King George II granted him a large tract of land.

Robeson Jr. was an officer in the American Revolution, the marker says, a state senator, and a member of several provincial congresses. His fame rests on two events, one that occurred while he was alive, the other after his death. At the Battle of Tory Hole, he commanded the Whig forces, who fought in and around a deep ravine that slopes from Main Street in the center of Elizabethtown to the Cape Fear River. The battlefield is a fraction of the size of the slaughterhouse complex; today it lies entirely within Tory Hole Park, across the street from the Bladen County Courthouse. There the Whigs surprised nine hundred Tories one late September dawn and sent them fleeing or tumbling into the ravine that would be named for them, where they were cut down or captured. Four years later, Colonel Robeson was dead, and two years after that Robeson County was sliced from Bladen County.

One hundred feet west of Robeson's Tar Heel road marker stands a stately, two-story, Greek Revival mansion. I read in several places that you could see George II's original deed to Thomas Robeson Sr. hanging in its hallway. The mansion, built around 1855 by Colonel Robeson's great-grandson, James Robeson Sr., is said to be the third manor house to stand on or about the spot where Colonel Robeson built his original home, and to resemble it. The whole plantation has been called Walnut Grove for the last 250 years. I was told by the head of the Bladen County Historical Society that sixth-generation Robesons were still living there and that the house had been listed on the National Register of Historical Places since 1975.[13]

Walnut Grove was once filled with black slaves. African slaves were first brought to North Carolina in 1526, along with five hundred Spanish hopefuls under the command of Lucas Vasquez de Aiello, all attempting to settle Cape Fear. They failed.[14] Sixty years later, Sir Francis Drake deposited a parcel of slaves he had captured from a Spanish vessel on Roanoke Island; of them we know nothing more.[15] African slavery arrived in British North America when a Dutch man-of-war sold twenty blacks to Jamestown's John Rolfed in August 1619.

Of 54,000 European slaving voyages, 13,500 were British or British North American. These ships delivered 11 million African slaves to the Americas—half a million to British North America and the fledgling United States.[16] Slaves trickled into northeastern North Carolina as their masters filtered south from Virginia. From Albemarle, one early settler wrote, "we may have a quantity of Hogs flesh who will soonest come to bare to send to Barbados wch will p[ro]duce us Negroes and Sarvts: to raise a plantation."[17] Because Carolina's eight Lords Proprietors well understood the commercial possibilities of a slave colony, their 1669 "Fundamental Constitution" provided that "[e]very Freeman of Carolina shall have absolute Authority over his Negro Slaves, of what opinion or Religion soever."[18] Carolina's first governor, Sir John Yeamans, brought black slaves with him from Barbados in 1669.[19] By 1699, Carolina was trading in slaves directly with Africa.[20] In 1700, 400 slaves were living in Carolina—one-twenty-fifth of the population.[21]

Between 1740 and 1750, almost 60,000 of the 200,000 slaves ferried to America in British ships disembarked in Virginia and the Carolinas.[22] North Carolina's slave population mushroomed to 6,000 in 1730, to 20,000 in 1755, then to 40,000 in 1767. Slaves constituted one-quarter of the entire population at the outbreak of the American Revolution; their numbers grew to nearly 30 percent, about 140,000, by 1800. Most were concentrated in the Lower Cape Fear area, primarily on larger plantations like Walnut Grove.[23] During the Revolution, 98 percent of Lower Cape Fear slaves were owned by masters of ten or more slaves, and 73 percent by masters with twenty or more.[24] By 1790, almost one-third of all North Carolina's families owned slaves.[25] On the eve of the Civil War, slaves constituted a full third of the state's population.[26] In 1757, Bladen County's population reached 2,040, of which 654, or 31 percent, were blacks.[27] The 1763 county tax list shows that 25 families or other entities owned as many as 49 black slaves apiece.[28] By 1767, the county's population had increased to 4,596, with its black population surging to 1,353, or 34 percent.[29] I would discover that some of them worked the land that was once part of Walnut Grove that now lies beneath the slaughterhouse complex.

Beneath any artifacts of Tar Heel's black slaves would lie remnants of Native Americans from what anthropologists call the Southeastern Culture Area—the land that stretches southward from the Carolinas to the Gulf of Mexico and west to Louisiana and Texas. Indians have been living there for twelve thousand years; Bladen County is rich in Archaic sites that date from 8000 BC to the birth of Christ. Lying closest to any slave artifacts might be coiling clay bowls, triangular projectile points, stone, shell, and bone knives and axes, stone and clay tobacco pipes, shell or stone beads, drills, scrapers, hoes, spades, mortars, pestles, grinding stones, tortoise shells, gourds, and stone masks dating from the later Woodland Period. This stretched from the birth of Christ to the moment when North America's natives burst into the light of history at their first "Contact" with Europeans who could write.[30] These later artifacts would be Siouan, perhaps Waccamaw, whose villages lay near the Cape Fear River.[31]

The Waccamaws dispersed as far south as South Carolina's Winyah Bay and as far north as the Neuse River, which flows fifty miles to the northeast of Bladen County.[32] Some Waccamaw Siouans call themselves "the People of the Fallen Star." Lake Waccamaw, near the border of Bladen and Columbus Counties, was created, they say, when a gigantic, blindingly bright meteor tore out a crater that filled with water.[33] Waccamaws and the other Southeastern Culture Area tribes cultivated crops, constructed mounds in village centers, used tobacco and gourd ladles, built rectangular, thatched, gabled houses and houselike storage structures, and created complex art.[34] Though they spoke three distinct languages, Siouan, Algonquian, and Iroquoian, their cultural similarities were so strong that after the Europeans brought, or encouraged, war, Indian slave raids, and disease, the pitiful remnants of many Southeastern tribes were still able to fuse, more or less readily, into workable communities.[35]

North Carolina's Indians lived in village clumps separated by swaths of uninhabited landscape. More than a dozen major trading trails crisscross the original Bladen County, with the Wilmington, High Point, and Northern Trails cutting through present-day Bladen County, following the Cape Fear River to pass near or through Tar Heel.[36] The largest tribe was the Cherokee. In 1600, six to eight thousand Cherokees nestled within the western Blue Ridge Mountains, part of a Cherokee population of thirty thousand that controlled much of what would become half a dozen American states. Nomadic, Algonquian-speaking tribes—the Bear River, Chowan, Hatteras, Moratok, Nachapunga, Pamlico, Secotan, and Weapomeos—clung to the Atlantic shore. The larger Siouan-speaking tribes—the five thousand members of the Coree, Meherrin, Neuse River, and Tuscarora—shared the central Piedmont Plateau east of the mountains and west of the sea with the seven to eight thousand Siouan-speaking Waccamaws, Catawbas, Enos, Waxhaws, Sugarees, Conarees, and a dozen others, who numbered five thousand. Other Siouan speakers contributed an additional seven or eight thousand, so that perhaps twenty-four thousand Indians in all spoke Siouan at its height.[37]

We have no idea how many Waccamaws lived before Contact. Pre-Contact American Indian estimates are always notoriously dicey. Population estimates for both Americas range from 8 million to 120 million; conservative North America population estimates fall as low as 4 million to 7 million.[38] North Carolina's estimates are equally iffy, ranging from fifty thousand to several hundred thousand.[39] We cannot be sure how many Waccamaws were living after Contact, for the early colonists sometimes mixed their tribes up. But it seems that the Waccamaw, Wocoon, and Cape Fear Indians, whom the colonists counted as three tribes, were probably one and the same, or closely related.[40] We also know that Indian artifacts from the late Woodland Period, around the sixteenth century, are devilishly hard to find. This suggests that a rapid depopulation occurred not long after the Spanish began cruising the Lower Cape Fear.[41] It has been claimed that Waccamaws numbered 900 in the year 1600.[42] In 1715, 610 were actually counted. Just 350 remained five years later.[43]

Native Americans and Britons did not just make "Contact." They "Collided." Violently. In many ways they differed. The English embraced constitutional monarchy, individual freedom, and patriarchy. Indians governed by consensus, lived in a subsistence economy, disdained the acquisition of wealth, granted substantial power to women, and subsumed the individual's welfare to that of the community.[44] But there was a similarity. Each believed North America pregnant with some "Unseen" that ruled their world. And there the similarities ended. In the next chapter, we will see that Waccamaw Siouan cosmology was unlikely to have led to the Walnut Grove plantation house, or the Tar Heel slaughterhouse, or the industrial farm. European cosmology, based on the Bible as it was then commonly understood, did lead to the near-extermination of the Indians, to the slave plantation, to the slaughterhouse, and the industrial farm.

Today we acknowledge that our genocide of Native Americans was wrong—that the Bible was misinterpreted. Today we agree that we were wrong to enslave millions of blacks and to mistreat them after they became free—that again, the Bible was misread. Today global climate change and other environmental catastrophes we continue to cause are leading us to a new understanding of how the Bible instructs us to act toward all of God's Creation—including the pigs of Bladen County. Our certainty as to the rightness of the genocide of Indians, and our subsequent about-face, our certainty as to the rightness of our enslavement and mistreatment of blacks, and our subsequent about-face, and our certainty of the rightness of the present system of industrial farming and slaughter of pigs, and how we are beginning to turn from that as well, are what the rest of this book is about.

CHAPTER TWO

Carolina Magic

Once upon a time man and animals talked with
one another on this continent.
—*Calvin Martin,* Keepers of the Game *(1978)*[1]

No nation in all history was ever founded by people
so dominated by the Bible as America.
—*P. Marion Simms,* The Bible in America *(1936)*[2]

INDIAN SPIRITUAL BELIEFS were remarkably homogenous throughout North Carolina, the American Southeast, indeed in North America.[3] The Indians' relationship to the natural world was everywhere embedded in a complex cosmology that colonists found impenetrable, unfathomable, ungraspable, and, above all, ridiculous. Europeans "misconstrued the character of native spirit-beings, comparing them to deities on the order of the Christian God, and puzzled over stories of spirits that appeared as animals. None of the English commentators came close to comprehending the distinctive character of native spirituality on its own terms."[4] Indian beliefs bore little relation to their own, and difference denoted inferiority. A Puritan, for one, "could not reasonably imagine the existence of native societies that were physically distinct from his own without being morally inferior. . . . The native inhabitants . . . were both enemies of God's people and pawns in God's plan to remind His people of their superiority."[5]

One dramatic difference between the two worldviews was that Native Americans exhibited "a genuine respect for other life forms."[6] They killed game animals for food, but their universe "was above all else an articulate universe" in which they did not distinguish between the natural and the supernatural.[7] Everything had *manitou*—roughly meaning "spirit" or "soul."[8] The anthropologist Calvin Martin defines manitou as "the spiritual potency associated with an object (such as a knife) or a phenomenon (such as thunder) . . . it was the force which made everything in Nature alive and responsive to man."[9] Every species had a "boss," a "guardian spirit," a "chief," a "master," an "owner," or a "keeper of the game" whose life and experiences summed up the lives and experiences of every species member.[10] The manitou of animals obliged Indian hunters to show them the greatest respect.[11]

Woven into Indian culture was the belief that "animal forms are as sentient and evolved as human."[12] Indians saw animals as spiritual kin and credited them with sophisticated intellectual, emotional, and spiritual characteristics similar to their own.[13] Many believed animals more skillful, more intelligent, even more powerful than humans. Animals were not separate from Indian society but part of it, so that even "the events of killing and eating them [were] experienced and talked about as so many ongoing instances of social interaction."[14]

Indians and animals shared the world equally. From Southeastern Indians chasing white-tailed deer to Northern Indians pursuing beaver and Plains Indians hunting buffalo, all considered their prey powerful, "inherently deserving" of respect, able to demand what they deserved—in short, North American Indians looked on animals as "persons."[15] Subarctic Indians generally "considered animals to be persons with whom humans could talk and enjoy other forms of social intercourse."[16] Any being, whether human, animal, or spirit, that the Ojibwa believed capable of social relationships could be a "person."[17]

A Respectful Covenant

Calvin Martin explains that "when Indians referred to other animal species as 'people'—just a different sort of person from man—they were not just being quaint. Nature was a community of such 'people'—'people' for whom man had a great deal of genuine regard and with whom he had a contractual relationship to protect one another's interests and to fulfill mutual needs."[18] Thus, the Plains Indians' "relations with other-than-human beings like buffalo, bear, other animals, plants, and so on were regulated by expectations and obligations similar to those that governed relations between kin or allies."[19] Once they had "conversed with, fought, killed, had sexual intercourse with, shared food with, and were kin" to buffalos and other animals; now they believed them to be "animated other-than-human persons."[20]

In Indian tales, animals often "reside in lodges, gather in council, and act according to the norms and regulations of kinship. In these tales, as in those of many peoples, man and the animals are depicted as engaging in all manner of social and sociable interaction: they visit, smoke, gamble, and dance together; they exchange wisdom; they compete in games and combat; and they even marry and beget offspring."[21] North Carolina's Indians saw their own social order reflected in the social organization of animals, who similarly divided themselves into tribes with chiefs, councils, and townhouses and lived an afterlife in the spirit world.[22] Indians never considered owning animals, not even the semidomesticated dog. Instead, they believed that everyone, human and animal, lived intertwining lives marked by balance, reciprocity, and "mutual courtesy: intelligent animal beings and intelligent human beings had contracted long ago not to abuse one another."[23]

The heart of the agreement between humans and animals was economic. Animals willingly gave themselves to humans for fair exchange. In return, they demanded that humans respect them, not insult or ridicule them, and never, ever, torture them.[24] "Never speak you ill of a beaver!" warned a woman in one Ojibwa tale returning to her village after spending years as a beaver's wife.[25]

Before Contact, Indians strained to comply with the contract they had made with the animal world.[26] One way was through a strict adherence to numerous taboos that could be broken only at great risk, for these "connoted a sense of cautious respect for a conscious fellow-member of the same eco-system who, in the view of the Indian, literally allowed himself to be killed for food and clothing."[27]

North Carolina Indians in particular observed certain rituals to avoid offending the animal tribes and to ensure successful hunting. They believed that animals did not really die but that their spirit returned to the "owner" or head of their particular animal clan. The Saponi, for example (like the Waccamaw, a Siouan-speaking tribe), carefully set aside and burned the bones of game animals, believing that if they did not do so, the game would leave the country. Other tribes kept animal bones out of the way of dogs or hung the skulls of certain animals in trees and honored them with prayers and ceremonial smoke offerings.[28]

Sometimes Southeastern Indians blamed sickness on retaliation by insulted animals.[29] Cherokees "believed that animals, like humans, acted on emotions such as desire for vengeance against those who contravened the rules of behavior."[30] That vengeance might take many forms. A hunter who tortured, or was cruel to, an animal might return empty-handed from hunts, then starve after the other animals learned of his disrespect.[31] He might suffer crippling rheumatism, or his family might sicken.[32] The offended animal would not return to life with a whole and healthy body. Any Slavey hunter who clubbed a trapped animal generally suffered bad luck.[33] A Koyukon hunter who violated a wolverine or marten taboo was said to trigger someone's early death—perhaps his own, perhaps a relative's or an unborn child's. Violation of a beaver taboo invited sickness; breaking a mink, beaver, or otter taboo led to scarcity.[34] Maltreatment of bears caused female sterility, triggered weakness in men, and brought rheumatism and starvation to each gender.

The anthropologist Antonia Mills writes that

> in contrast to the Buddhist/Hindu/Jain and Judeo-Christian traditions for peoples who are hunters and gatherers and fisher-folk there was no injunction that "thou shalt not kill." Instead the ethics of tribal peoples are a set of injunctions about properly respecting the spirit of the life forms that are taken. Among North American Native peoples, the taking of human as well as animal life was not proscribed as a damning act that inhibited one's spiritual evolution, but as an act which entailed consequences in both the human/animal and spirit realms for both the person taking the life and the person whose life was taken.[35]

Both human hunter and prey were believed to understand their role in the hunt. The hunter pursued, while the prey was "resigned to its fate" but neither feared nor resented it, because the animal's death was only temporary and he might receive certain goods he desired.[36] Ojibwa hunters were required to offer goods that made animals happy and wealthy; beavers, it was known, were fond of tobacco.[37] Most Indians thought that the dead animals were reincarnated: while the covenant between humans and animals required the animals to die so the human hunter and his family might live, they were believed to be reborn a short time later within another nearly identical animal, so long as the hunter observed the proper rituals and taboos and did not abuse the animal.[38] Mills, who studies American Indian reincarnation beliefs, has "not heard of any North American . . . Indian society that did not hold such a belief."[39]

Tramping Carolina's wild backcountry at the beginning of the eighteenth century, John Lawson recorded that "[a]ll the Indians hereabouts carefully preserve the Bones of the Flesh they eat, and burn them, as being of opinion, that if they omitted that Custom, the game would leave their Country, and they should not be able to maintain themselves by their Hunting."[40] Traditional Ojibwa tales reaffirm that "when the men fulfill their obligations faithfully, their animals will give themselves willingly to the hunter to be killed. . . . The apparent harshness of this requirement is mitigated by the notion that the death of animals killed under the proper circumstances is not final; rather they will come back to life to enjoy the offerings they receive."[41] Twentieth-century Rock Cree Indians informed anthropologist Robert Brightman that a lynx and two foxes they removed from traps were the "same one[s]" killed within the previous two winters.[42]

Cherokee medicine men believed that every animal was assigned a specific number of lives, often four or seven, that could not be ended prematurely.[43] Once an animal was killed, its body "immediately resurrected in its proper shape from the blood drops, and the animal continued its existence until the end of the predestined period, when the body is finally dissolved and the liberated spirit goes to join its kindred spirits."[44]

A Broken Covenant

As the sixteenth century turned, 85,000 deerskins were being exported from Carolina and Virginia annually. Sixty-five years later, that number had jumped to 400,000. Because Southeastern deer populations were not large enough to sustain this rate of slaughter, the century closed on woods nearly emptied of deer.[45] This tragedy recapitulated the Northeast Indians' near-total slaughter of the beaver and foreshadowed the Plains Indians' destruction of the buffalo.[46] "The record seems emphatic . . . the post-contact Indian wasted game with gusto," wrote Calvin Martin.[47] The question is: why?

Some have claimed that the Indians' slaughter of the animals can be harmonized with their traditional cosmologies.[48] Many North Carolina tribes thought that their forests were inhabited by dwarves who protected game animals and retaliated against hunters who killed them without showing the proper respect. When game animals became scarce because of overhunting, the Piedmont Tuscaroras decided that the dwarves had taken the animals deeper into the forest where the Indians could no longer find them.[49] Some have argued that Indians could not possibly waste an animal's body by, say, eating just the tasty tongue if the animal did not mind, and that the animal would not mind so long as his physical body was treated with the required degree of respect. However, the human hunter could waste an animal's soul by killing the animal, then treating his body so scandalously that he could not, or would not, reincarnate.[50]

Many regard this sharp turn away from sustainable and respectful hunting toward uncontrolled slaughter as a sea change in how the Indians related to the natural world.[51] Perhaps some Indians simply rejected the spirit world entirely, engaging in what Martin calls "the despiritualization of the material world," and opted for a Stockholm Syndrome–like embrace of the religion of the newcomers who were devastating them.[52] Martin cited one example of the "pathos of this transformation of attitude and behavior." Near the end of the seventeenth century, the Jesuit Chrestian Le Clerq recorded Micmac Indians saying that they would "cease to make war upon [the beaver] if these would speak, however little, in order that they might learn whether the beavers were among their friends or their enemies."[53] But the beaver had fallen silent, and the Micmac knew it. According to Martin, "Nature—the universe—[seemed] to have become inarticulate and the dialogue between human persons and animal persons [to have] ceased."[54]

There was another possibility. A missionary, John McDougall, wrote of the mid-nineteenth-century Cree Indians that, when they hunted buffalo, "not one buffalo is allowed to escape. The young and the poor must die with the strong and the fat, for it is believed that if these were spared they would tell the rest, and so make it impossible to bring any more buffalo into a pound."[55] In the late 1620s, the missionary Joseph de la Roche Dallion observed that the Neutrals (French-named for their neutrality in Huron and Iroquois wars) living in southern Ontario, western New York, and southeastern Michigan "have this maxim for all kinds of animals, whether they need them or not, that they must kill all they find, for fear, as they say, that if they do not take them the beast would go and tell the others how they had been hunted and that then in times of want, they would not find any more."[56] Professor Brightman speculates that the Neutrals believed that any animal a hunter refused to kill would complain of this rejection to the rest. This harmonized with the general Algonquian belief that hunters were required to take what was offered and that insulting rejections jeopardized future hunts.[57] Killing animals who offer themselves "is an act of love and gratitude. If a hunter is 'offered' much, it is obligatory to take much."[58] If hunters were having problems locating game because of steep population declines, it was the fault of the game bosses or rulers for refusing to reincarnate the dead animals.

In 1978, Calvin Martin posited a novel and controversial hypothesis.[59] In the decades after Contact, virulent European diseases began carrying most Indians away. All the Indian shamans could do was repeatedly demonstrate their impotence against these diseases. Indians knew that disease was one way in which wronged animals punished them for breaching their contract. But they believed that they had not violated that contract. Therefore, in the diseases brought upon them they detected a widespread animal conspiracy and struck back. This ensuing holy war was designed to wipe out the chief offenders, especially the bear and the beaver. "Wildlife had broken the compact of mutual courtesy. The dialogue between man and animal became acrimonious and then simply ended."[60] In turn, the animals considered the Indians' unrestrained slaughter both presumptuous and insulting. It was true that they had long permitted Indians to kill them, but only to the extent necessary for survival. This wholesale slaughter "would have been resented by the animal kingdom as an act comparable to genocide and would have been resisted" as a breach of the contract that had existed between humans and animals since time out of mind.[61]

In 1587, Thomas Hariot described his encounters with North Carolina's Indians: "Some religion they haue alreadie, which although it be farte from the truth, yet beyng at it is, there is hope it may bee the easier and sooner reformed."[62] Eventually the Indians' religion was reformed, indeed extinguished. When that happened, the Indians lost their traditional spiritual moorings and adopted prevailing Christian principles grounded in the Bible. Then they began to slaughter the animals in earnest.

"THE POINT OF REFERENCE IN ALL THEIR THINKING"

The continuing robust presence of the Bible in Bladen County was brought home while I was digging through musty real estate records in the courthouse located in Bladen's county seat, Elizabethtown, population 3,900. Occasionally I required some ancient document stored in the Superior Court across the hall. Once, while waiting, I noticed two copies of Zondervan's King James Version lying facedown on the counter. I initially thought a citizen using the courthouse had forgotten them, though in thirty years of haunting courthouses I had never stumbled upon a single forgotten Bible, never mind two. Curious, I picked one up and turned it over. Embossed in gold on the cover were the words "The Judicial Department." North Carolina law does require court witnesses and jurors to take their oaths in one of three ways. They may say, "So help me, God." They may make a nonreligious affirmation. Or they may place their hand on "the Holy Scriptures." Perhaps that was what these Bibles were for.[63] Perhaps.

American Christianity sprouted from the pages of Protestant Bibles like the ones lying on the Superior Court counter.[64] These were often the only books many colonists carried to America from England. These newcomers scrutinized their Bibles, then tried to live in harmony with what they understood they were being told.[65] This was something new. Until then, the common English men and women got most of their religion by staring at religious stained-glass paintings, attending the performances of sacred plays, and listening to sermons. Now the Bible could be read in English.

Initially, the Church of England vehemently opposed the Bible's translation, claiming the common person had no business interpreting God's raw language.[66] It was just in 1455 that the Bible had first been mass-produced using movable type. These were Vulgate editions, translated by Jerome in the fifth century, the Old Testament from the Hebrew, the New Testament from the Greek. A handful of Wycliffe Bibles, English translated from the Vulgate, had appeared in the 1380s, but were promptly suppressed.[67] Then, in 1523, Martin Luther translated the Five Books of Moses, of which Genesis was the first, from Hebrew into German, and a handful of Anglophones began thinking about repeating this feat in their own native tongue.

The first Bible in English appeared in 1526. Within a quarter-century, most British households possessed at least one well-thumbed copy; it was read aloud so often that readers, even illiterate hearers, would often memorize huge chunks.[68] Two million English Bibles were printed between 1525 and 1640, at a time when the English population totaled just six million souls.[69] These Bibles were intended to act as a guide to daily devotions, to be read silently or aloud to an attentive family or in public gatherings, and to be used by ministers. For most seventeenth-century Britons, the Bible "was their point of reference in all their thinking . . . the source of virtually all ideas," religious, economic, political, and moral.[70] Accordingly, "Bible reading was present in every moment of existence."[71] That is why "the pioneering men and women who tried to cling to life at Roanoke and Jamestown were Bible people. They could hardly be anything else, coming from Jacobean England."[72]

To follow God's will, one must hear him accurately. Until the middle of the seventeenth century, the most popular Bible—the one favored by the Puritans—was the Geneva Bible. There were others—Matthew's Bible of 1537, Miles Coverdale's first complete English Bible, the Great Bible of 1539—all of which were, at heart, Tyndale Bibles, which we will get to in a moment. During Shakespeare's half-century of life, which spanned the reigns from Henry VIII's daughter Bloody Mary to James I, 142 Geneva Bible editions were printed.[73] Geneva Bibles dominated early Virginia.[74] Recall from chapter 1 that George Durant was one of North Carolina's earliest settlers; we have his deed for land purchased along the Albemarle Sound in 1662. He arrived in North Carolina carrying the 1599 Geneva Bible he had imported from England.[75] One of the oldest English colonial Bibles of which we know, and one of the first books toted into North Carolina, Durant's Bible may be seen today at the University of North Carolina at Chapel Hill.[76] A 1620 "Mayflower" Geneva Bible that belonged to Governor William Bradford is on display in Pilgrim Hall in Plymouth, Massachusetts; Pilgrim John Alden's Geneva Bible is preserved in the Dartmouth College library.[77]

The first Geneva Bible appeared in 1560, published by English Protestant exiles riding out Bloody Mary's Catholic reign in Geneva, Switzerland. It would become the most important book available in English for the next century. Extensively annotated, the first half of its Old Testament was lifted nearly intact from William Tyndale's Bible.[78] Tyndale was extraordinary. His original Bible translations transformed English.[79] Much of the verb-centered, monosyllabic cadence and plain Saxon that forged the beauty of the

King James Version of the Bible—"take up thy bed and walk," "let there be light," "salt of the earth," "my brother's keeper," "blessed are the peacemakers"—beg to be read aloud and were cribbed from Tyndale. Shakespeare knew Tyndale's work well.

Tyndale learned Hebrew, a rarity for an Englishman, just so he could translate the Old Testament.[80] He finished most of it too, but before he could finish it all he was jailed by Catholic authorities in Antwerp. "Lord, open the king of England's eyes," he cried as he was being strangled.[81]

King James did not like the Geneva Bible's annotations. He believed that God ordained kings, such as himself, to rule in His name, and he was displeased at Geneva's suggestion that the yoke of tyrant kings and queens—remember hated Bloody Mary—could, like other yokes, be unhitched.[82] He decided to replace the Geneva Bible with one more friendly to the divine rights of kings and appointed several dozen translators and half a dozen committees to write it.[83] The 1611 King James Version, which lacked annotations, incorporated fully 83 percent of Tyndale's New Testament and 76 percent of his Old Testament. But nowhere did it contain the word "tyrant."[84]

The King James Version would become the most popular and influential book ever published, helped along by James's 1616 prohibition of any further Geneva Bible publication in Britain.[85] It could still be imported from Holland, if anyone dared, but even that loophole was closed by the Archbishop of Canterbury after James's death.[86] Its readership pruned, the final Geneva edition was published in 1644. It remained popular with anyone who could find one—certainly the Puritans looked—and the two editions battled for supremacy in the New World over the next century and beyond; the Geneva stood for Parliament and the Puritans, the King James Version for monarchy and the Church of England. Eventually, the increasingly scarce Geneva Bibles simply drowned in the rising tide of King James Versions.

CHAPTER THREE

The Genesis Disaster for Native Americans

For them the arrival of the Europeans marked the
beginning of a long holocaust, although it came not in
ovens, as it did for the Jews. The fires that consumed the
American Indians were the fevers brought on by newly-
encountered diseases, the flashes of settlers' and soldiers'
guns, the flames of villages and fields burned by the
scorched earth policy of vengeful Euro-Americans. The
effect of this holocaust of North American Indians, like
that of the Jews, was millions of deaths.

—*Russell Thornton,* AMERICAN INDIAN HOLOCAUST AND SURVIVAL *(1987)*[1]

I subjoin some observations with regard to the animals,
vulgarly called Indians. . . . They have the shapes of men
and may be of the human species, but certainly in their
present state they approach the character of Devils.

—*Henry Hugh Brackenridge,* INDIAN ATROCITIES *(1853)*[2]

The Anti-Christ in the Forest

European settlement of the New World opened a new and critical theater in the unceasing battle between God and the Devil. Or so Christians imagined. Historian Jorge Cañizares-Esguerra explains:

> Although Europeans had been confronting Satan for millennia and thought that demons hovered over the entire world, their battle with them in the New World was thought to be qualitatively different. It was not that the New World was afflicted with more demons than Eurasia. Europeans believed that there were millions of good angels and bad angels, organized in armies, all over the world. The problem was one of entrenchment. The devil and his minions (read Indians) had exercised uncontested sovereignty over the New World for 1,500 years, ever since Satan took a group of Scythians, his own elect, to colonize the empty land that was America right after or around the time the Gospel began to spread in Eurasia. Thus the devil had had time to build "fortifications" in the New World and set deep roots both in the landscape and among the people.[3]

The Devil may have begun to grip the New World even earlier, for the Bible "made it perfectly clear that Satan had been allowed by God to rule the world's wilderness area after Adam's and Eve's original disobedience to God in the Garden of Eden."[4]

For Christians, North America was a spiritually perilous and treacherous land, "full of unchallenged evil."[5] Walter Raleigh saw the Devil lurking, with his Indians, behind Carolina's trees, on the edges of its fields, and along its waterways. John Smith encountered the same situation in Virginia. William Bradford was certain that Cape Cod's Indians had once spent three days sending the Devil against his Pilgrims.[6] Samuel Sewall, Salem Witch Trial judge and future Chief Justice of the Massachusetts Superior Court of Judicature, wrote that, when the Puritans arrived, "Satan was here in his House strongly Fortified and well Moted in. . . . Here he had his headquarters, his Palaces; his Throne, kept his Court; exercised an Universal, unlimited Unquestioned Jurisdiction."[7] In a dazzling display of theological detective work, Boston's Cotton Mather discovered that Satan had arranged his New World kingdom in a vicious parody of the Bible's, complete with perverted Trinity, anti-Christ, twisted baptism, and raising of the dead.[8] Like New England's Puritans, Virginia's and Carolina's Protestants regarded their part of the New World as the site of an epic confrontation between God and Satan.[9]

SATAN'S PARTY

Because the Puritans were compulsive writers, we know much about them. But I highlight them for other reasons as well. The Puritan influence throughout British North America was immense.[10] Many of us automatically think of the *Mayflower*, Plymouth Rock, and Thanksgiving when we think of English colonists. The 102 years from 1558, the year of Queen Elizabeth's coronation, to the Restoration of King Charles II have been called England's "Puritan Century."[11] The ten thousand Puritans who fled to the New World in the 1630s formed the core of "a spiritual movement . . . which covered the colonies like a blanket."[12] And their influence was lasting. The Protestant religion that dominated the colonies by the Revolution evolved into an Americanized Anglicanism "deeply colored by Puritan convictions," with Congregationalists, Presbyterians, Baptists, and similar dissenters providing the moral and religious background for three-quarters of the Americans who declared independence, and perhaps as many as 90 percent.[13] If, over the last four hundred years, morality, religion, and law intertwined in the United States, it was because Puritans demanded that religion be moral, that morals be religious, and that religious morals be law. We are their spiritual heirs.[14]

English Protestants could see only darkness awaiting them in the New World; devils and Satan himself, aided by his Indian emissaries, would be ceaselessly testing their faith. Historian Alfred A. Cave explains that "the Native American was cast, in a radical sense, into the role of the 'Other,' the living example of what civilized men had transcended and of all that Christians must resist in their encounters with the wilderness and its denizens."[15] Puritan writings, literary scholar Sacvan Bercovitch concludes, "tell us, in effect . . . that there are two parties in the new world, God's and the Devil's; and that God's party is white, Puritan and entrusted with a world-redeeming errand, while Satan's party is dark-skinned, heathen and doomed."[16] "In killing the Indians in massive numbers . . . the English were only doing their sacred duty," writes historian David Stannard, "working hand in hand with the God who was protecting them."[17]

We do not inflict holocausts on ourselves, on "Us."[18] We inflict holocausts on "Others," on "Them." But who is "Us" and who is "Them"?[19] We divide and subdivide the world into many "kinds"— political, religious, family, geographical, national, class, educational, occupational, ethnic, racial. Our brains are restless kind-dividing machines, judging, always judging. The distinction between "Us" and "Them" need not follow species lines: within nonhuman kinds, there might be companion animal kinds, such as dog and cat kinds, and there are noncompanion animal kinds, such as pig, elephant, chimpanzee, parrot, and wolf kinds.[20]

Modern thinkers reject the folk idea that the differences we insist upon creating actually reflect something true and "essential" about the world, that these differences are innate, obvious, unchanging, universal, and commonsensical, and that all we need to do is look! Our categories may not correspond, yours and mine, but we still embrace them with equal fervor, we stoutly resist every attempt to change them, and don't confuse us with the facts. "[W]hen statistical reasoning meets essentialism," David Berreby writes in *Us and*

Them, "it's essentialism that wins, almost always."[21] Not always, or Europeans would still be murdering Waccamaw Indians, slaves would be picking cotton on Walnut Grove, and my wife would be sitting home on election day. But almost always.

We categorize with profound consequences. We eat pigs, but not dogs or Catholics. One essential, and historically decisive, category has been race. But today many argue that race has no meaning. Professor Jared Diamond writes that

> science often violates simple common sense. Our eyes tell us that the earth is flat, that the sun revolves around the earth, and that we humans are not animals. But we now ignore that evidence of our senses. We have learned that our planet is in fact round and revolves around the sun, and that humans are slightly modified chimpanzees. The reality of human races is another commonsense "truth" destined to follow the flat earth into oblivion.[22]

Our categories reflect nothing essential because they "aren't facts," says Berreby. "They're thoughts: mental actions that you take to cope with your current circumstances." Kinds need not be true or rational; they just need to work for us. We categorize people based on how we relate to them, what we want from them, and how we feel about them.[23]

Slavery has not always been based on race. Whatever characteristic was used, "masters have been consistent in the way they have described slaves throughout the world, from ancient Rome to medieval England to antebellum North America to dynastic China. The consistency is not in the slaves, who come from every sort of religion, culture, and race. Nor is it in the masters, who ranged from Caligula to Thomas Jefferson. The shared thread was the *relationship* of master to slave."[24] The stronger we *feel* about the kinds we create, the more powerfully we believe the categories are correct.[25]

Berreby explains that "getting you to feel that my cause is morally right . . . is a matter of getting you to feel that you belong to the same kind as the people (or animals, or grasslands, or sculptures) that I want to help. Not because you're similar on the surface (though similarity helps) but because, underneath appearances, you and the others are all a part of the community of the ethical."[26]

If we want to undermine an anachronistic category or kind, we had better understand the cultural certainties that permitted us to create it in the first place. Well into the early twentieth century, Christians believed that Anglo-Saxons descended from Japheth, one son of Noah, and that Native Americans and blacks came from his brother Ham.[27] Genesis 9:20–27 tells the story:

> And Noah began to be a husbandman, and he planted a vineyard: And he drank of the wine, and was drunken; and he was uncovered within his tent. And Ham, the father of Canaan, saw the nakedness of his father, and told his two brethren without. And Shem and Japheth took a garment, and laid it upon both their shoulders, and went backward, and covered the nakedness of their father; and their faces were backward. And they saw not their father's nakedness. And Noah awoke from his wine, and knew what his younger son had done unto him. And he said, cursed be Canaan: a servant of servants shall he be unto his brethren. And he said, Blessed be the Lord God of Shem: And Canaan shall be his servant. God shall enlarge Japheth, and he shall dwell in the tents of Shem; and Canaan shall be his servant.

Noah's Curse, also known as the Curse of Ham, runs deep. Europeans early regarded Ham as the father of all the unfree. By the sixteenth century, both the Spanish and the French thought the New World natives cursed; the English joined them in this opinion in the seventeenth century.[28] The Boston wit and public intellectual Oliver Wendell Holmes, father of the Supreme Court Justice, orated of the

American Indian in 1855 that "the white man hates him, and hunts him down like the wild beasts of the forest, and so the red-crayon sketch is rubbed out, and the canvas is ready for a picture of manhood a little more like God's own image."[29] Theodore Roosevelt speechified in 1886: "I don't go so far as to think that the only good Indians are dead Indians, but I believe nine out of every ten are, and I shouldn't like to inquire too closely into the case of the tenth."[30] As the twentieth century opened, the popular southern Episcopal theologian Benjamin Palmer offered a homily in segregated New Orleans in which he rejoiced that "the Indian [was] practically extinct; the vast forests in which he pursued his game leveled to the earth, and the fertile bosom of the soil receiving culture and yielding its fruit a thousand-fold to the industry of man. Instead of the warwhoop of the Indian, we hear the chimes of Sabbath bells, and songs of praise issuing from myriad of Christian homes to the glory of God . . . in the just judgment of a righteous and holy God . . . the Indian has been swept from the earth, and a great Christian nation . . . rises up."[31]

"Vacant Soyle"

The Puritans were certain that God had guided them to the Indians precisely to show them what they could become, and to allow them to glimpse the glories of eternal salvation. Puritan occupation of Indian land, they believed, was therefore a boon to the Indians, for it gave them the opportunity to observe the Puritans frequently and at close range, often on what had lately been Indian land. The English were determined to transfer to the Indians every aspect of what they believed to be their superior culture, especially their religion, but also their law, and even their agriculture. And the Indians were thirsting for all of it, or so the Puritans believed, as they designed the Seal of the Massachusetts Bay Colony to depict an Indian holding a bow in his right hand and an upside-down arrow in his left. He was beseeching the English to "Come Over and Help Us."[32]

The Indians certainly needed help with their agriculture, so the English believed. The way any culture feeds itself can reveal much about its values.[33] The contrast between how the Indians and colonists fed themselves was dramatic. Indians did not try to transform or subdue the land; they celebrated it as central to their sense of who, where, and what they were, then left it much as they found it.[34] They often ate by hunting and gathering, neither of which the English thought qualified as agriculture, much less civilization.[35] When the English hunted, it was often for sport.[36] And they lacked the category of "ownerless livestock." Every pig, every lamb, every cow belonged—*had* to belong—to someone. In contrast, Indians lacked the category of "owned live animals"; no Indian owned an animal unless he killed her.[37] These abstract conceptual differences inevitably led to real conflicts in Indian squash fields and the forests surrounding colonial homes.[38]

Indians did farm—or Indian women did. That was why the Waccamaw and other Woodland Period North Carolina Piedmont Indians settled near streams, for there the alluvial soil was rich and easily worked. Southeastern Indians had been cultivating squashes and pumpkins for 2,500 years, corn for 1,400 years, and beans for 1,200 years, along with edible sunflowers, sunweeds, chenopodium, pigweed, knotweed, giant ragweed, and canary grass, by the time the Europeans came.[39] In western North Carolina's mountains, the Cherokees had absorbed the more politically and religiously organized Mississippian culture that began to develop around AD 700 and turned even more vigorously toward a more settled village life and farming; the more eastern tribes, such as the Waccamaw, were less affected.[40]

North American Indians did not domesticate animals. Every medium and large American mammal—the horse, mammoth, and camel—had vanished ten millennia before. South and Central American Indians domesticated a few smaller species, such as turkeys, llamas, alpacas, Muscovy ducks, and guinea pigs.[41] But North American Indians had only hawks and maybe dogs, although those bony canines would have appeared feral to us. They certainly did to many early English observers, who found them closer to wolves than the canines they had known back home. Or they were seen as part wolf and part fox. A Virginian colonist, Peter Wynne, wrote that "there was nothing tame about" the dogs kept by Virginia's Powhatan Indians; John Smith claimed that "thye cannot even barke but howle."[42]

The Indians may have understood that humans were simply one species of animal. Certainly no colonist recorded any generic Indian name for "animal."[43] The English bifurcated "animals" into humans and everyone else, with the pig being the fulcrum around which agriculture had long revolved. Pigs resembling the wild boar, "a long-legged, razorbacked, dark brown, and bristly beast with bad manners," roamed everywhere in Britain.[44] One seventh-century *doom*, or law, of King Ine of Wessex determined the value of an illegally burned mast-producing tree by counting the number of pigs it would have sheltered.[45] The Domesday Book, that comprehensive survey of English assets ordered by William the Conqueror in 1086 to more efficiently tax his Saxon subjects, often classified woodland areas according to the number of pigs those areas could support. Pig-keeping evolved into an important and lucrative occupation in the medieval English countryside. Pig flesh could be better preserved than cow flesh or sheep flesh, while pig lard was an important source of fat in an age when fat was hard to get, and pigs could easily be raised on non-arable land or even loosed into the forests to feed on acorns and wild nuts until winter threatened and they were gathered in to have their throats cut.[46]

By the seventeenth century, two million pigs inhabited England and Wales—one for every two humans.[47] As that century closed, the average English man or woman was consuming almost 150 pounds of red meat each year, mostly pork, beef, and mutton. When the First Fleet arrived in Australia's Botany Bay a century later, bearing its unhappy load of convict-settlers, sailors, and marines, it carried the usual seafarer's daily meat allotment: four pounds of beef and two pounds of pork.[48] By the start of the nineteenth century, England boasted the second-highest animals-to-human ratio in Europe (after the Netherlands), counting one sheep for every three humans and one pig and three cows for every English man and woman.[49] In 1845, Friedrich Engels spied pigs penned "in almost every interior court" in Manchester, and there were three pigs for every human in 1854 Kensington.[50]American colonials treasured their pigs for good reason. Pigs reproduced easily and in large quantity, would eat anything, and could defend themselves against hungry forest wolves and bears. Hogs often roamed the countryside, just as they did in England, rampaging through Indian fields, until the colonists decided that they were ready for slaughter, just as in England. Then the hogs would be hunted down and killed.[51] Livestock husbandry was not just a way to make a living—it was a way of life. "Done properly," notes historian Virginia DeJohn Anderson,

> it reinforced a set of behaviors that seventeenth century English people regarded as normative and emblematic of civilized existence . . . [and it] personified an English agrarian ideal. They were prudent and well-organized, following rigorous daily and seasonal routines dictated by climate, habit, economic goals, and their livestock's needs. They were economical, saving table scraps for hogs and manure for their fields, as well as experimental, adopting new agricultural techniques if they promised significant benefits. . . . As Christians they exemplified divinely sanctioned dominion over animals. They were, in short, everything Indians were not.[52]

"Replenish the Earth and Subdue It"

The newcomers wasted little time in rooting out the devils in the forests. Captain John Underhill commanded the Massachusetts Bay

Colony's slaughter of Connecticut's Pequot Indians at the "Mystic Massacre," a critical part of the Puritans' genocidal 1636–37 Indian war. Underhill put one thousand Indians to the sword—men, women, and children, old and young, infirm and robust—explaining that "sometimes the Scripture declareth women and children must perish with their parents. . . . We had sufficient light from the Word of God for our proceedings."[53] North Carolina's Tuscaroras were decisively defeated after a sharp and bitter war that began in 1711. Tribal remnants migrated north to New York and Pennsylvania and became the sixth member of the Iroquois Confederacy.[54] According to Baron Christopher de Graffenreid, founder of New Bern, North Carolina, one of the war's chief causes was "the harsh treatment of certain surly and rough English inhabitants who deceived them in trade, would not let them hunt about their plantations, and under this excuse took away from them, arms, munitions, pelts or hides, yes, even beat an Indian to death."[55] With the Tuscaroras, long the most powerful tribe in Piedmont North Carolina, out of the way, the English could continue pushing west.[56]

Bladen County's natives were decimated in the usual ways. The Eastern Cherokee anthropologist James Mooney listed them.

> The chief causes of decrease, in order of importance, may be classed as smallpox and other epidemics; tuberculosis; sexual diseases; whiskey and attendant dissipation; removals, starvation, and subjection to unaccustomed conditions; low vitality due to mental depressions under misfortune; war. In the category of destroyers, all but wars and tuberculosis may be considered to have come from the white man, and the increasing destructiveness of tuberculosis itself is due largely to conditions subsequent upon his advent.[57]

The Europeans had nothing against the Indians, so long as the Indians traded with them but otherwise left them alone. Certainly some sought to convert Indians to Christianity. But most just wanted the Indians' land and didn't scruple to kill or remove any original inhabitants who resisted.[58] It was the Christian thing to do. Anytime a Puritan exploited an Indian, he notched a victory in the worldwide struggle of God's Chosen People, the Elect, the Saints (the Puritans called themselves many things) against Satan.[59] The Indians did not see it that way. John Lawson, the first Englishman to explore Carolina's mountainous west, wrote that the English

> daily cheat them in every thing we fell, and esteem it a Gift of Christianity, not to fell to them so cheap as we do to the Christians, as we call our selves. Pray let me know where is there to be found one Sacred Command or Precept of our Master, that counsels us to such Behaviour? Besides, I believe it will not appear, but that all the Wars, which we have had with the Savages, were occasion'd by the unjust Dealings of the Christians towards them.[60]

Especially in "Virginia and the Carolinas . . . Indians were meaningless to Europeans except as occupants of coveted land or as non-Christian slaves."[61] Taking the Indians' land was not stealing, for it was not the Indians' in the first place. As far as the English were concerned, any acreage the Indians did not regularly farm was *vacuum domicilium*—vacant land that anyone could possess who settled and worked it, land that belonged to no one until then. This encompassed nearly the entire continent, which conveniently no one had owned before the Europeans arrived. Since the Indians regularly farmed only a small number of tiny fields, that was the only portion that was theirs. Thus the Massachusetts Superior Court of Judicature ruled that "what landes any of the Indians, within this jurisdiction, have by possession or improvement, by subdueing of the same, they have just right thereunto, according to that Gen. 1:28, chap 9:1, Psa: 115, 16."[62] That the Indians had hunted the land for centuries was irrelevant. God had commanded the sons of Adam to subdue the land—the Geneva and King James Bibles both used the word "subdue"—not run atop it chasing animals.[63] "Subdue" is a grimmer word than "dominion," the power God gave man over the animals, harsher and more brutal. It connotes a greater use of force. It is a command to enslave, to conquer militarily. It is an order to wrestle the land down.[64] "By what warrant have we to take that land, which is and hath been of long tyme possessed of others the sons of Adam?" John Winthrop asked in 1629.

> This savage people ruleth over many lands without title or property; for they inclose no ground, neither have they cattell to maintayne it, but remove their dwellings as they have occasion, or as they can prevail against their neighbours. And why may not christians have liberty to go and dwell amongst them in their waste lands and woods (leaving them such places as they have manured for their come) as lawfully as Abraham did among the Sodomites?[65]

As Winthrop and other Massachusetts Bay Company members prepared to depart Southampton for the New World in 1630, Reverend John Cotton reminded them that

> where there is a vacant place, there is liberty for the sonnes of *Adam* or *Noah* to come and inhabite, though they neither buy it, nor ask their leaves. . . . [It] is a Principle in Nature, that in a vacant soyle, hee that taketh possession of it, and bestoweth culture and husbandry upon it, his Right it is. And the ground of this is from the grand Charter given to Adam and his posterity in Paradise, Gen. 1–28 *Multiply, and replenish the earth, and subdue it.* If therefore any sonne of *Adam* comme and find a place empty, he hath liberty to come, and fill, and subdue the earth there. This Charter was renewed to *Noah*, Gen. 9.1 *Fulfill the*

earth and multiply. So that it is free from that common Grant, for any to take possession of vacant Countries.[66]

Making Room for the Elect

"The major initial effect of the Columbian voyages was the transformation of America into a charnel house," writes the historian Alfred Crosby, who coined the term "Columbian Exchange."[67] The Indians got the worst of the "Exchange." Syphilis returned on the ships to Europe. But two centuries later, the Indian population had been reduced to just 5 percent of its pre-Contact strength.[68] The lethal slurry of microbes harbored by the Spaniards, French, and British, their African slaves, and the miserable pigs, cows, sheep, and horses they penned or roped for weeks below decks killed most, inflicting them with dysentery, malaria, yellow fever, smallpox, measles, the plague, cholera, typhoid, pleurisy, scarlet fever, diphtheria, mumps, whooping cough, colds, gonorrhea, chanchroid, pneumonia, flu, and typhus.[69]

Pigs were effective agents of microbe dispersal, harboring novel and virulent strains of anthrax, brucellosis, leptospirosis, trichinosis, tuberculosis, and influenza. The ones that followed Hernando de Soto's tiny army on its epic four-year journey through the Southeast may have ignited pandemics among the numerous Indians and complex societies it encountered. Populous and thriving villages were decimated, which may explain why so few Indians remained when the English arrived a century later.[70] Most of the Cherokees, whose population of 22,000 may have controlled more than 100,000 square miles in or near Appalachia in 1650, were soon gone, swept aside by at least four epidemics of influenza, bubonic plague, and typhus.[71] Smallpox would soon halve the survivors.[72] The Pamlico Indians, who lived east of Bladen County, simply evaporated in one epidemic.[73]

The Columbian Exchange, running full throttle through the sixteenth and seventeenth centuries, devastated Bladen County. In

1587, the English who settled Roanoke Island wrote that when they encountered an Indian village,

> within a few dayes after our departure from everies such townes, that people began to die very fast, and many in short space; in some townes about twentie, in some fourtie, in some sixtie, & in one six score, which in trueth was very manie in respect to their numbers. . . . The disease also was so strange that they neither knew what it was, nor how to cure it; the like by report of the oldest men in the countrey never happened before, time out of mind.[74]

John Lawson wrote of the Indians in 1701 that smallpox and rum "have made such a Destruction among them, that, on good grounds, I do believe, there is not the sixth Savage living within two hundred Miles of all our Settlements, as there were fifty Years ago. These poor Creatures have so many Enemies to destroy them that it's a wonder one of them is left alive near us."[75] Anthropologist Russell Thornton explains that "the diseases did not merely spread among American Indians, kill them, and disappear. On the contrary, they came, spread, and killed again, and again, and again. There may have been as many as 93 serious epidemics and pandemics of Old World pathogens among North American Indians between the early sixteenth century to the beginning of the twentieth century."[76] One and a half percent of New England's Indians died every year.[77]

The evidence is in the increasing absence of reference to Indians in colonial records. After 1730, North Carolina's records rarely refer to Indians again.[78] In 1729, the Scots and French Huguenots who settled Heart's Creek, near Fayetteville, twenty miles north of Tar Heel, detected "a large tribe of Indians" living along the Lumber River swamps, near Lumberton, in present-day Robeson County. These Indians may have looked like "a tribe" to the Europeans, but they were not. Carolina tribes rarely endured long after Contact. Most fractured under the pressures of these exotic diseases, as well as encroachments and attacks. But, in the swamps, survivors from all three major linguistic groups—Waccamaw, Tuscarora, Saponi, Hatteras, Keyauwee, Eno, Shakori, and Mattamusket—were re-forming new tribes that incorporated descendants of European indentured servants and escaped black slaves. The object was mutual protection.[79]

The Indians had given up their traditional religion. To become Christians, farmers, and slave owners. Some spoke an archaic form of English and lived in a European style.[80] "In order to be great like the English," an elderly Lumbee would explain in 1864, "we took the white man's language and religion, for our people were told they would prosper if they would take white man's laws."[81] Cherokees absorbed the dazed remnants of the Delaware, Natchez, Creek, and Chickasaw.[82] Then, in 1830, Congress enacted the Indian Removal Act, which President Andrew Jackson used to pressure the Cherokees to trade their eastern land for western land. Thousands of dead Cherokees would line the 1838 Trail of Tears.[83] But some Cherokees evaded the troops and stayed in North Carolina, though by 1890, fewer than three thousand eastern Cherokees remained, and half of these were holed up in the mountains of what had once been Bladen County.[84]

Some of the English viewed the massive Indian die-off as powerful "evidence of God's favor to them, His chosen people."[85] When New England's Puritans stepped off the *Mayflower* onto land picked nearly clean by the pandemic of 1616 and 1617, they thanked God for His "wondrous work . . . [in] wasting the naturall Inhabitants with deaths stroke" to make room for His Elect—that would have been themselves.[86] Later Cotton Mather would rejoice that the New England landscape had been cleared "of those pernicious creatures, to make room for better growth."[87] Governor Bradford would attribute one pandemic to "the good hand of God," which "favored our beginnings" by "sweeping away great multitudes of the natives . . . that he might make room for us."[88] Cotton's father, Increase, referred to a 1631 epidemic as occurring at just the time "the Indians began to be quarrelsome touching the Bounds of the Land which they had sold to the English, but God ended the Controversy by sending the Smallpox among the Indians of Saugust, who were before that time exceedingly numerous."[89]

Even as they were disappearing, North Carolina's Indians began exterminating the Carolina white-tailed deer with whom they had lived in harmony for so long. Southeastern Indians had always hunted deer in moderation. Calvin Martin argues that the Indians turned on the animals after concluding they had betrayed them and that this slaughter was facilitated by the destruction of the natives' religion and their embrace of European Christianity.[90] Anthropologist Charles Hudson Jr. disagrees, claiming that the Indians wanted guns and the way to get them was by trading deerskins.[91] "When the bases of their survival changed, they did what they had to do in order to survive," he argues.[92]

But the Indians did not survive. At Contact, the Southeast brimmed with deer who ran in herds of hundreds.[93] Soon deerskins and, for some while, Indian slaves became the primary British tools for reducing the natives to dependency.[94] Indians had long enslaved a few war captives. Now the British wanted large numbers of Indian slaves to labor alongside black Africans. And so Indian began to war on Indian in order to furnish captives for the English to turn into slaves.[95] When that stopped, the slaughter of deer continued. Eighty-five thousand deerskins were shipped from Carolina and Virginia near the end of the seventeenth century. Half a century later, Southeastern Indians were killing one million deer a year.[96] That could not go on, and eventually the forests of Bladen County fell silent, both deer and Indians gone.[97]

CHAPTER FOUR

The Genesis Disaster
for Black Slaves

No other passage in the Bible has had such a disastrous
influence throughout human history as Genesis 9:17–27.
—*David Brion Davis*, INHUMAN BONDAGE *(2006)*[1]

The whole Southern mind with an unparalleled unanimity
regards the institution of slavery as righteous and just,
ordained of God, and to be perpetuated by man.
—*William H. Holcombe, "The Alternative: A Separate Nationality,
or the Africanization of the South" (1861)*[2]

I SPENT SEVERAL DAYS in the Bladen County Register of
Deeds in the Elizabethtown courthouse puzzling out the relationship between the Walnut Grove slave plantation in Tar Heel
and the slaughterhouse complex. I pored over musty grantor and
grantee indexes and old deeds and plats, trying to determine the
metes and bounds that Walnut Grove had encompassed so I could

answer the question of whether any part of the plantation had been sold to somebody, who had sold to somebody, who had sold to somebody, who had sold to the Smithfield Packing Company.

It was hard to start from the beginning, for Bladen County's land records were incomplete, the courthouse having been ravaged by fire in 1770, 1800, and 1893. I had to wrestle with eighteenth- and nineteenth-century deeds—written in barely decipherable back-woods penmanship with casual spelling—that described some parcel of land as being next to another parcel whose location I didn't know, or as being a few rods south of a pine tree or a large stump that had rotted away when Jefferson was president, or as being a mile north of a fork in a river whose name had changed three times. Eventually I surrendered to the enigmatic and began to work back-ward from Smithfield's purchase of the slaughterhouse land in the 1990s. That was easier, though not by much. Walnut Grove had first expanded, then contracted so many times over two centuries, been divided and subdivided into ever-shrinking pieces, that I came to admire the grit of the Smithfield lawyers who must have had to fig-ure out who owned what, and when. I left the courthouse per-suaded, mostly, that the Tar Heel slaughterhouse complex had been stitched from land that had once been part of Walnut Grove.

I wanted to ask the sixth-generation Robesons who, I had been told, were occupying the manor house what they knew of Walnut Grove's history. Having read that the owners sometimes gave tours, I telephoned the head of the Bladen County Historical Society to ask where I could sign up for one. He said that he doubted whether Emily Averitte, the great-great-great-granddaughter of Colonel Robeson, was still permitting those tours.[3] She was, he said, a very private person.

A Tar Heel Plantation

I set off in 104-degree heat for the Wilson Library at the Univer-sity of North Carolina at Chapel Hill to examine its trove of Robeson family papers. After a day squinting at faded, ancient, slightly comprehensible official documents, yellowed newspaper clippings, and Robeson flotsam, I found "A Historical and Genealogical Account of Andrew Robeson of Scotland, New Jersey, and Pennsylvania and of His Descendants from 1653 to 1916, begun by Susan Stroud Robeson, assisted by Caroline Franciscus Stroud, Compiled, edited and published by Kate Hamilton Osborne Press of J. B. Lippinscott Company, Philadelphia 1916, Updated by Suzanne Olivia Sanborn Rushing from 1992 to 1998, assisted by Mary Doris Lyon Sanborn." It was typed, and I learned later that it was a summary of a much larger book. Deep within its pages of names, birth dates, death dates, marriage dates, and summaries of lives led, appeared the name "Priscilla Finch Carpender." Born in 1963, it said, she lived in Charlotte, North Carolina. She was, it said, an "animal right" activist.

My quest turned toward Priscilla Finch Carpender. But I couldn't find her. Finally, a computer search turned up the fact that Anne Carpender, Priscilla's mother, had passed away in early May 2007. The *Charlotte Observer* maintained an electronic guest book in Anne Carpender's memory for anyone to sign and leave comments. Priscilla Finch Carpender had signed the guest book, and I could contact her through it. After hesitating, I signed the guest book too, with apologies for the intrusion.

Priscilla and I failed to get off on the right foot. It wasn't that I had contacted her through the guest book. But next morning I received a fax in which she informed me that, when she opened my e-mail, her computer had crashed and she was therefore reporting me to the authorities. And who was I? I explained by fax who I was and what I wanted and assured her that I didn't know how to crash her computer. Eventually she realized that it had crashed without my assistance, apologized, then wanted to know what I wanted to know about her family. She would be happy to help, though she worried about how any information I received might reflect on the Robeson name: "Folks still tar-and-feather down here," she warned. My wife

Gail, and I flew to Charlotte to meet Prissy Carpender at a Buca di Beppo restaurant in Pineville.

Gail and I figured we were at the right place when we pulled alongside a car standing nearly alone in the Buca di Beppo parking lot that was festooned with bumper stickers saying, STOP ANIMAL TESTS, FRIENDS DON'T CHAIN FRIENDS—BRING DOGS INSIDE, ABOLISH SLAVERY—BOYCOTT THE CIRCUS, TO NEUTER IS CUTER, and LIBERATE LABORATORY ANIMALS. Inside, Prissy handed me some Robeson family books, provided a thumbnail sketch of her life and Robeson family history, then invited us to her home to view Robeson family memorabilia. After regaling us with stories about the many Robeson family reunions she had attended at Walnut Grove, she gave us Mrs. Averitte's telephone number and told us to use her name.

On Thomas Robeson Sr.'s death, most of the Walnut Grove plantation passed to Thomas Jr., as elder son, with the balance going to his younger brother, Peter. Thomas Jr. moved into the manor house, while Peter built a home directly across the Cape Fear River. I located a copy of Thomas Jr.'s will in the tiny Elizabethtown public library. It confirmed that Walnut Grove had been a slave plantation: its house and outbuildings and an out-kitchen, dairy, smokehouse, barn, well, old frame, and scalding vat had all been at least partially built and worked by slaves.[4] I also found a 1930s newspaper story that noted that while Walnut Grove's "old kitchens were in use small negro boys were employed to carry the hot dishes into the main dining room, and today on the walls of these ancient cook rooms can be seen graduated marks made from greasy heads of the boys as they waited to 'start' the dishes."[5]

Dated June 1, 1780, Thomas Robeson Jr.'s will began:

In the Name of God "Amen" . . .

I, Thomas Robeson of Bladen County, now in health and perfect mind and memory thanks be unto God for the same and calling to mind the mortality of body and knowing that it is appointed for all men once to die do make and ordain this my last Will and Testament. . . .

I give and recommend my soul into the hands of God that gave it and for my body I recommend to the earth to be buried in a decent Christian like manner at the discretion of my Executors nothing doubting but at the general resurrection I shall receive the same again by the mighty power of God, and as touching such worldly estate wherswith it hath pleased God to bless me with in this life, I give, devise and dispose of the same in manner following. . . .

The fifth paragraph provided the unmistakable evidence:

Fifth: I give and bequeath all the rest and remainder part of my estate, lands, negroes, stock of all kinds and moveable estate to be equally divided among my children, Bartram, Jonathan, William, Elizabeth, and Sarah, to and amongst them and by them freely to be enjoyed.

Captain Peter Robeson's will echoed his brother's and provided equally certain evidence that his home across the Cape Fear had also been a slave plantation.

Fifth: It is my will and desire that my daughter Mary have two acres of land laid off to her from a piece that I have lying in the town of Fayetteville and two hundred acres laid off to her out of some lands lying in Lord Neck, and also an equal share with my three sons of moveable estate such as negroes, stock and all kinds of household and kitchen furniture and plantation tools.

Sixth: It is my will and desire that my three sons have the remainder part of my lands equally divided among them whenever my Executors may think it most convenient it is my desire also that my three sons have an equal share in all my moveable estate such as negroes, stock of all kinds, household furniture and plantation tools, and by them fairly to be possessed and enjoyed.[6]

Colonel Robeson's wife was Mary Bartram, daughter of William Bartram Jr.[7] Mary's uncle, John Bartram, and his son William became America's most famous eighteenth-century naturalists. With the aid of the Waccamaws, John Bartram was the first to explore Lake Waccamaw. William journeyed through the Southeast for four years, beginning in 1773, and published his *Travels* in 1791 to international acclaim; his portrait would be painted by Charles Wilson Peale, who captured Jefferson, Washington, and Lewis and Clark. William Bartram's book included a great deal about the Southeast's surviving Native Americans but little about North Carolina's Indians, except for describing the Cherokees' rearguard fight against the ceaseless encroachment of the "Virginians" (their word for any European) on their mountainous western backcountry lands.[8] He noted that the Muscogulgee Indians "wage eternal war against deer and bear, to procure food and clothing, and other necessaries and conveniences; which is indeed carried to an unreasonable and perhaps criminal excess, since the white people have dazzled their senses with foreign superfluities."[9]

After the death of her father, William Jr., in 1771, Mary's mother, Elizabeth, drafted a will in which she left Mary's sister, Sarah Brown, wife of General Thomas Brown, "all my negroes [as follows:] Old Jack, Old Cloe, Billinder, Lonzo, Shicles, Joe, Amy, Little Chloe, Florah & her 3 children, viz.—Dick, Nan, Toney."[10] By will dated 1815, Thomas Brown bequeathed his slaves Amey, Clarissa, and Murray to his wife Lucy, and other slaves—Thomas, Old Alonzo, Virgil, Hamlet, William, Cato, Hester, and Harvey—to his son Thomas.[11]

Marjory Bartlett Sanger's "interpretative biography" of William Bartram relates a Christmas 1776 meeting with his cousin Mary

Bartram Robeson at the Bartram family home, called Ashwood. (A historical marker notes that Ashwood stood two miles east of where NC Route 87 crosses the Cape Fear River north of Tar Heel.) Mary called to her servant Cezar to bring a pitcher of punch and some fruitcake that Old Betty had baked that autumn and stored in a metal chest in the root cellar.

> "Cezar and Old Betty are Robeson slaves," Billy commented.
>
> "Well, I'm a Robeson now," Mary said simply.
>
> Billy remarked that he would have expected to find Old Chloe and Little Chloe and Lonzo at Ashwood, where they had always been.
>
> "Mother left all to Sarah," said Mary, as simply as before.
>
> "All of her slaves?" Billy asked, astonished.
>
> "All of everything: land, stock, slaves, silver."[12]

Bladen County's 1763 tax list reveals that a "Robbison Thos. Sen." owned nine slaves, while a "Robison Thos. Jun." owned three.[13] Three volumes of the "Abstracts of Early Deeds of Bladen County, North Carolina" are devoted almost entirely to recording the sales of land and slaves. On April 14, 1798, we find "William G. McDaniel to William Robeson [a son of Thomas Robeson Jr.]— 120 pounds—a Negro named Isaac about 14 years old," and on October 25, 1797, "Jonathan Robeson [another son of Thomas Robeson Jr.] (Robins) to Richard & James Salter, Esq. 150 pounds current money & . . . a negro slave named Jack."[14]

I found original, handwritten, North Carolina 1790 census notes on microfilm at the University of North Carolina at Chapel Hill. I could not make them out, however, and was thankful to locate a typed copy in the Elizabethtown library.[15] It reported that Bladen County had 837 free white males above the age of fifteen, 830 free white males below the age of sixteen, 1,683 free white females, 58 other free persons, and 1,676 slaves. No "Robesons" were listed, but I knew that they were present in disguise. As always, the spelling was not rigorous—Noah Webster's *Blue-Backed Speller* appeared only in 1783—and census takers spelled what they heard.[16] There were Robinsons reported. In Bladen County today, I hear "Robeson" pronounced "Rob-es-sun," and it would be easy to hear an implied internal "n." The census information on the "Robinsons" seemed to match what we know about the Robesons. The family of "Batrum Robinson" was listed in the census as consisting of two free white males over fifteen years old, two free white males below the age of sixteen, three free white females, and twenty-four slaves. The family of "Jonathan Robinson" was made up of just himself. The family of "Peter Robinson" (presumably Thomas Jr.'s brother) had one free white male over the age of fifteen, two free white males below the age of sixteen, three free white females, and twelve slaves. The 1820 census recorded six Robesons: Catherine, Charles, two Johns, Margaret, and Samuel. Together they owned twenty-seven slaves. The household of "William Robinson," likely the son of Thomas Jr., and the owner then of Walnut Grove, consisted of five free white males, seven free white females, and twenty-five slaves.

On the drive to Tar Heel from Charlotte, just before we were pulled over by a local police officer who accused us of ferrying large quantities of illegal drugs in the trunk of our rental car and claimed never to have heard of Bladen County, Gail telephoned Mrs. Averitte, mentioned Prissy, and received permission to visit Walnut Grove. Having managed to persuade the officer that we were law-abiding visitors and that there was such a county as Bladen, Gail and I were able to drive to the Walnut Grove manor house early the next morning. There we encountered Mrs. Averitte. She gestured that we should park in the rear of the manor house, near the out-buildings. She was in her early eighties, formidable and erect. I was disappointed to find that King George II's original deed to Thomas Robeson Sr. was not hanging in the hallway. After some small talk in the living room, I asked whether the deed was still in the house and was politely ushered into an adjoining parlor. There it was, with an impressive seal. I could barely make out a word. Eventually I got round to asking Mrs. Averitte the question I wanted answered: did the Tar Heel slaughterhouse complex stand on land that had once been part of Walnut Grove?

Yes, she said, without hesitation. *Everything* in Tar Heel had once been part of Walnut Grove—the Subway, Allen's Tire, Clark's Chapel AME, Zion Church, Minuteman Food Market, Tienda Hispania, the Faith Deliverance Ministries, Tar Heel Middle School, Tar Heel Realty, the U.S. post office, the Smithfield Family Medical Center and Pharmacy, the Smithfield Employment Center, the Tar Heel Rural Volunteer Fire Department, Tar Heel Treasures and Gifts, and the entire Tar Heel slaughterhouse complex. All of it stands on land once worked by the Robeson family's black slaves.

"To Render the Submission of the Slave Perfect"

Black slaves were routinely neglected and abused in North Carolina. In her travels through the state before Independence, Janet Schaw noticed that slaves subsisted on just "a quart of Indian corn per day" and whatever they could raise or steal.[17] After the Revolution, Johann David Schoepf, a former Hessian surgeon, attended a public auction in front of the Wilmington courthouse, sixty miles southeast of Walnut Grove. There,

> negroes were let for 12 months to the highest bidder, by public cry as well. . . . The keep of a negro here does not come to a great figure, since the daily ration is but a quart of maize, and rarely a little meat or salted fish. Only those negroes kept for house-service are better cared for. Well-disposed masters clothe their negroes once a year, and give them a suit of coarse woollen cloth, two rough shirts, and a pair of shoes. But they who have the largest droves keep them the worst, let them run

naked mostly or in rags, and accustom them as much as possible to hunger, but exact of them steady work. Whoever hires a negro, gives on the spot a bond for the amount, to be paid at the end of the term, even should the hired negro fall sick or run off in the meantime. The hirer must also pay the negro's head-tax, feed him and clothe him. Hence a negro is capital, put out at a very high interest, but because of elopement and death certainly very unstable.

The sales often broke up families.

The father was put up first; his anxiety lest his son fall to another purchaser and be separated from him was more painful than his fear of getting into the hands of a hard master. "Who buys me," he was continually calling out, "must buy my son too," and it happened as he desired, for his purchaser, if not from motives of humanity and pity, was for his own advantage obliged so to do. An elderly man and his wife were let go at 200 Pd. But these poor creatures are not always so fortunate; often the husband is snatched from his wife, the children from their mother, if this better answers the purpose of buyer or seller, and no heed is given the doleful prayers with which they seek to prevent a separation.[18]

Even the most callous slave master had little to fear from the law of North Carolina. The chilliest judicial defense of slavery's brutality in our nation's history flowed from the pen of Judge Thomas Ruffin of North Carolina's Supreme Court in 1828.[19] Elizabeth Jones had hired her slave Lydia to John Mann of Chowan County, 150 miles northeast of present-day Bladen County. When Lydia annoyed Mann, he shot her. She lived. Convicted of assault and battery, Mann was fined five dollars. He appealed. Judge Ruffin, the most prominent American state court judge of his generation, reversed Mann's conviction. Slavery's end, Ruffin wrote, is the profit of the master, his security and the public safety; the subject, one doomed in his own person, and his posterity, to live without knowledge, and without the capacity to make any thing his own, and to toil that another may reap the fruits. . . . The power of the master must be absolute, to render the submission of the slave perfect. . . . The protection afforded by several statutes, that all-powerful motive, the private interest of the owner, the benevolences toward each other seated in the hearts of those who have been born and bred with each other, the frowns and deep execrations of the community upon the barbarian, who is guilty of excessive and brutal cruelty, to his unprotected slave, all combined, have produced a mildness of treatment, and attention to the comforts of the unfortunate class of slaves, greatly mitigating the rigors of servitude, and ameliorating the conditions of the slave.[20]

Harriet Beecher Stowe observed that "no one can read this decision so fine and clear in its expression, so dignified in its earnestness, and dreadful in its results, without feeling at once deep respect for the man and horror for the system."[21]

In the 1930s, some of North Carolina's former slaves recalled their torments. Ann Parker was born near Raleigh, at the northern edge of what was once Bladen County. Her master, Abner Parker, owned one hundred slaves. "I ain't never liked him much," Parker said, "'cause we had to work hard and we ain't got much to eat."[22] Thomas Hall was also born on the northern edge of old Bladen County, in Orange County. The conditions and rules of slavery were terrible, he recalled; punishments were severe and barbarous, slaves were burned at the stake, and families sold apart.[23]

North Carolina's escaped slaves provided some of America's richest slave narratives. One slave, Moses Roper, was born in 1820s Caswell County, also outside Bladen's northern boundary, 150 miles northeast of Tar Heel. His master's bastard, Roper was sold and swapped throughout the South, returning to Bladen County's

Fayetteville and Charlotte. He was brutally and repeatedly flogged, sometimes nearly to death, beaten and starved, weighted with a ball and chain so heavy that he could scarcely move, though he was still expected to labor, burned, his fingernails squeezed off, and his toenails smashed off. He witnessed many other slaves suffering similar fates, and worse.[24]

Moses Grandy was born in Camden County, North Carolina, 230 miles northeast of Tar Heel, in 1786. He recalled the day his younger brother was sold: "My mother, frantic with grief, resisted taking her child away: she was beaten and held down: she fainted; and when she came to herself, her boy was gone. She made much outcry, for which the master tied her up to a peach tree in the yard and flogged her."[25] Sold to one master after another, Grandy was repeatedly beaten with whip and shovel, and routinely starved. His feet froze in winter for want of shoes, and he possessed just a few articles of clothing. After his bride of eight months was sold away, he never heard of her again. He rarely had bedding or a bed. "In all the slave states," Grandy wrote, "there are men who make a trade of whipping Negroes: they ride about inquiring for jobs of persons who keep no overseer; if there is a negro to be whipped . . . this man is employed when he calls, and does it immediately; his fee is half a dollar. Widows and other females having negroes, get them whipped in this way. Many mistresses insist on the slave who has been flogged, begging pardon for her fault on her knees, and thanking her for the correction."[26]

Thomas Jones was born in 1806 on John Hawes's plantation, between the Black and South Rivers near Wilmington, North Carolina, along the western edge of Bladen County.[27] Hawes, Jones wrote, "owned many slaves on a large plantation and regarded them as barely sentient draft animals."[28] They were overworked, underclothed, and underfed. At age nine, Jones was sold to a new master forty-three miles away who whipped him. He was not permitted to visit his family for thirteen years. "And, then, at the age of twenty-two, was I permitted to revisit my early home. I found it all desolate; the family all broken up; father sold and gone; [brothers and sisters] sold and gone. Mother, prematurely old, heart-broken, utterly desolate, weak and dying, alone remained."[29] His future masters, all in eastern North Carolina, would prove equally brutal.[30]

The most famous North Carolina slave narrative remains that of Harriet Jacobs. Born to vicious masters in 1813 Edenton, two hundred miles northeast of Tar Heel, Jacobs was frequently threatened with rape by a master who reminded her that, as his property, she was required to submit to his every desire. She sketched scenes of neighboring plantations. "Various were the punishments resorted to [by Mr. Litch, who had six hundred slaves]. A favorite one was to tie a rope round a man's body, and suspend him from the ground. A fire was kindled over him, from which was suspended a piece of fat pork. As this cooked, the scalding drops of fat continually fell on the bare flesh. . . . Murder was so common on his plantation that he feared to be alone after nightfall."[31] Then there was Mrs. Wade. "At no hour of the day was there cessation of the lash on her premises. Her labors began with the dawn, and did not cease till long after nightfall. . . . An old slave of hers once said to me, 'It is hell in missis' house. 'Pears I can never get out. Day and night I prays to die.'"[32] Jacobs described being beaten, thrown down a flight of stairs, and watching her jealous master hurl her infant across the room.[33] She was finally hidden in a dark, airless, nine-by-seven-foot garret room with a steeply sloping roof no more than three feet high. She lived there for seven years before she was able to escape to the north.[34]

NOAH'S CURSE

The Robesons of Walnut Grove were devout Presbyterians; sixteen of them lie buried in the cemetery of the abutting Beth Car Presbyterian Church.[35] They did not own black slaves *despite* being devout

Presbyterians; they owned slaves *because* of their religious beliefs. "By all accounts, white southerners in the nineteenth century were among the most devoted Christians in the Western world, but their faith seems only to have strengthened their determination to hold another people in bondage."[36] Recall that the Genesis story of Noah and Ham helped rationalize the Christian oppression of the American Indians. But that story's greatest New World contribution was to underpin African slavery, racial discrimination, and racial segregation in the American South for more than three centuries. Boston abolitionist Theodore Weld thought "this prophecy of Noah . . . the *vade mecum* (something a person regularly carries with them) of slaveholders, and they never venture abroad without it."[37] This is why antebellum abolitionists accused the Christian churches of being "the bulwarks of American slavery."[38]

Noah's Curse was far from the only biblical support for slavery. In 1850, the Virginia Southern Baptist minister Thornton Stringfellow lovingly documented the mass of favorable biblical references to slavery, beginning with Abraham's.[39] But Noah's Curse was preeminent. Stringfellow wrote:

> The first recorded language which was ever uttered in relation to slavery is the inspired language of Noah. In God's stead he says, "Cursed be Canaan: a servant of servants shall he be to his brethren." "Blessed be the Lord God of Shem: and Canaan shall be his servant." "God shall enlarge Japheth, and he shall dwell in the tents of Shem; and Canaan shall be his servant." Gen. ix. 25, 26, 27. Here language is used, showing that the *favor* which God would exercise to the posterity of Shem and Japheth, while they were holding the posterity of Ham in a state of *abject bondage*.[40]

In short, he concluded, "*God decreed slavery*."[41]

Stringfellow wasn't trying to sanction slavery in general but only African slavery, and that is where the Noah story proved its worth.

The ninth chapter of Genesis also explained how humanity had come to occupy the entire world: "of them [Noah's sons] was the whole earth overspread."[42] Before the seventeenth century, one son, Japheth, was often associated with Europe, another son, Shem, with Asia, and the third, Ham, with Africa. By the 1670s, those associations had stabilized.[43] Religious studies professor Stephen R. Haynes explains:

> Even if we assume that Christian advocates of slavery knew the Bible lacked any explicit justification for the "enslavement of Africans, and only Africans in particular," this only confirms the central role of Noah's curse in the proslavery argument. The curse became indispensable precisely because, according to culturally sanctioned views of the Bible, history, and society, it could be regarded as providing the justification for black slavery missing from other texts. If the majority of antebellum proslavery intellectuals failed to emphasize the racial dimensions of Genesis 9:20–27, it is not because they were embarrassed by their inability to prove Ham was the ancestor of black slaves. Rather, they considered Ham's negritude to be . . . self-evident. . . . Proslavery Southerners were drawn to Genesis 9:20–27 because it resonated with their deepest cultural values. . . . For proslavery intellectuals Ham's act of gazing on his father's nakedness and Noah's subsequent curse of the descendants of Ham and Canaan to be "servants of servants" were held to be definitive proof that the enslavement of black Africans was God's will.[44]

Writing in 1852, the scholar, writer, college professor, Episcopal priest, and free black Alexander Crummell thought the curse of Noah

> a general almost universal, opinion in the Christian world. . . . During the long controversy upon the slavery question which

has agitated Christendom, no argument has been so much re-
lied upon, and none more frequently adduced. It was first employed in vindication of the lawfulness of the slave trade.
When the slave trade was abolished, and philanthropists commenced their warfare against the system of slavery, the chief
pro-slavery argument brought forward in support of that system was this text. The friends of the Negro race have had to
meet it when asserted by statesmen in the Legislature, and they
have had to contend against the earnest affirmation of it by
learned divines. And now, although both slavery and the slave
trade are condemned by the general sentiment of the Christian
world, yet the same interpretation is still given to this text, and
the old opinion which was founded upon it still gains credit
and receives support. . . . It is found in books written by learned
men; and it is repeated in lectures, speeches, sermons, and
common conversation.[45]

Crummell gloomily concluded that "so strong and tenacious is
the hold which [slavery] has taken upon the mind of Christendom,
that it seems almost impossible to uproot it."[46] Yet slavery was up-
rooted, everywhere, and I save the implications of that uprooting for
the end of our story.

CHAPTER FIVE

Wilbur

And all that moveth vppon the erth havynge
lyfe shall be youre meate.
—*Genesis 9:3 (William Tyndale, trans., 1530)*[1]

Pigs are wonderfully accommodating. They enjoy
company, even that of other species, and they are not
territorial. They are willing to move when we do and to
look after their own large litters. They don't need to be
herded and are easily trained to come and go, responding
to the sound of a horn or call. And they are smart. Show
any pig something just once, and it gets it.
—*Lyall Watson*, THE WHOLE HOG *(2004)*[2]

I T WAS HOT at summer's end, 2007. Just after the heat broke,
Wilbur was born in a farrowing barn outside Tar Heel. Huge
ventilating fans pushed the triple-digit-degree air through the barn.
At least that was what likely happened. I wasn't there. Probably no
human was, and if any were, none would have noticed. In the second

chapter of Genesis, God brought the world's animals to Adam to be named. It was his duty. A named animal is a unique individual. I named this piglet Wilbur. Wilbur's keepers gave him no name. Instead, they cut a number into his body, using a standardized system of ear notching.[3] A numbered animal is merely a unit of production, worth what the market will bear.

A sow can have from six to thirty teats, though some may not work. Wilbur's mother possessed the more usual twelve. Soon after birth, Wilbur, blind, struggled to his feet and instinctively began trying to locate one of his mother's nipples by smell. Wilbur's first social lesson was "teat order." He learned which teat was his and stuck to it, which reduced intrafamily conflict. Piglets who haven't staked a claim to a working teat, preferably one up front, usually die within a few days.[4] So long as the number of working teats exceeds the number of piglets, things usually go all right for every piglet, and things went all right for Wilbur. He found his teat, staked his claim, and began gaining the five and a half ounces of weight per day that a newborn piglet usually gains during the first week of life. He made six and a half ounces a day during his second week of life, and half a pound each day of the third.[5]

North Carolina pioneered the industrial, or factory, farming of pigs.[6] Wilbur was just one of a crop of 1 million piglets born in 2007 in Bladen County, one of 5 million born in Bladen, Sampson, and Duplin Counties, one of 10 million born in North Carolina, and one of 100 million born in the United States. Use of the word "crop" may seem inappropriate when applied to a group of animals. But it's a standard term in the factory farming industry and is routinely used by governments. According to North Carolina's Department of Agriculture and Consumer Services, that state's 2007 "pig crop" was 20.4 million.[7] The word "crop" surfaced in one famous English case from the 1990s. McDonald's Corporation (U.S.) and its British subsidiary, McDonald's Restaurants Ltd., sued a former minibus driver and a postman in a London court for defamation over statements they made about the way McDonald's treated its animals. McDonald's expert witness, Neville Gregory, testified that broiler chickens were grown together as a "crop." A Mr. Bruton, who made his living catching the unfortunate broiler chickens whose time was up, explained that the birds were often injured in the catching process, and testified even the "injured birds with broken legs or wings or scabs were loaded for slaughter," because the farmers told him that "they are all part of our crop; it goes to the factory."[8] The presiding judge commented that "crop" "is an appropriate term because their mass cultivation appears, superficially at least, to be closer to plant cultivation than traditional animal husbandry."[9]

WILBUR'S GENEALOGY

Wilbur was a member of the subspecies *Sus scrofa domesticus*. His family likely descended from one of the couple dozen subspecies of wild boars that evolved in different parts of the world in response to local conditions. They are not native to the Americas; every American pig is either born outside the hemisphere or is descended from one who was. DNA studies reveal that humans domesticated wild boars at least seven times—in northern India, central Europe, Italy, southeastern Asia, and the islands of southeastern Asia. Archaeological evidence shows that pigs were being domesticated nine thousand years ago in China and Turkey. Everywhere pigs were domesticated, they escaped. Today pigs live wild on every continent but Antarctica and roam wild through most American states. Eventually they will populate every state.[10] Modern European pigs are all descended from the European wild boar, which probably replaced an earlier domesticated subspecies that had arrived in Europe from the Near East during Neolithic times.[11] Because large numbers of smaller, lighter, fast-maturing Chinese and Southeast Asian pigs were imported to Europe in the eighteenth century and bred there with the native European boar, there are probably no pigs left who are entirely descended from the European wild boar.[12]

Round-backed and long-legged, with a coarse brownish coat, tusks formed from upper canines, sharp lower canines, and a long tail, wild boars everywhere resemble one another. Although they prefer deciduous forests, especially river valleys and marshy places, they survive in tropical rain forests, grasslands, scrub, and near-deserts.[13] Biologist Juliet Clutton-Brock writes that wild pigs "are much more like dogs and people than they are like cattle or sheep."[14] For one thing, they scavenge. For another, they are extremely social and like to huddle and rub against each other. They build nests with twigs and grass and branches in which to give birth to their young. They are gregarious, with six to twenty of them forming a herd or "sounder."[15] Piglets are born immature and stay near their mother and her nest for a few weeks. When they leave the nest, mother and children stay in frequent contact by touching noses and engaging in what Clutton-Brock calls "a complicated series of vocalizations." They remain together as a family, often with other mothers and their children, and an adult male.[16] They forage for food four to eight hours a day, during which time they may travel six miles. They may wander 40 square miles and travel 150 miles in a year. They eat omnivorously—fruits, fish, reptiles, amphibians, mammals, grass, roots. They are clean and prefer to rest away from the places in which they eat and defecate. They may live to the age of twenty.[17]

Pigs have an exquisite sense of smell. That is why male and female together produce odors from nine glandular areas.[18] They can detect aromas from seven miles away and from twenty-five feet below the earth. The truffle manufactures a chemical named 5-alpha-androstol, which happens to be the testosterone that boars produce in their salivary glands during mating season. When sows smell it, they start digging furiously.[19]

The biologist Lyall Watson writes that pigs

> are fastidious and sensitive in every sense of the word. They all
> have an acute sense of smell. In truth they are built for it. The
> snout is at the same time arm, hand, spade, and primary sense
> organ: a probe that makes it possible to travel, feed, drink, and
> interact with others, even in the dark. In tests of acuity pigs
> have proven that plastic cards, once nuzzled by them, can be
> picked out from a pack days later—even after being washed.
> The olfactory bulb of pig brains is well-developed and is served
> by an extensive area of sensory cells at the back of the large
> nasal cavity. This direct chemical connection to the forebrain
> deals with the recognition and memory of odors, making it
> possible for newborn piglets to locate, not just their dam, but
> the one teat of hers that they have adopted as their own. In ad-
> dition to this primary sense of smell, pigs have a functional sec-
> ond system, beginning with the vomeronasal or "Jacobsen's
> organ" on either side of the nasal septum. This is sensitive to
> pheromones, airborne hormones that provide information
> about social and sexual states, and it sends news of these to the
> limbic system—that part of the pig's hindbrain that deals with
> the coordination of basic behavior such as sex and aggression.[20]

Remember, there were no large domesticated animals in the
North America in which the Europeans first stepped. Some odd and
puzzling bones suggest a lost history of pigs in America.[21] One Texas
pig skull was found embedded with a prehistoric projectile, while a
two-to-four-millennia-old pig skeleton has been pulled from an Indian midden in Arkansas. But we know nothing more. The first historical North American pigs were dumped by Columbus over the
gunwales of one of the seventeen ships that made his 1493
Caribbean voyage. Once these Iberian pigs pulled themselves onto

the shore of Hispaniola, they began running wild, reproducing with abandon. Less than a quarter-century on, Cortez introduced pigs to the mainland; dozens followed his little army north, reproducing madly and feeding his soldiers, to the Aztecs' sorrow. In the 1530s, Francisco Pizarro ferried pigs to Peru. Later the French would take pigs to Quebec, the Dutch West India Company would bring pigs to New Netherlands, and the English had them on Roanoke Island.[22] In May 1539, Hernando de Soto sailed with three hundred pigs from Cuba to Charlotte Harbor, Florida.[23] A year later, two months into their three-year, 3,100-mile march through the American South and Southeast, de Soto's army arrived in the mountains of western North Carolina. They had hundreds of pigs in tow. The expedition dined daily on pig meat, presented pigs by the dozen to friendly Indians, and suffered the theft of hundreds more. Still, more than seven hundred pigs were following de Soto's army when it reached the Mississippi in 1543. Some of them escaped, and their feral descendants can be found today in many American states.[24] By the 1700s, feral hogs were more numerous in North Carolina than in any other English colony.[25] Most wild North Carolina boars are today confined to its western mountains. But some have been reported around Bladen County's Green Swamp, fewer than twenty miles northeast of Tar Heel.[26]

WILBUR'S MOTHER, OR, THE LIFE OF A BREEDING SOW

Wilbur's appearance marked the eighth time his mother had given birth over the past three and a half years. Sows gestate for just under three months. During each of her eight pregnancies, Wilbur's mother had been confined to a seven-foot-by-two-foot metal "gestation crate." The "farrowing crate" in which she nursed her piglets was built somewhat larger to accommodate them all, but not much larger: it was five feet by seven feet. Weighing more than four hundred pounds and stretching the length of the crate, she could scarcely stand and was prevented by the iron bars from moving about or building nests, as would have been part of her innate drive before giving birth.[27]

She was thin and lame. The number of piglets she was producing had been decreasing since her fourth litter. That could mean only one thing for a profitable hog-producing operation. According to the Farm Animal Health and Resource Management Department of the College of Veterinary Medicine of North Carolina State University:

> An important measure of profitability of a swine enterprise is the number of pounds of pork marketed at or above the basis. Market price times pounds marketed yields gross income from which production costs must be subtracted to calculate enterprise profit. . . . Management practices employed in the farrowing house have a major impact upon the pounds of pork marketed, and therefore enterprise profitability. Obviously the number of weaned (successfully produced) is essential to maximizing the number of pounds of pork marketed, but so too is the average weight at which the pigs are weaned.[28]

As explained in the *Proceedings of the North Carolina Healthy Hogs Seminar*, a farrowing barn should constantly be striving to increase its number of "pigs weaned per sow per year," or PWSY. The PWSY is calculated by multiplying the "number of pigs weaned per litter" by the "number of litters farrowed per sow per year."[29] Profit also varies with the maximum number of "functional teats." The Animal Health and Resource Management Department folks are unequivocal about how to fix the problem of a sow's declining PWSY: "Cull old . . . sows that do not wean large numbers of piglets." Rigorous culling combined with replacement by a sow with a larger PWSY is the key to profitability.

> Replacement decisions are usually based on biological and economic considerations. There are two types of culling that occur in breeding herds. Involuntary culling is the removal of females

from the breeding herd for reasons such as death, anestrous, sterility, abortion, lameness, farrowing difficulties and old age. Voluntary culling is the removal of females from the breeding herd based on performance criteria such as numbers of pigs farrowed and weaned, weaning weights, days from weaning to rebreeding, production indices, and size or condition.[30]

In case the reader misses this rose among the thorns, the authors spell out five "take-home points": "Maximizing the average number of functional teats per sow will increase the number of pigs weaned per litter. Maximizing functional teat availability is accomplished by strict selection of gilts (that is, breeding sows), use of maternal genetics, and culling older sows that wean low numbers of piglets."[31] It takes about 500 sows with reasonably high PWSY to produce a weekly truckload of 200 pigs for Tar Heel, 5,000 sows to keep Bladen County's finishing barns filled with 2,000 pigs a week, and 400,000 sows to keep Tar Heel humming at a kill rate of 32,000 pigs a day.[32] The bottom line is that the number of pigs produced per sow per litter per year (PPSY) must be kept as high as possible for maximum profit. Some experts predict that the most efficient commercial hog farms will soon be producing 25 PPSY, with the most productive reaching more than 26 PPSY.[33] That will heavily burden sows.

Say a sow gives birth to 11 piglets on an average of 2.3 times a year. She will annually give birth to 25.3 piglets, live and dead. To reach 26 PPSY, she will have to give birth more often than 2.3 times a year. Or she will have to produce more than 11 piglets per litter. Or do both. Not every piglet is born alive. If she averages just half a stillborn piglet per litter and loses fewer than 10 percent of her litter before weaning, both good numbers, she will fall below 22 PPSY. The factory hog-farming industry today considers 20 PPSY good production to wring from a breeding sow. Less efficient farms produce fewer than 14 PPSY.[34]

A factory hog farmer is limited in the ways he can increase a sow's PPSY. Eight variables contribute to sow productivity. The two most important are the number of a sow's "nonproductive days"—those wasted days when she is neither pregnant nor lactating—and the weaning age of her piglets.[35] Today's most efficient sows are nonproductive nearly 60 days a year. Fewer than 20 nonproductive days a year trespasses the biological absolutes of even an uber-sow: it assumes 2.3 litters a year and a mere seven days' lapse from last wean to first estrus.

Two factors more modestly influence sow productivity: farrowing rate, or the rate of conception, which is currently about 80 percent, and the number of piglets born alive, which exceeds 10.[36] Pork scientists are working hard to increase both. In 2003, North Carolina State University scientists demonstrated that they could select for increasing litter size over nine generations and increase the number of pigs born by 0.83 pigs a litter.[37] *Pig Production*, a textbook published in 2003, assures us that "new research in breeding and genetics has identified breeds and at least one specific gene that codes for a high number of pigs born. With less than 10% preweaning mortality and fewer than 1.0 stillbirths, the farm that has 14 pigs born (that is 14 piglets born in each litter) will wean over 27 PPSY. If a herd has 14 total pigs born and low stillbirths and preweaning mortality the unit could potentially wean 30 PPSY!"[38] Fourteen piglets born per litter times 2.3 litters a year means that 32.2 piglets could be born per sow per year. If preweaning mortality and stillbirths together total less than 7 percent, then there you go—30 PPSY.

"A Quantum Leap in Pig Productivity"

That prediction is coming true. Today sows in the United Kingdom are weaning an average of 20.5 piglets a year, French sows 23.9, Dutch ones 24.3, and Danish sows 24.7.[39] In 1992, Smithfield

Premium Genetics (SPG) acquired exclusive American rights to the genetic lines of lean pigs that Britain's National Pig Development (NPD) Company, in the business of genetically modifying pigs since 1969, had developed. Companies sell purebred pigs to commercial producers, such as Smithfield, as "seedstock" that buyers cross with other lines in hopes of producing piglets with more desirable characteristics. They may produce more muscles more quickly; their meat may be more tender, juicy, or flavorful. They may have higher rates of conception and increased litter sizes, a greater resistance to disease, higher sexual drive, lower aggression, fewer abnormal behaviors such as tail-biting and navel-sucking, and more desirable handling responses.[40]

NPD began importing the traditional Chinese Meishan pig into Britain in the 1980s. Executives were enthralled with the number of the sows' teats, but little else. "It's fatty, the meat on the damn thing is terrible, and it's ugly," complained Roger Widdowsen, an NPD general manager. The Meishan's folds of skin, the way its long ears obscure its eyes, and its thick and bristly black hair moved one NPD employee to describe the animal as looking like a "pile of old coats."[41] NPD soon crossed Meishans with its own Large White and Landrace breeds, then rigorously selected them to produce cuter pigs with less fat, more teats, and a higher libido. One line became the Manor Meishan, which NPD unveiled in 1992 and called a "quantum leap in pig productivity" that would "take the world pig industry into the 21st century."[42] "With all that in the way of what pig people call 'motherability' going for it, the Manor Meishan is reckoned to be able to produce 30 piglets per annum versus 25 for the best of other breeds," reported the *International Herald Tribune*.[43] For starters, the Manor Meishan sow was engineered for eighteen teats. "It's no good producing 18 piglets if you have only got 14 teats," explained Rosetta Nicholson, NPD's public relations person.[44] By 2006, Stephen Curtis, an NPD founder, by then managing another pig-breeding company, ACMC, had created the Meidam breed. It has sixteen teats, gives 15 percent more milk, and farrows thirty pigs a year; one Yorkshire farmer's Meidam gave birth to forty piglets in 2004.[45]

Smithfield flew three thousand lean British NPD "nucleus animals" to four American farms.[46] From three breeds it planned to develop "Smithfield Lean Generation Pork" breeds. By the late 1990s Smithfield owned more than 300,000 NPD breeding sows and was producing 3.3 million NPD pigs.[47] The following year, Smithfield added more nucleus farms and a fourth breed. "By exercising complete control over genetics and nutritional regimen," Smithfield produced 700,000 sows who were churning out 13 million piglets in "the leanest hog in large-scale commercial production in the United States."[48] Pigs like Wilbur were members of Smithfield's "Lean Generation."

Choice Cuts

Some claim that cooked meat and fat from sexually mature pigs smells or tastes of "boar taint." It's a mixture of two naturally occurring compounds, androsterone, a pheromone produced in pig testicles and stored in the fat surrounding their muscles, and skatole, derived from the Greek word for "dung," which is created in the digestive tract. Females and castrati can metabolize skatole, but uncastrated boars can't, and so it accumulates in the fat.[49] That's why Wilbur was castrated at the age of two weeks. The *New Pork Industry Handbook* tells us how that should be done.

1. Hold the piglet by both hind legs with its head down.
2. Using the thumb, push up on both testicles.
3. Make an incision through the skin of the scrotum over each testicle in the direction of the tail.
4. Be sure the incisions are made low on the scrotal sac to allow for fluid drainage.

5. It does not matter if you cut through the white membrane of each testicle or not.
6. Pop the testicles through each incision and pull on them slightly.
7. Pull each testicle out while pressing your thumb against the piglet's pelvis.
8. Thumb pressure on the pelvis is important to ensure that the testicular cords break off at the point of your thumb rather than deep inside the body, which may promote development of a hernia.
9. If necessary the testicle may be cut free of the cord using a scraping motion.
10. Cut away any cord or connective tissue protruding from the incision and spray the wound with antiseptic.[50]

As often happens, a few hours after Wilbur was castrated inflammation set in, and he began to suffer. No one noticed.[51]

Wilbur's eight baby teeth were clipped to the gums hours after birth to stop him from sinking them into his mother's nipples.[52] Hours later, all but two-thirds of an inch of his tail was cut away to prevent the other piglets, desperate to chew on something, from gnawing his tail and perhaps infecting it.[53] Then he was given the first of numerous vaccinations.[54]

Wilbur's ears were notched at age three days so that he could be identified. Each notch was cut one-quarter to three-sixteenths of an inch deep. This procedure is often performed last because it's a bloodier business than tail-docking, teeth-clipping, or injection.[55] The right ear of every piglet in a litter—known as the "litter ear"— is given the same series of notches. Each left ear is given a unique set of notches. When the whole thing is finished, each ear carries no fewer than one and no greater than nine notches; no more than two notches may be made in each quadrant. It takes practice to read ears. Different areas of a piglet's ear stand for the numbers 1, 3, 9, 27, and

81. Every number from 1 to 161 can therefore be notched on each ear. The numbers on the right ear add up to the litter number. Combined, the numbers on the left ear identify each individual pig. Wilbur's right ear was notched nine times: twice in the 1, 3, 9, and 27 areas and once in the 81 quadrant. His left ear was notched twice in the 1 area and twice in the 3 area. His unique number was therefore 161–7; he was the seventh pig notched from that factory farm's 161st litter for that year.

A pasture piglet is weaned at the age of six to ten weeks. When piglets began to be factory-farmed, their weaning age was dropped to four to five weeks. Then it was lowered again. Wilbur was lucky. On some factory farms, he would have been separated from his mother less than two weeks after birth, sometimes one week, because the shorter the time from birth to wean, the sooner a sow can be returned to production. Wilbur received three weeks of mother's milk. Then he was taken to the nursery.

He slept poorly that first night in the nursery. On the second and third days, he suffered minor injuries from tussles with the more aggressive of the twenty-three piglets in his pen as each struggled to find his place. No one could move around much, for the eight-foot-by-nine-foot pens were jammed. But that was intentional, for crowding produces a higher profit. Although the weight gain of some of the piglets might be slightly reduced, all the piglets taken together tend to accumulate more weight in a crowded pen.[56] Wilbur had just three square feet of space. He was so cramped that it was impossible for him to create the separate areas for sleeping and eating, defecating and urinating, and escaping that is normal for pigs. The more dominant piglets attacked him. He instinctively needed to suck and, in his deprivation, began "belly-nosing," that is, massaging the bellies of piglets with his snout.[57] Other piglets belly-nosed him until he became so uncomfortable that he tried to escape. But there was nowhere to go. The other piglets would chase him, and sometimes he had to confront, and even fight, his pursuer when cornered.[58] He fended them off as best he could. His injuries weren't noticed by any human. He just didn't feel like eating for a couple days. Then, suddenly, he felt hungry and began to gorge.[59] Diarrhea struck and gripped him for several days. Other piglets suffered the same. Some died. Some nearly died. Wilbur survived.[60]

But he never saw his mother again. Factory-farmed piglets never see their mothers again. None of Wilbur's seventy sisters and brothers and half-sisters and half-brothers ever saw their mother again. For three weeks, she had functioned as a frustrated, breathing milk machine for Wilbur and her other children. But after weaning, she was always returned to the gestation barn where, a week later, she would resume being stressed by boars into estrus. This time she was not returned.

A breeding sow may be culled for many reasons, most of which concern her failure to reproduce adequately. Remember, PPSY is the key to factory farm profitability. A sow can fail in many ways to maintain an appropriately high PPSY. She may begin to have trouble conceiving. That happens about one-eighth of the time. A quarter of breeding sows become diseased. One in twenty sows begin producing too little milk. The same percentage begin aborting or taking too long to return to estrus. She may begin producing too few piglets each litter. One-seventh of them do that.[61]

Wilbur's mother's PPSY had been dropping for almost a year. The farm manager had decided to cull her a litter ago, then changed his mind. The question now was not whether she would be killed; the question was whether she would be fattened and sold for meat, then killed, or simply killed and tossed on a heap to rot.

Her thinness, from feeding her piglets, didn't necessarily disqualify her from a trip directly to the Tar Heel slaughterhouse. The *National Hog Farmer* explains that

> some healthy sows with superior performance in lactation will leave the farrowing crate quite thin. These sows may be good candidates to feed. Obviously, sows that are thin because they

are not healthy (possible ulcer or respiratory conditions) or are lame usually are not good candidates to feed for additional weight gain. Similarly, sows with shoulder sores may not be good candidates for further feeding, depending on how severe the sore is or if it appears to be causing lameness. The relatively unthrifty and lame sows should be sold as quickly as possible or be euthanized in a timely, humane manner.[62]

Wilbur's mother was not fattened. Instead, a stockman spray-painted a scarlet KILL on her back, which marked her for destruction, then left to feed some piglets. When he returned for her, she must have sensed something was wrong, for she resisted. He stuck his thumb into her eye, and when she dug in her hooves, cuffed her twice on the head with an iron gate rod until she was too stunned and helpless to prevent him from dragging her from her stall into a side yard. There he shot her in the forehead with a captive bolt pistol about twenty-five millimeters above her eyes. The penetrating bolt angled down toward her gullet. Mercifully, the distance to the killing ground had been a matter of only a few yards, she was exhausted, her resistance, though determined, was feeble, her killer's arms were strong, the pistol was in good working order, and his aim was true. Except for the piglets in her final litter, Wilbur's mother had outlived all her children, each of whom had lived, or would live, for almost exactly six months.

DOMESTICATION AND SLAVERY

Yale slavery historian David Brion Davis has observed that "the truly striking fact . . . is the antiquity and almost universal acceptance of the concept of the slave as a human being who is legally owned, used, sold, or otherwise disposed of as if he or she were a domestic animal. This parallel persisted in the similarity of naming, branding and even pricing slaves according to their equivalent in cows, horses, camels, pigs, and chickens."[63] In the 1930s, a former

American slave reminisced about Ole Merrill, a slave trader who would "buy and sell niggers just like hogs."[64] Mesopotamian slaves were disfigured to identify them three thousand years ago, and were branded like livestock.[65] The first African slaves shipped to Lisbon in the fifteenth century "were stripped naked and marketed and priced exactly like livestock."[66] The Englishman Samuel Purchas wrote of African slaves in 1613 that "the Portugals doe mark them as we doe sheepe with a hot Iron."[67] South Carolina newspaper advertisements of the eighteenth and nineteenth centuries identified escaped slaves by their brand, often the initials of their owner.[68]

That Wilbur, his mother, his sisters and brothers, and Cezar, Old Betty, Old Chloe, and Little Chloe should be treated in a similar way in Bladen County, more than a century apart, is no coincidence. Juliet Clutton-Brock writes that a domesticated animal—and that could be an animal of any species, including *Homo sapiens*—"has been bred in captivity for purposes of economic profit to a human community that maintains total control over its breeding, organization of territory, and food supply."[69] Domesticated wild animals share characteristics that lend themselves to slavery. They are strong, adaptable, and gregarious. Their social groups are based on a hierarchy that accepts human dominance. They eat versatile diets, are gentle and easygoing, breed readily even when confined or closely herded, and reproduce easily, and in large numbers, while in captivity.[70]

Domestication, says Clutton-Brock, may originally emerge from a relationship of trust in which humans and nonhumans share resources. Then it is transformed into one of "total human control and domination. . . . In order to be domesticated animals have to be incorporated into the social structure of a human community and become objects of ownership, inheritance, purchase and exchange."[71] For the historian Karl Jacoby, there is

> the central position of force in both institutions. Slaves and domesticated animals exist in relationships of domination requir-

ing a master as much as a servant. In theory, the master commands; the servant obeys. But in the real world . . . a master's
control over either domestic animal or slave derives from the
willingness to use violence when necessary to make animals
and slaves comply with one's wishes. Whips, chains, castration,
and branding are ultimately all means to enforce a common
control by the master. . . . In fact, since *homo sapiens* is a social
animal, like nearly every creature successfully domesticated by
humans, one can interpret slavery as a little more than the extension of domestication to humans.[72]

Lyall Watson thought that "domestication, as far as pigs were
concerned, was a good deal—their own idea almost, or at worst a
treaty between consenting intelligent parties who entered into an
agreement in a spirit of mutual self-interest."[73] However, any uber-
boar who "chose" domestication nine thousand years ago would
have failed to anticipate the factory farm and the Tar Heel slaughterhouse. The writer Stephen Budiansky claims that certain animals "chose" domestication toward the end of the last ice age,
when they "exchanged elaborate defenses for dependence, adult-
hood for perpetual adolescence."[74] "Perpetual adolescence" refers to
"neoteny," the fact that humans often select for such juvenile characteristics in their domesticated animals as a shorter jaw and facial
bones, crowded mouths, smaller teeth, larger heads and eyes as
compared to the body and face, fatter legs and feet, and submissive,
fearless, and curious personalities.[75] Unlike wild boars, for example,
domestic pigs deposit fat under their skin and possess curly tails, "a
short muzzle, crowded teeth and a steep forehead."[76] David Brion
Davis explains that "neoteny, the development of childlike characteristics in slaves, was clearly the goal of many [human] slaveholders."[77] But not just slaveholders. "In patriarchal societies, women
were treated like domesticated or petlike animals in order to ensure
their dependence and submission; they not only worked in the
fields, but reproduced, augmenting the size and wealth of tribes

and lineage."[78] Every attempt to domesticate human slaves failed, not for want of trying, but because there wasn't enough time for the necessary biological changes to occur. By using traditional breeding techniques and genetic manipulation, we have succeeded with the pig.

CHAPTER SIX

The Smell of Money

Older agricultural instructors (and even some younger
ones) may say to their students, when the smell of the
pigs reaches their noses on the first day of swine class at
the farm, "Take a deep breath, everyone;
that is the smell of money!"

—*John McGlone and Wilson Pond,* PIG PRODUCTION *(2003)*[1]

In the United States, where NPD [National Pig
Development Company] signed an exclusive franchising
arrangement with one of that country's largest pig
producers, the average size of a pig herd was no more
than 500. Now NPD's ultraefficient American franchisee,
Smithfield Foods, is raising them in farms housing up to
10,000 animals. In its concern for animal welfare, said
Robert (Bo) Manley Smithfield, executive vice
president, "we lag behind Britain and I hope
we continue to do so for some time."

—*Eric Ipsen, "The Next-Generation Pig" (1992)*[2]

> We think the typical production system's designs
> and operations are very animal-friendly.
>
> —*Steven Cohen, spokesperson for the National Pork Producers Council*[3]

E IGHT THOUSAND PEOPLE work full-time in North Carolina raising hogs. The jobs of another sixteen thousand depend on them—in retail, wholesale, transportation, and agricultural
manufacturing. Eleven thousand more slaughter hogs. Another
eleven thousand work in associated industries. In total, the raising
and slaughtering of hogs keeps nearly fifty thousand North Carolinians working and accounts for $7 billion in annual sales.

WHERE DID THE HOG FARMS GO?

In 1998, professors from the University of North Carolina's School
of Public Health pinpointed the locations of all 2,514 factory hog
farms then on file with the state's Division of Water Quality. The
hog farms turned out to be located primarily in North Carolina's
poorest and blackest areas, such as Bladen County, which is just 70
percent as wealthy as the rest of North Carolina, and 75 percent
blacker.[4] The county's industrial hog farms are easy to spot from the
air. They're the long, white structures situated beside small green lagoons. I hoped to get onto one of these farms and expected no trouble finding them. I was wrong. They weren't situated next to major
roads, nor even minor ones, or at least not the roads I turned down.
Frustrated, unable to find them, I contacted folks I thought might
be able to help. But they couldn't. Everyone assured me, "They're
everywhere—you'll find them." But I couldn't find them.

I had an idea. Experts claim that one hog produces two, four,
some say even ten times as much waste as a human does.[5] In 1997,
Bladen County's 758,000 hogs were producing at least 1.4 million
tons and 350 million gallons of waste.[6] Home to an additional

100,000 hogs in 2007, Bladen County was by then expelling nearly as much waste as all 9 million human residents of the Tar Heel State put together. That's a lot of muck to store in open-pit manure lagoons, which might stretch the length of several football fields. If I jumped in one, I would have trouble touching bottom.

Open-pit manure lagoons have had their problems in North Carolina. In 1995, one ruptured and dumped 25 million gallons of raw sewage into the New River, which flows toward the Atlantic Ocean three counties east of Bladen. Ten million fish died, and 364,000 acres of coastal wetlands were closed to shellfishing.[7] In the wake of flooding caused by Hurricane Floyd in 1999, a Department of the Environment and Natural Resources spokesperson estimated that there had been fifty or sixty lagoon spills.[8] Murphy Family Farms was fined $40,000 for thirteen violations that involved dumping 1.5 million gallons of muck into a tributary of the Cape Fear River.[9]

As the public health professors realized, factory hog farm producers must obtain a permit from the Division of Water Quality if they want to raise more than 250 pigs. I decided to pull those permits in the hope that the addresses of Bladen County's industrial hog farms, and the number of pigs raised on each, would be printed on them. I began corresponding with the North Carolina Division of Water Quality's Aquifer Protection Section and asked to meet with a representative when I traveled to Raleigh in August 2007.

My pen pal at the Aquifer Protection Section turned out to be Jaya Joshi, who worked inside a boxy government building near the intersection of Interstate 440 and U.S. Route 1 in Raleigh. He seemed pleased that I had turned up. He walked me down a short hallway to a large, open, low-ceilinged room filled with filing cabinets containing water permits for all the factory hog farms for all of North Carolina's one hundred counties. I said that Bladen County's permits would be quite sufficient.

He pointed to two large cabinets. I randomly opened a drawer and plucked out a permit. He took it and explained how to figure out what it meant. I said I thought it was going to take me a long time to go through every permit, which was a shame, as I was just seeking the address of each farm and the number of pigs on them. If *that* was all I was looking for, Mr. Joshi said, he could pull that information up on his computer and print it out. Soon I would be on my way. Over the next half-hour he did just that. That night I studied his printouts in my hotel room alongside my *Delorme North Carolina Atlas and Gazetteer* and local MapQuest printouts and tried to determine anew where the factory hog farms were located. Next morning I drove to Bladen County.

I wasn't sure what I was going to do when I found a factory hog farm. I decided I would knock on the door of the nearest long, low, white building that stood beside a stinking lagoon and ask whoever appeared to show me around. But try as I might, I still couldn't find a single factory hog farm, and supposedly I had their addresses. Four times that August I found the roads on which hog producers had informed the Aquifer Protection Section their farms were located, and four times I came up empty. The really irritating part was finally locating the indicated road, but not being able to find the farm, even though I would drive up and down the road searching for it. Eventually I returned home without having set foot on a single factory hog farm.

INSIDE A "LARGE CONCENTRATED ANIMAL FEEDING OPERATION"

I located two men who had managed to get inside one. One was Matthew Scully, who had been a special assistant to, and senior speechwriter for, President George W. Bush. He had written speeches for Vice Presidents Cheney and Quayle and would pen the stem-winder that Sarah Palin delivered at the 2008 Republican Convention in her unsuccessful bid for the vice presidency. He was also a contributing editor to the conservative political journal *Na-*

tional Review. Scully told me that Smithfield Farms had made certain incorrect assumptions about his attitude toward nonhuman animals merely from the fact of his conservative politics, and he had felt under no obligation to correct them.[10] In his beautifully crafted book *Dominion*, Scully had written about his visit to Farm 2149, a Duplin County hog production facility near Warsaw, about sixty miles northeast of Tar Heel.[11]

I never learned the other man's name. In the late fall of 2007, I read that an undercover investigator had been working in an industrial hog farm located halfway between Tar Heel and Warsaw in Sampson County, the next county east over from Bladen. I contacted his employer, People for the Ethical Treatment of Animals (PETA), to seek permission to speak to him. PETA wouldn't give me his name or tell me anything about him, but said he would call me if he felt like it. PETA also sent me CDs that contained videotape that he had shot while working undercover. Because the investigator wanted to continue his undercover work, I agreed not to ask his name. I decided to call him "Mr. Nikita." I spoke with Mr. Nikita three times. He said he had begun working as a "herd technician 1" at the Murphy Family Ventures Garland Sow Farm on September 13, 2007. That was about the time Wilbur was born. Mr. Nikita said that the Murphy Family Ventures Garland Sow Farm contained about 3,500 sows and a dozen boars. It sold about 2,000 piglets a week. That made it a "Large Concentrated Animal Feeding Operation," as defined by the U.S. Environmental Protection Agency under the Clean Water Act.

PETA dispatched Mr. Nikita to Sampson County after it received information that hogs were being abused at a Murphy Family Ventures facility. First, he needed to get onto the farm. He drove to the Murphy Family Ventures headquarters on Highway 117 in South Wallace, about an hour and fifteen minutes southeast of Tar Heel.[12] Murphy Family Ventures is an independent contract hog producer for Murphy-Brown LLC, which is a livestock production subsidiary of Smithfield Farms. According to Smithfield, "Murphy-Brown LLC is the world's largest hog producer."[13] Murphy Family Ventures says it "is committed to employing and retaining people who want to apply their talents to the production of quality pork for the national food chain."[14]

According to the textbook *Pig Production*:

> Modern technology and efficient pen and barn design have made such advances that one person can care for up to 8,000 pigs in a day. . . . To spend 8hr/d caring for 8,000 pigs or 1 hr/1,000 pigs and to provide good animal care requires an alert, well-trained individual. Assuming that ½ hr. is spent treating individual pigs or equipment problems, the worker must look at 33 pigs/min, or about 2 sec/pig. . . . The dedicated stockperson has the following features:
>
> - A good work ethic
> - Job satisfaction and a positive attitude
> - A healthy positive attitude toward pigs
> - A basic understanding of pig biology
> - The ability to develop skills in providing animal care
> - The ability to develop interpersonal skills useful in people management
> - The ability to plan complex tasks[15]

Pigs and humans share similar anatomies and physiologies. Our hearts, lungs, livers, kidneys, and spleens are about the same size. Our digestive systems, kidneys, livers, pancreases, skin, and other organs work about the same way. In biomedical research, "pigs are utilized as a model species in cardiovascular, skeletal, urinary, nervous, and digestive system function and in dermatology, alcoholism, teratology (the study of the processes that lead to abnor-

mal development and birth defects), ethology, reproductive biology, immunology, anesthesiology, surgical studies, and develop-
mental biology."[16] I asked Mr. Nikita if he knew anything about
pigs or pig biology or animal care when he applied for the job. He
said he hadn't a clue.

He sprouted stubble, then drove to South Wallace, where he
completed Murphy Family Ventures' standard employment application. Apparently, his application was faxed around, for the manager
of the Murphy Family Ventures Garland Sow Farm called to offer a
job. Mr. Nikita drove to Garland the next day. It wasn't near the
farm that had been the subject of PETA complaints, but he signed
on anyway. I asked whether he believed that he had worked on a
typical eastern North Carolina factory hog farm. He thought he
had. The farm manager said he had a position open in the breeding
department but wanted first to ensure that Mr. Nikita would get
along with him and his future coworkers. When he was satisfied Mr.
Nikita could, the manager showed him around the barns and explained what he would be doing as a herd technician 1. As I would
do, the farm manager asked Mr. Nikita if he had any experience
working with pigs. He replied that he had never been around pigs in
his life. No matter—he got the job.

I never met Mr. Nikita, though I interviewed him for hours by
telephone. He is soft-spoken, intelligent, and articulate. Had he
graduated from college? He had, but omitted that fact from his application. He jotted down the name of the high school from which
he had graduated nine years before and left it at that. When the
farm manager asked him if he had attended college, he said no. A
college degree would have entitled him to begin work at a higher
pay rate instead of the $7 an hour he was initially offered. The me-
dian household income for Sampson County was $33,824 in 2004;
the last census reported that 69 percent of county residents over the
age of twenty-five possessed a high school degree, while 11 percent
had a college degree—fewer than half the nationwide percentage.[17]

It is unlikely that many baccalaureates work inside factory hog farms. He would have stood out.

I repeatedly tried to get inside the Tar Heel slaughterhouse. When every attempt failed, I was advised to apply for a job there and observe incognito, as one *New York Times* reporter had done. Unlikely. A fifty-six-year-old, white, gray-haired, Boston-educated lawyer would have presented quite a spectacle at the Smithfield employment office. What about a twenty-eight-year-old, college-educated animal rights activist who was clueless about pigs? Mr. Nikita laughed. He had worked real hard, he said, to "dumb myself down" and didn't shave for a while before he applied. He ended up working alongside a manager, an assistant manager, a breeding department manager, two stockpersons who assisted with breeding, and three others who helped with farrowing. I asked him what education his coworkers had achieved. He didn't know for sure, but doubted that most of them had finished high school.

Mr. Nikita was never instructed on any aspect of animal husbandry. His training consisted entirely of watching what his coworkers did. He could find no materials on the factory farm to consult. For the first couple of days, he shadowed his farm manager in an attempt to learn how to artificially inseminate sows, for that was to be his major job. Twice he went to Murphy Family Ventures' main location, once to learn about the dangers of slipping and falling and about wearing eye protection, and once to get generally oriented to the company. All the other employees at the orientation meeting, he said, were cleaners.

Professor Paul H. Hemsworth has been studying the interaction between hogs and factory farmers for decades. It can have a significant impact on the well-being of pigs. "High levels of fear of humans," he writes, "may be a major limiting factor to the reproductive performance of commercial pigs."[18] Pigs begin to fear keepers who display poor attitudes toward them or who physically interact with them in a negative way. Hemsworth concludes that "there may be considerable opportunity for the pig industry to improve the performance, and possibly the welfare, of pigs by selecting and training stockpersons on the basis of their attitude and behaviour towards pigs."[19] Another expert points out that "when pigs fail to move the way the stockperson intends, the stockperson should ask, 'What am I doing wrong?' Often stockpeople wonder instead, 'What is wrong with these pigs?' The answer to the second question is that nothing is wrong with the pigs. They are responding naturally to the stimuli the stockperson is providing."[20]

One example: what is the proper way to empty pigs from a pen? A commonsense approach is to open the gate, get behind the pigs, and drive them out of the pen using their natural flight zone to propel them forward. However, pigs are naturally reluctant to explore new territories when pressured from behind. Because pigs feeling pressure are likely to keep its source in sight, they tend to circle past the open gate and around to the back of the pen behind the handler. The more pressure the pigs feel, the more likely they are to seek the safety of the back of the pen, without realizing that the open gate offers relief. A different approach to emptying the pen is grounded on pigs' natural curiosity and their "follow the leader" instincts. A handler who quietly opens the pen gate and stands to the side of the gate will draw the attention of the most curious pigs. Curiosity will bring those pigs toward the handler and the open gate. After exploring the stockperson for a few seconds, the lead pigs will see the open gate and usually go through it to the alleyway. As the first pigs exit, the next most curious pigs follow, and soon the group instinct draws even the most reluctant pigs through the gate to join their penmates.[21]

I was able to observe Mr. Nikita's manager instruct him on the proper way of dealing with sows, thanks to Mr. Nikita's having captured the lecture on videotape.[22] It wasn't easy to understand. The manager's mouth was always full of tobacco, Mr. Nikita explained. Here is what he said:

You can't beat the shit out of them. I ain't gonna lie to you. I've done it. My temper is that long. I get fucking frustrated, and I have knocked the shit out of them. Like that one who bit me the other morning, that motherfucker, he didn't need an ass whipping, but I cut the shit out of his Goddamned nose with a fucking gate rod. I didn't beat the fuck out of him, but I hit him one good Goddamn lick, and that, that was wrong. Goddamn motherfucker bit me. Goddamn, I was gonna bite the mother-fucker back any way I could.

This lesson was typical of the stockmanship that Mr. Nikita said he observed at the Murphy Family Ventures Garland Sow Farm. The behavior of such employees results in one of two evils, according to one expert.

The willingness of an owner or manager to allow animals to suffer on a farm tells employees that pain and suffering is not of the same importance as ensuring that feed is properly mixed or that pigs are sorted correctly. As a result, sick and injured pigs must cope with their afflictions, while employees are forced to cope with the sight of compromised animals. Employees who are unable to deal with this workplace environment terminate their employment, while other workers desensitize themselves to the needs of the pigs.[23]

The bioethics professor Bernard E. Rollin writes that

the nature of animal use changed quickly and dramatically at mid-twentieth century. Historically, the major use of animals . . . was agriculture. The key to agricultural success was animal husbandry, from the old Norse word *hus/bond*—bonded to one's household. Animal husbandry betokened an ancient and symbiotic contract between humans and domestic animals, perhaps best expressed by . . . "we take care of the animals and they take care of us." . . . Animal husbandry was about putting square pegs into square holes and round pegs into round holes, and creating as little friction as possible. . . . [On the other hand, animal] science is about efficiency and productivity. The husbandman put the animal into optimal conditions of the sort the animal was evolved for, and then augmented the animal's natural ability to survive and thrive by providing the animal with food during famine, water during drought, medical attention, help in birthing, help during natural disasters, and so on. The animals gave us their products, their toil, and sometimes their lives; we gave them better, more comfortable lives.[24]

Rollin, who teaches in Colorado, says that western ranchers practice cow husbandry today, and he relates how one rancher jumped into a partially frozen pond to save the life of a calf who had broken through the ice. "Confinement swine producers," he writes, "do not jump into ponds to save animals. In fact, they don't even treat sick animals; rather they knock them in the head, since the value of each animal is too small to bother with. Although each animal may be miserable, the operation as a whole is economically solvent."[25]

Mr. Nikita photographed sows miserable with sores and skin eruptions, and reported that the sick were sometimes left untreated for days. He never saw a veterinarian at the farm. Sometimes coworkers treated sick hogs by swabbing iodine on a wound, injecting antibiotics, or ultimately firing a captive bolt to the temple. At Farm 2149, where Matthew Scully visited, the sick and the lame and the halt were dragged to the cull pen, its injured hogs "never examined by a vet, never splinted, never even noticed anymore." As for the old and sick, Scully writes:

If the ailment threatens a particular production unit's meat-yielding capacity, like the vaginal and urinary tract infections apparent from discharge stains on some of the sows, that'll get treated. *That* can be justified by the return on labor and costs—though only if the unit isn't too old to even bother, "old" meaning three or four years instead of one or two. Otherwise it's a quick cull and sale to the renderer. There is no sick ward here. For most, it's either Kopertox [the antibiotic used] or the cull pen.[26]

The animal sciences Ph.D. whom Scully encountered at Farm 2149 told him that "the ones with disease don't go to Smithfield at all. These are, like, trash."[27]

Mr. Nikita filmed stockpeople at the Murphy Family Ventures Garland Sow Farm snaring huge sows, even injured ones, by their snouts, dragging them, hitting them, kicking them, jabbing them, gouging them, kneeing them, slapping them, poking them, smashing them, pushing them on their backs, on their faces, in their eyes, by their ears, on their faces and heads and torsos, sometimes into the metal bars of their crates, until they were bellowing, squealing, screaming.[28] They hit the sows with everything they had. They bashed them with long, thick iron gate rods. They struck them with two-inch-thick red handling boards, pieces of hard plastic that resemble cutting boards. Sometimes they threw the boards at the sows. One stockperson dug his fingers and thumb into the sows' eyes to encourage them to move. He pulled their ears. Unable to get enough time around livestock during the week, the man said he traveled to Virginia to bet on weekend cockfights. Matthew Scully could tell just how long a sow had lived at Farm 2149: "Some of them are still defiant, roaring and rattling violently as we approached. Some of them are defeated, motionless even at the touch. Some of them are dead."[29]

Smithfield's glossary of animal welfare terms explains that "thousands of farmers, including [Smithfield's] contract growers, depend on [gestation crates] to house their sows to ensure the safety, welfare and health of each and every pig. Opinions vary on the use of gestation crates, but we believe that to prohibit sow stalls in the absence of superior alternatives would be negligent and ultimately harmful to the health and welfare of pigs."[30] Of the sows in Farm 2149's gestation crates, Scully writes that "confinement doesn't describe their situation. They are encased, pinned down, unable to do anything but sit and suffer and scream."[31] Many were lying in their own shit or blood, sometimes covered with sores, bruises, and two-inch pus pockets, their legs swollen from sprains or fractures.[32] Mr. Nikita found three gestation buildings on the Murphy Family Ventures Garland Sow Farm that housed a total of 3,500 sows, all confined to twenty-two-inch-wide crates. Breeder sows may weigh 500 pounds and are permitted to survive three, four, occasionally five years. The sows on this sow farm were forced to lie in metal stalls able to contain their quarter-ton bodies only if they thrust their hooves between the thick, round iron slats. Somehow the sows managed, legs splayed, bellies protruding through the iron bars, until not an inch of filthy floor could be seen. Outside the farrowing crate, they stood shoulder to shoulder and were never let out of their cages except to be moved to a farrowing crate, or shot.

Mr. Nikita watched his coworkers yank these doomed, worn, used-up, sick, screaming, squealing sows out of their stinking iron pens by their ears, noses, heads, some with the word KILL sprayed in crimson on their pink backs, through the scum and bedlam into a side yard. There the stockperson would press the barrel of a captive bolt pistol to the sows' foreheads and pull the trigger.

A captive bolt pistol does not fire a bullet, but a retractable stainless steel shaft powered by gunpowder or compressed air. One type of bolt penetrates the sow's head and destroys some of her cerebrum and cerebellum, or at least that's what it's supposed to do. The nonpenetrating, mushroom-shaped type of bolt simply smashes against her forehead. Both are intended to cause immediate unconsciousness, with the penetrating type generally having greater success. Mr.

Nikita's videos revealed that, at pistol crack, the sows slump. Some
lie on their sides violently convulsing and kicking. I could hear Mr.
Nikita asking why the hogs were still shaking after falling to the
ground. Were they still alive? "That's the nerves," he was told. "The
nerves." And sometimes the stockpersons would laugh and spasti-
cally shake their arms and legs to imitate the dying or dead hogs
twitching at their feet. Boars have thicker skulls than sows do, Mr.
Nikita was told, and at least one boar was shot twice. The second
time he let out a loud grunt or groan. "Nerves," Mr. Nikita was told.
"Nerves. He was dead after the first shot."

Stillborn piglets or the piglets crushed to death were tossed into a
large garbage bucket. In a video, I could see their tiny, bloody bodies
half-filling the garbage bucket. The confused or the slow or the sick
began to starve. Spotted piglets, greasy piglets, piglets too small or
too sick, or piglets who failed some buyer's criteria were killed. Like
the sows who died in their pens, they never met the captive bolt pistol. Scully says that at Farm 2149 the unwanted piglets were simply
knocked on the head. Mr. Nikita said that when stockpersons, men
and women, encountered piglets too small, overly spotted, or too
greasy-looking to be profitably sold, they picked them up by their
rear legs, swung them high in the air, and slammed the backs of
their heads onto the concrete floor. He saw men and women do it
and said the crushed piglets would sometimes shake violently for
half a minute, sometimes up to five minutes. He asked why the
piglets shook. "That's the nerves," they replied.

Those pigs who were dispatched quickly by the captive bolt pistol
or had their skulls crushed against concrete were luckier than those
who quietly keeled over in their iron cages from injury or disease,
then had to be winched onto dead sleds and dragged from the barn.
But the most unfortunate were those marked for death just for
being sick or injured or unproductive. Mr. Nikita saw a stockperson
hit two of these doomed gilts with a board. It didn't matter, the man
said, the hogs were going to die anyway. Better to pull or push the
living animal out of the crate to the killing ground rather than

winch out a quarter-ton of dead weight from its narrow crate and drag it outside. If the sows could stagger out, so much the better. If not, the stockperson might attach a snare to the ears or snout and pull it tight, and the disabled and terrified hog would scream violently and long, and she was pulled to her death.

Wilbur was castrated to rid his body of the stink of boar taint when it was eaten. "These are assembly-line castrations," Mr. Nikita told me. "Each lasts only about five seconds." While castration may lessen the chance of boar taint, it has its economic downsides. Wilbur would convert feed to meat less efficiently. He would develop more fat and grow more slowly. His wounds might become infected. And castration hurts.[33] One moment he would be lying in his farrowing crate, and the next moment a stockperson—it always was a woman on the Murphy Family Ventures Garland Sow Farm—would grab him by his hind legs and swing him to chest level. As he struggled, upside down, screaming and wriggling, she would dig her scalpel deep into his scrotum, slice open the sac, twist out the tiny testicles, spray on an iodine solution, and toss him back in the pen. There would have been no anesthesia.

Since half of the two thousand piglets that the Murphy Family Ventures Garland Sow Farm sold each week were males, that meant about one thousand castrations performed each week. One castratrix told Mr. Nikita she thoroughly enjoyed her work: it unstressed her. Sometimes she would dangle piglets before him, then laughingly castrate them while making fun of his unease. When Mr. Nikita protested the castration procedures, his assistant manager explained that pigs have tougher skin than humans do. Scrotum cuts don't bother them, he said.

Sow Stressing and Boar Collection

Sows are usually "stressed" back to estrus, and that requires a boar. Matthew Scully reports that, at Farm 2149, groups of boars were released from their cages and allowed to stampede past the crated sows.[34] Sow stressing was done differently at the Murphy Family Ventures Garland Sow Farm. Mornings, Mr. Nikita might place a collar and leash on a seven-hundred-pound boar, then parade him in the faces of the sows, who were so closely confined to their crates that they couldn't turn away. Most had been returned to the gestation barn just within the previous week. If a boar decided to make a run for it, there was little Mr. Nikita could do. He said it was like trying to haul back a frisky, determined, seven-hundred-pound dog. He either had to drop the rope or run alongside the boar while a coworker closed off gates until the boar realized he was trapped. Then he would be led back to the business of stressing sows.

As Mr. Nikita displayed a huge boar to the sows in the front aisle, a coworker moved down the rear aisle, methodically determining which sows had returned to estrus, usually by sticking a hand into the vagina. Mr. Nikita learned this procedure by following a coworker down the rear aisle. The technician would press thumb to forefinger to demonstrate the stickiness that heralded a sow's readiness to be impregnated. Or the technician might scrutinize the sow's vulva to see if it was sufficiently red and inflamed.

After lunch, Mr. Nikita and his coworkers would move all the sows in estrus into the same section. Then it was time to inseminate them. In the morning Mr. Nikita and another herd technician would have tested them to determine which sows were ready. Temple Grandin, an autistic professor of animal science who believes that "autism is kind of a way station on the road from animals to humans," finds that

> breeding pigs commercially is an art. I talked to a man who had one of the most successful records for breeding sows out there and he told me things that no one's ever written in a book as far as I know. Each boar has his own little perversion the man had to do to get the boar turned on so he could collect the semen. Some of them were just things like the boar wanted to have his dandruff scratched while they were collecting him.

(Pigs have big flaky dandruff all over their backs.) The other things the man had to do were a lot more intimate. He might have to hold the boar's penis in exactly the right way that the boar liked, and he had to masturbate some of them in exactly the right way. There was one boar, he told me, who wanted to have his butt hole played with. "I have to stick my finger in his butt, he just really loves that," he told me. Then he got all red in the face. I'm not going to tell you his name, because I know he'd be embarrassed. But he's one of the best in the business—and remember, this is a business we're talking about. The number of sows successfully bred by the boars translates directly into the profits a company can make.[35]

I read Grandin's paragraph to Mr. Nikita. He had heard that Murphy Family Ventures had boar farms where fresh semen was collected in a sort of sleeve after they masturbated the boars; his farm manager had joked that he would never do that job, and Mr. Nikita had never seen it done. After he and a herd technician from the Murphy Family Ventures Garland Sow Farm estimated the number of sows who would be coming into heat that day, they would place an order for delivery of the proper amount of semen. Another Murphy Family Ventures sow farm lay nearby, and the two farms alternated picking up the semen. Mr. Nikita never did it, but was told that the sow farm employees scored their semen from the boar farm employee each day in a Wal-Mart parking lot.

Semen must be injected into a sow's vagina. Left alone with a sow, boars usually find a way. Professor Wayne L. Singleton of Purdue University explains that from age eight-and-a-half months to age twelve months, a boar can be productively mated once a day, five days a week. But natural conception is so unpredictable, so inefficient—so twentieth-century—that most commercial pig breeders use artificial insemination, called "AI." Singleton says that young AI boars can be "collected, that is masturbated, twice a week," but he recommends collection every ten days to improve the odds of successful insemination.[36] A couple times, just for the hell of it, Mr. Nikita and his coworkers tried to inseminate the sows almost naturally, by helpfully inserting a boar's penis into a sow's vagina. But they never got him to ejaculate. Grandin knows that there is a psychology to pig sex and pig pregnancy and that success in the tricky business of ejaculating boars and impregnating sows requires a thorough grounding in porcine passion. Grandin's boar-masturbator friend had it. Mr. Nikita, alas, did not, and so each of his inseminations was artificial.

Large producers may operate their own boar farms. It's also the business of companies with such names as International Boar Semen (IBS) ("AI Innovators Since 1976"), now a division of Universal Pig Genes, Inc. ("First in All the Ways That Count"). IBS ships fresh and frozen boar semen, in individual bottles, in cochettes, or in what IBS calls the "SEMBAG." Five billion sperm cells a dose are guaranteed at a cost as low as $5.[37] For those in need of porcine sex education, IBS offers a video and CD. Its "How to Use Artificial Insemination: Using Fresh Boar Semen" demonstrates heat detection, semen collection and storage, proper handling, and artificial insemination procedure.

We should not overlook the sows. They need to be excited too if they are going to produce twenty-five or more PPSY. Grandin says that if a sow is not completely aroused, or if she is fearful, fewer eggs will be fertilized and she will produce smaller litters. A sow, she says, is ready to be injected when her ears "pop"—that is, when she stands erect—and she experiences back pressure similar to an act of intercourse with a boar. Then she will "stand for the man," stand stock still so she can be penetrated and injected by either penis or syringe. When a breeder employs a syringe, he may sit on her back to simulate the weight of the boar, or place weights on her back.[38]

Mr. Nikita was never trained in the techniques of artificial insemination. But, after watching others perform for a few days, he was deemed ready. This is what he did. The semen would arrive fresh from the Wal-Mart parking lot in a five- or six-inch-long, plastic-tipped plastic bag. He would break off the tip and insert the end into an artificial boar penis that was attached to a thin plastic tube about eighteen inches long. Then he would place a boar in a small, remote-controlled crate and roll him along the rear aisle in order to stimulate the sow and get her ready to "stand for the man."

Once directly behind a sow's vagina, the stalls were too narrow for the sows ever to turn. He would place a harness around her waist, just above a rear leg, and clip the bag of semen onto the harness so that it would simulate a boar's touch on her back. Then he would press the end deep into the vagina and inject. Each sow received three injections: the first during the afternoon of the day she returned to estrus, the second and third on the morning and afternoon of the day following.

Mr. Nikita was on probation for the first months of his employment. Employees at the Murphy Family Ventures Garland Sow Farm received bonuses based on the number of live pigs sold. The entire purpose of Mr. Nikita's job was therefore to maximize the number of piglets conceived, born live, and weaned. He would have been eligible for a bonus of $500 when he quit on November 2, 2007. But he was thinking that his colleagues had begun to suspect him. For one thing, they were commenting openly about how nice he was to the hogs. For another, when they told him to hit the hogs or hit them harder, he refused, and he was the only one. The hogs were really smart, he told me, each with a unique personality. Skittish when they first met him, the hogs learned to trust him and stopped running away. Finally, his two female farrowing barn coworkers had begun joking that he must be an animal rights person. "We know who you are," they said. "You're a spy."

I FIND A FACTORY HOG FARM

I returned to Bladen County in November 2007, a week after Mr. Nikita quit his job at the Murphy Family Ventures Garland Sow Farm. This time I brought my Spanish-speaking wife, Gail. We resumed the search for industrial hog farms that I had abandoned a couple months before, focusing on the Elizabethtown area, which seemed to have more factory hog farms than did Tar Heel. Using the information I had obtained from the Division of Water Quality, we kept locating what appeared to be the correct roads. But no matter how far we drove them in either direction, we were unable to find a factory hog farm. Eventually we had to break off our searches to meet slaughterhouse workers at local fast-food joints.

After we finished our interviews, we tried again. We took a right off a four-lane highway, another right off a two-lane highway, a left, a right, then a left onto dirt that barely formed a road, and then . . . we really got lost. Our map was wrong. The numbers were wrong. The Division of Water Quality's records were wrong. We started driving aimlessly, randomly taking lefts and rights. Until, suddenly, we found ourselves on a road that matched the name of a road upon which there was supposed to be a factory hog farm. It was in a residential area with numbered mailboxes. We came to a mailbox with a number that matched a number in a Division of Water Quality record. But it stood in front of a neatly clipped ranch house. We couldn't see a factory hog farm. To the right of one of the houses was either a long, winding dirt road or somebody's long driveway, so long that it disappeared over a rise. We took it.

Whatever we were on twisted and turned until, after more than half a mile, it opened onto a flat vista. Before us sat twelve low, white buildings that, from pictures I had seen, appeared to be factory hog buildings. We parked the car alongside a building and I got out. No one was around. I yelled, "Hello! Anybody here!" No one answered. I walked fifty yards to the nearest building to see if I could locate anyone. I couldn't. So I walked behind the building.

Then I was facing a large body of liquid. From the smell, the tarry look, and the size, color, and shape, I knew I was staring at a hog manure lagoon. The place reeked. I walked up to a building. "Hello," I called at the locked door. "Anybody there?" I could hear movement inside, lots of movement. But nobody called back. Neither could I see what was making the noise, for the building was buttoned up, its windows covered by a tough, whitewashed, fibrous canvas pulled so tight that I could not wedge a finger into it. I couldn't see a crack. I was finally able to pry open the canvas a sliver. "Anybody in here?" I called. I put an eye to the sliver and ignited a stampede. The building was filled with piglets. They weighed perhaps thirty pounds apiece and were crammed twenty or thirty to a stall. They were piling up against each other in their eagerness to get as far from me as they could.

I heard a noise and looked up. A small cloud of billowing dust was settling on the long dirt driveway. Perhaps someone had driven by. I walked around the building. Gail was speaking to a large bearded man wearing a baseball cap and sitting in a large brown-and-green golf cart. I walked over and asked if he owned the land. He said he did. I asked if he owned the pigs. He said he did not, all in a friendly tone.

He had just finished telling Gail that someone had called him to report that the farm's silent alarm had been set off. He had decided to call 911, then changed his mind when he saw Gail. "You must be lost" was the first thing he said. We were at the end of a half-mile-long, twisting dirt driveway, off a dirt road that was about three miles from any major road.

I gave him my name and said I was a writer interested in Bladen County's hog farms. Might I have a tour of his farm? He hesitated and asked what I wrote about. Before I could explain, he asked: had I placed the ad in the local newspaper that week seeking to interview slaughterhouse workers? I said I had, and that was the key that unlocked my tour of a Bladen County industrial hog farm.

He mentioned that his wife had written a book, but she hadn't had much luck getting it published. I asked if she had an agent, and he said she did not. That was about all he knew: "I'm not up on book stuff." But he couldn't wait to tell her that he had met "book people." He wasn't a book person himself, he said, but his son was, and so was his wife. On vacation, they always ended up in bookstores. "I've published some books," I said. "If you show me around your farm, I'll sit down with your wife, look at her book, and tell her how I think she might get it published." "Okay," he said. "Come back tomorrow morning, about nine o'clock."

Gail and I stayed the night at Elizabethtown's Days Inn, then returned up that long, winding, dusty driveway again about 8:45 the next morning. He was waiting for us. He waved, then ushered us into a dark makeshift office, where he took a chair and gave us a thumbnail sketch of the history of his farm. It had been his parents' farm. He and his two brothers had purchased the entire six hundred acres from them and then, in the middle of the 1990s, decided to start raising hogs. They hadn't had much money, so he and another brother took jobs. His job was at a hog finishing farm just across the County line. After a year, he started managing the farm. Then the finishing farm gave him a job that involved driving a truck between farms and he didn't like that. The brother who had stayed to manage the hog farm didn't like his job either; he wanted to drive a truck. So my friend persuaded his employer to hire his brother in his place, and he took over the job of running the family hog farm, which he had been doing ever since. The brothers eventually decided to go their separate business ways and split up the farm. As there were twelve pig houses, each brother took four.

He said hog-raising has three steps. The first takes place at the sow barns where the pigs are born and stay for three weeks. Then he gets them, when they weigh about twelve pounds and have been putting on almost half a pound a day. He keeps them at his nursery barn for eight, sometimes nine, weeks. When they leave they weigh fifty pounds or more and are adding a pound a day. He ships them to a finishing barn, where they stay another thirteen weeks and pack on another two hundred pounds at the daily rate of a pound and a half at the end. He always keeps one of his four barns vacant for maintenance and cleaning, as do his brothers. Once a week a truck delivers sow barn piglets, and another trucks them out to the finishing barn. He said the three brothers have about 1,600 pigs in each barn, which means that they are caring for over 14,000, among the three of them, at any one time. More than 100,000 pigs rotate through their barns every year. He said he spends about half a day with the pigs every morning, making sure they have enough water and food. Any unhealthy-looking piglets he treats or isolates. He was obviously struggling financially. I asked if he was an independent producer. No, he had been contracted to Smithfield for many years. It wasn't a good deal for him, he said, but he felt he had little choice. He only knew one independent producer. I asked to see the inside of the barns.

On the way, we passed the manure lagoon. He said that the state had placed a moratorium on building hog farms unless they were accompanied by waste treatment facilities that he couldn't come close to affording. He knew the place stunk. He took me to the two barns into whose windows I had tried to peer, but wouldn't let us go more than a step or two inside. I could see now that there were no glass windows in the building, just translucent shades that let light in. The barns were bisected, about twenty stalls to each room, in two lines of ten, each stall holding about forty pigs. He said finishing barns are much larger than this, with each room being about the size of one of his buildings. As soon as he opened the door, the frenzy I heard the previous day resumed. I peeked through the doorway. The place was crawling with skittish, floppy-eared, pink piglets who would alternately freeze then pile up against a wall. Huge ventilation fans were whirring.

After an hour and a half, he took us to meet his wife. Five dogs met us outside his home, a collie, a show Labrador, and three I couldn't label. They jumped all over him all the way to the house. Inside, his son was sitting in a chair, reading. He looked up and took his book down the hallway. The farmer introduced us. His respect for his wife was as plain as his love for the dogs. She shyly handed me her manuscript. I spent twenty minutes reading. It was terrific. She said she had been turned down thirty or thirty-one times. I said that she needed an agent and told her how she could get one. Then it was time to leave. The dogs jumped all over the farmer all the way to the car. I scratched the collie behind the ears and whispered my congratulations for not being born a pig.

CHAPTER SEVEN

River of Death

One could not stand and watch very long without being
philosophical, without beginning to deal in symbols and
similes, and to hear the hog-squeal of the universe. . . .
Each of them had an individuality of his own, a will
of his own, a hope and a heart's desire; each was full of
self-confidence, of self-importance, and a sense of
dignity. And trusting and strong in faith he had gone
about his business, the while a black shadow hung over
him, and a horrid Fate waited in his pathway. Now
suddenly it had swooped upon him, and had seized him
by the leg. Relentless, remorseless, all his protests, his
screams were nothing to it. It did its cruel will with him,
as if his wishes, his feelings, had simply no existence at all;
it cut his throat and watched him gasp out his life.
—*Upton Sinclair,* THE JUNGLE *(1906)*[1]

Killing was a relatively simple matter—a blow to the head,
a knife to the throat—complicated only by how much one
cared about the pain or terrors animals felt in dying. . . .
The animal also died a second death. Severed from the
form in which it had lived, severed from the act

> that had killed it, it vanished from human memory
> as one of nature's creatures.
> —*William Cronon*, NATURE'S METROPOLIS *(1991)*[2]

> You have just dined, and however scrupulously
> the slaughterhouse is concealed in the graceful
> distance of miles, there is complicity.
> —*Ralph Waldo Emerson, "Fate" (1860)*[3]

WILBUR WAS GOING to be killed at Tar Heel, and I wanted to know how. Actually, I didn't want to know how. I didn't want to hear his squeal or smell his fear or see his throat cut or watch the dull-eyed workers pierce, cleave, slice, crop, carve, chisel, and behead him. Years before, I visited a small bovine slaughterhouse in central Massachusetts. I watched cows and calves being killed for an hour and was seared. I remain seared. I didn't want to see or write about the Tar Heel slaughterhouse. I mentioned this to the writer John Coetzee. He replied, "I understand entirely. Just rehearsing certain acts in one's mind becomes a kind of butchery."[4] Recent neurophysiological discoveries support him. Mirror neurons within the human brain that appear to be linked to our ability to read others' emotions and states of mind and empathize with them fire the same way when we observe an action as when we act it.[5] I was seared because the slaughterhouse workers were disgusted, the animals terrified.

But Tar Heel existed, and I wanted to see what was going on there. Gail Eisnitz, author of *Slaughterhouse*, had traveled to Bladen County in the 1990s, but had been unable to get into the slaughterhouse. Matthew Scully managed initially to line up a tour. But after he met with Jerry Godwin, president of Murphy Family Farms, Smithfield realized they had misjudged their boy, and suddenly no one was available to conduct Scully about. Scully would pillory

Smithfield with what he saw on his factory farm visits and report
that, after Godwin told him there would be no slaughterhouse tour,
"I told him that if I ran a place like that, I wouldn't let people in
either."[6] Today Jerry Godwin is president of Murphy-Brown LLC, a
subsidiary of Smithfield Farms since 2000. I suspect he has not forgotten that conversation.

The Largest Employer in Bladen County

Smithfield is used to getting its way in Bladen County. In early
2007, Smithfield Packing Company became unhappy with the
North Carolina Division of Water Quality restrictions that limited
it to killing 176,000 pigs a week at Tar Heel—just 8,488,000 pigs a
year. Smithfield Packing asked the Division for leave to kill a whole
lot more. Smithfield pointed to its history as a good Bladen County
citizen. "The Tar Heel plant's management and staff have made a
concerted effort to become involved in the local community. Company personnel participate in activities such as the Keep Bladen
Beautiful Committee and NC Big Sweep program to help keep
local rivers, lakes, and public areas free of trash and debris. Tar Heel
staff work with local schools to provide environmental education
through events like the World Water Monitoring Day and as judges
for science fairs. In total, Smithfield Packing–Tar Heel participates
in and/or provides support to over 30 local organizations."[7]

Others pressed Smithfield's economic argument. One typed form
letter had had its [blanks] filled in by a "Robert Gooden":

> Hello. My name is [Robert Gooden] and I am a pork producer
> here in Bladen County. I raise market hogs on contract with
> Murphy-Brown and I have done so for the past [15] years. The
> animals I raise are shipped to the Tar Heel plant for processing
> and the continued successful operation of the Tar Heel plant is

vital to my farming operation, to my family's future and our financial well-being. I am proud to be affiliated with Smithfield and Murphy-Brown and place great value on our business relationship. They have always treated me fairly and they are important partners in the success of my farming operation. I am here in support of the proposed permit for the Tar Heel plant for the reasons I have stated here and I also believe the new permit will provide much needed new job opportunities for the citizens of our area.

A second typed form letter, its [blanks] filled in by Isaac Singletary, said:

Hello. My name is [Isaac Singletary] and I am a pork producer here in Bladen County. I have been in the hog business for [38] years and I raise market hogs which go to Tar Heel for processing. I am a contract grower for Murphy-Brown and my decision to contract with them to grow hogs has been one of the best business decisions I have ever made. . . . We need the Tar Heel plant here in Bladen County and it is vitally important to the economy of this county and the surrounding region. The proposed new permit will allow the Tar Heel plant to be more efficient and to process more hogs but will not require any expansion of hog farms. . . . The continued successful operation of the Tar Heel plant is vital to my farming operation, to my family's future and our financial well-being. . . . My contract hog operation has made it possible for me to build a successful business which I can pass down to my children, something which can keep them involved in agriculture and provide a sound financial future for their children. . . . I know there are a number of other contract growers here tonight who support the permit issuance. I would ask them and their families to stand and show their support. (Turn and recognize them.)

One Ellen D. Gause, who claimed she had worked in economic development in a ten-county area of southeastern North Carolina for over thirty years, wrote that the slaughterhouse "provides much needed employment opportunities for Bladen and the surrounding counties. Their 5,000+ employees receive fair wages and fringe benefits far superior to those of other companies in the area. As Bladen County's largest employer, the economic impact of this Company is enormous both in direct and indirect ways. . . . Even with the environmental and labor issues that have constantly plagued Smithfield, having the largest pork processing facility in the world is the best thing that has happened to Bladen County."[8]

Smithfield also inundated the Division with reams of water quality data it claimed showed that the increase would not lead to further pollution. A lot of folks disagreed. The Southern Environmental Law Center argued that Smithfield "should not be allowed to expand until it demonstrates its willingness and ability to comply with North Carolina's laws and appropriately conserve and protect the state's natural resources." The labor-related Research Associates of America in Washington, D.C., said that "for the sake of the residents of North Carolina and the men and women who work in the Tar Heel plant, we urge you to reconsider the permit." Cape Fear River Watch, Inc., of Wilmington, North Carolina, begged the Division of Water Quality to "please protect our natural resources and deny the draft permit." A spokesperson for the Neuse River Foundation urged that "for the health of the Cape Fear River and all those who enjoy her, I strongly oppose the renewal of the . . . permit." Some of Smithfield's disgruntled Tar Heel neighbors attested to "the negative impacts of the hog slaughtering industry. These impacts include air pollution, heavy truck traffic, noise, hiring of many illegal aliens, and of course water problems."[9] Still, the Division granted the request. Thenceforth, Smithfield Packing Company would be authorized to kill 195,000 pigs every week, to a maximum of 9.5 million a year.[10] One of those would be Wilbur.

PORKOPOLIS

The pigs of Bladen County are no more protected than once were the county's Native Americans and black slaves. Outside the slaughterhouse almost anything goes.[11] Because the Federal Animal Welfare Act and the North Carolina anticruelty statute do not concern themselves with factory-farmed pigs, they may be raised under almost any conditions imaginable.[12] The Federal Humane Slaughter Act does require that pigs be killed humanely and stipulates that conscious animals unable to walk cannot be dragged to slaughter. But Gail Eisnitz interviewed federal meat inspectors who told her that even the Humane Slaughter Act exists only on paper and is not enforced.[13]

Oliver Evans's 1783 invention of an automated grain mill powered by a water wheel marked the beginning of the long evolution in production that led both to Henry Ford's assembly line and to Tar Heel.[14] In the early nineteenth century, Cincinnati entrepreneurs pioneered the "disassembly line," which required workers to repeat motions again and again. It proved a major impetus in two races against decay. At that time, Ohio produced a lot of corn that had to be rapidly converted into pigs or whiskey, or rot, for time was short after slaughter. Unless they were salted or smoked, forty thousand dead pigs a year—about a day's work in Tar Heel—had to be rushed down the Ohio River to the Mississippi to market before their bodies decomposed.[15] Cincinnati slaughterhouses began to mechanize by introducing a large horizontal wheel from which eight freshly slaughtered pigs could be hung. Each worker performed the same task on each corpse, one splitting the hog, another removing the entrails, another taking out the organs, and another washing down the remains when it rotated in his direction.[16] The bodies were then taken down, sent to a cooling room, and cut into pieces.

It was a seasonal industry. Slaughterhouses operated only in late fall so that the autumn chill would lessen the rate of decay; they had

to halt operations when the rivers froze. There was such an overpro-
duction of pigs that only their hams, shoulders, sides, and lard were
not heaved as waste into the Ohio River.[17] By the 1850s, Cincinnati
had become the leading pork-packing city in the United States, calling itself "Porkopolis." Pigs were driven up a ramp to the uppermost
story of the new larger slaughterhouses. There they were smashed
on the forehead, stuck in the jugular vein, bled to death, then
hoisted onto an overhead rail. The potential energy their bodies
stored in their upward struggles was converted to kinetic energy as
gravity slowly pressed their bodies down.[18] It was still being done
that way half a century later in Chicago. Upton Sinclair wrote in
The Jungle that in Chicago's Union Stockyards the pigs climbed
high, "to the very top of the distant buildings; and Jokubas explained
that with refinement of cynicism they made the pigs literally clean
and dress themselves. They went up by the power of their own legs,
and then their weight carried them back through all the processes
necessary to make them into pork."[19]

By midcentury, Cincinnati was processing 334,000 pigs a year,
Chicago 20,000.[20] During the 1860s, overhead rail systems, whose
descendants are in use at Tar Heel, appeared in more midwestern
slaughterhouses.[21] Once packers learned how to store ice for use in
warmer months, things began to run year-round. Chicago became
the new pork hub and by the 1880s eclipsed Cincinnati, processing
more than one million hogs a year.[22]

The historian William Cronon explains that packing plants

> distanced their customers most of all from the act of killing. . . .
> The more people became accustomed to the attractively cut,
> carefully wrapped, cunningly displayed packages that Swift had
> introduced to the trade, the more easily they could fail to re-
> member that their purchase had once pulsed and breathed with
> a life much like their own. . . . As time went on, fewer of those
> who ate meat could say they had actually killed the animals

themselves. In the packer's world, it was easy not to remember that eating was a moral act inextricably bound to killing. Such was the second nature that a corporate order had imposed on the American landscape. Forgetfulness was among the least noticed and most important of its by-products.[23]

A Modest Request

In May 2007, I e-mailed James Hostetter, Smithfield's Vice President for Investor Relations and Corporate Communications, at his Park Avenue address in Manhattan. Might I visit the Tar Heel slaughterhouse and chat with a few workers? One Keira Ullrich promptly replied: "Smithfield Foods, Inc. does not grant plant tours due to bio security concerns after September 11, 2001."[24] I pointed out that Smithfield employs more than five thousand workers at the slaughterhouse, that these include many illegal immigrants and convicts, and that it suffers a 100 percent annual turnover rate. Every workday Smithfield must hire another twenty workers. According to the *New York Times*, to obtain them "the Smithfield plant will take just about any man or woman with a pulse and a sparkling urine sample, with few questions asked."[25] I doubted I constituted a significant bio-security risk in that crowd and asked again, politely, for a tour. Silence. I decided to knock on the door.

I imagined I would park my car on a lonely side road near the slaughterhouse, inconspicuously poke about the grounds, peer into a couple windows, and ask a few workers some questions as they left work. But when I Googled "Tar Heel slaughterhouse," I discovered that labor and management were warring not just against the pigs but against each other.

A website called SmithfieldJustice sketched the labor battleground as a colorful tableau of wildcat strikes, arbitrary employee terminations, visits by civil rights and religious leaders, racism, sexism, intimidation, union-busting, unfair labor practices, unsafe working conditions, filthy drinking water, injured workers, low pay, illegal Hispanic immigrant arrests by U.S. Immigration and Customs Enforcement (ICE) agents, municipal boycotts of Tar Heel's pork products, and a visit by a Democratic presidential candidate in support of a union.[26] The website of the United Food and Commercial Workers (UFCW) International Union added that Tar Heel was the only meatpacking plant in the United States to have its own police force: "Under a somewhat obscure North Carolina state law, Smithfield has created a company police force that patrols the plant, carries concealed weapons on and off duty, and has the power to arrest workers, and detain them in an on-site jail cell."[27] Organizations as diverse as the Revolutionary Communist Party, the Sierra Club, Robert F. Kennedy Jr.'s Waterkeepers, and Human Rights Watch joined in condemnation.[28] An administrative law judge had ruled that Smithfield committed widespread labor violations to prevent the plant from being unionized in 1997. The company had threatened to discharge union supporters and close the plant if workers chose union representation; threatened to report illegal immigrant workers if they chose union representation; threatened violence against workers engaged in organizing activities; threatened to blacklist union supporters; harassed, intimidated, and coerced union supporters; retaliated against union supporters; spied on union supporters; prevented workers from wearing insignia that supported unionization; and confiscated union literature.[29]

On October 17, 2007, Smithfield Foods and Smithfield Packing would charge the United Food and Commercial Workers International Union, the Research Associates of America, and some union organizers with federal racketeering and conspiracy in Richmond's U.S. District Court.[30] *New York Times* legal columnist Adam Liptak examined Smithfield's lengthy Complaint and concluded that Smithfield's claim of extortion "sounds quite a bit like free speech."[31] Certainly Smithfield's charge that Research Associates of America tried to prevent the North Carolina Division of Water Quality from issuing the water permit that would permit Smithfield to kill another nineteen thousand pigs a day (one million a year) because it would harm the environment sounds like free speech.[32] Liptak was especially impressed by Smithfield's claim that one defendant had engaged in illegal racketeering by declaring in a speech that "Upton Sinclair said it best: 'It is difficult to get a man to understand something when his salary depends upon his not understanding it.'"[33]

Inconspicuous prowling about the slaughterhouse complex seemed out of the question. Still I needed to learn what was happening inside. In December 2006, I watched the five-and-a-half-minute Public Broadcasting Service (PBS) video *A Day at the Plant*, which was shot in and around the Tar Heel slaughterhouse. What attracted senior correspondent Maria Hinojosa to Tar Heel was the unionization struggle. She said that her cameras were the first allowed inside the plant. But Smithfield severely circumscribed her ability to film. She was permitted to shoot just the "cut floor," about midway through the pig-processing operation. Mostly the video showed workers slicing large pieces of dead pigs into smaller pieces. She was prohibited from filming an entire hog, and for good reason: "It is not as disturbing to see slabs of meat as it is to film what I saw: hundreds of hogs recently shot and then bled out, hanging from hooks," she said.

I watched this video a dozen times, mesmerized by its antiseptic white images of the cut floor, its towering ceilings, the hundreds of workers decked out in white hairnets and purple hard hats, blue-and-white open-backed aprons, covered to their necks, knives slashing at the pig pieces that spun past, hundred-pound half-bodies suspended from hooks whirling a dozen feet above their heads. I imagined slowing the video and adding "It Goes as It Goes," the haunting theme song that opened the film *Norma Rae*, cotton wafting through the air in slow motion. That 1980 film was based on the life of Crystal Lee Sutton, who catalyzed the unionization of the J. P. Stevens textile plant 150 miles up Interstate 95 from Tar Heel: "Maybe what's good gets a little bit better. And maybe what's bad gets gone."[34]

I bought a plane ticket for Raleigh and headed back to Bladen County. Soon after I crossed the Cape Fear River, a sign indicated that the Smithfield Farms Environmental Division was sponsoring the next stretch of highway. I passed another sign that said SMITH-FIELD PACKING CO., stopped at a red light, and looked right. The Division of Water Quality had described the Tar Heel slaughter-house as "a pork packing plant that currently harvests up to 32,000 hogs per day weighing approximately 260 lb/hog. The primary products are fresh primal cuts. By-product operations include blood and hair collection, viscera handling and inedible rendering. The plant operates about two shifts five or six days a week." Now there it was, all 973,000 square feet.[35]

To my right loomed several enormous, whitewashed, windowless boxes, between two and a half and three stories high. I couldn't tell at first whether they were separate buildings or connected. But the complex was hundreds of yards long. I wondered which building had been the one where Maria Hinojosa filmed the cut floor. As I sat waiting for the light to change, a triple-decker truck turned left in front of me on its way into the slaughterhouse complex. Pink ears and pink snouts were poking through the numerous small openings in the steel trailer in which perhaps 250 pink bodies rode. The noise of the truck's acceleration into the complex drowned out the squeals. An identical truck followed closely behind, and another followed that. Then the light turned green. Seven hundred and fifty pigs had passed in twenty seconds, twenty minutes of inside work.

It took some while to drive the length of the complex. There were at least four entrances, one for employees and trucks, one for main-tenance, one for the Smithfield main office. A couple thousand cars jammed the parking lots. Warrens of pipes clustered along the building tops. Four orange wind socks fluttered. Then I was past the sign announcing Tar Heel's city limits. It had a picture of the bottom of a foot with a black smudge on the heel.

At the southern edge of town, I made a U-turn and headed slowly back toward the slaughterhouse. I had abandoned any idea of parking on a lonely lane, for there were no side streets near the slaughterhouse complex. Behind it, to the west, was nothing but swamp. I logged onto Google Earth and looked around the slaughterhouse complex from outer space. All I could see was swamp. I had also given up on the idea of peeping through the slaughterhouse windows; there were no windows. Two of the large whitewashed buildings appeared connected, forming a single building perhaps a quarter-mile long. I decided to knock on what I guessed was the front door.

In the parking lot of the main office building, beside spaces reserved for the USDA, I stepped into a stench. On either side of the entranceway stood a carved black piglet, back sliced away, its open cavity filled with sand and snuffed cigarettes. Inside the small lobby was a sofa. A coffee table was piled with magazines with titles such as *Meatingplace*. A large painting of an ecstatic pig basking on a piece of sunny farmland hung on one wall across from the receptionist. She was glaring at me. I rolled up a copy of *Meatingplace* and casually stuffed it into the rear pocket of my cargo shorts. The receptionist ordered me to take it out of my pocket and place it on the desk.

"My name's Steve Wise. I'm researching a book about Tar Heel and this processing plant. How do I arrange a tour?"

"There aren't any tours."

"Oh, there must be. Who do I speak to about it?"

"That would be Miss Sally."

"And where might she be?"

A severe-looking woman with chiseled reddish hair walked up the hallway. Miss Sally, I presumed. I wondered if the receptionist had summoned her with a silent alarm.

"Is that her?" I asked, perhaps unnecessarily.

"Yes."

"I'm Steve Wise," I said, trying to sound pleasant. "I'm research-ing a book about Tar Heel and this plant. I'd like to take a tour."

"Only Joseph Luter the Fourth can authorize that," Miss Sally said, looking at the receptionist.

"And where's he?"

"He's president of Smithfield Farms." She took a yellow sticky note from the receptionist. "Here's his phone number and his secre-tary's name. Call and say what you want, and they'll call you back with a yes or no." She wrote it all down and handed me the yellow sticky. I reached for the copy of *Meatingplace.*

"Can he take that?" the receptionist asked.

"It's okay," Miss Sally said. I strolled back into the stench, the magazine rolled in my back pocket.

When I telephoned President Luter's office, his secretary for-warded me to the office of Dennis Pittman, the public relations spokesman for Smithfield Foods in Tar Heel. I left a polite message. A week later, I received a phone call from Joyce Fitzpatrick. She asked me to e-mail her the names of my prior books, the names of everyone else I was interviewing, and an explanation of what the book was about, "so we can see how we can help you." I Googled Ms. Fitzpatrick, who, I discovered,

> is the founder and president of Fitzpatrick Communications, Inc. and has more than 25 years experience helping clients with public relations. Fitzpatrick has implemented successful and award-winning public relations strategies for corporations, law firms, universities, museums and nonprofit organizations. Her expertise in crisis communications allows her to provide valu-able counsel to clients during times of major change. Fitzpatrick has lectured on corporate communications at MIT, The Kenan-Flagler School of Business, George Washington University and

the Georgetown University. She is a master's degree candidate in English/creative writing at NC State and is an adjunct professor at UNC–Chapel Hill.[36]

Ms. Fitzpatrick had also been inducted into the North Carolina Journalism, Advertising, and Public Relations Hall of Fame.[37] I was very ready to be related to and communicated with.

On October 22, 2007, I sent her my first e-mail.

> I am writing a book that follows the history of Bladen County, North Carolina. I have been researching the Native Americans, Colonists, slaves, and hogs there. That has lead me to seek interviews with, among others, descendants of the Indians of Bladen County, descendants of the Robeson family, whose manor house is just outside Tar Heel, present and former workers in the hog industry and slaughterhouse at Tar Heel, and regulators in Raleigh. As I intend to write about the slaughterhouse, which I understand is the largest in the world, I would like to have a tour of it and meet with people from Smithfield to discuss it, so that I can place whatever they have to say, without editorial comment, into my upcoming book. I would like to interview Joe Luter, IV, too.
>
> I have written three books. Two concern animal rights law, *Rattling The Cage—Toward Legal Rights For Animals* (2000) and *Drawing The Line—Science And The Case For Animal Rights* (2003). My last book focused on the trial of a slave in London in 1772 and was entitled *Though The Heavens May Fall—The Landmark Trial That Lead To The End Of Human Slavery* (2005).
>
> I look forward to hearing from you and hope that my requests will be granted.

Four days later she replied:

I am in the process of advancing your request. Who is your publisher? I need to know who else has been or will be interviewed for this book. What the working title is. Who you are talking to in the hog industry other than Smithfield. Is this book a true history of Bladen County or is it specifically about the hog industry only? Are you speaking with growers, too?

Terrific. I responded on November 2.

My publisher is Da Capo Press, part of the Perseus Books Group. To date, I have interviewed, or have sought interviews with, public officials in Raleigh, descendants of the Robeson family from Tar Heel, descendants of Bladen County Indians, in particular Lumbees, Tar Heel slaughterhouse workers, and food science professors. I am trying to speak to growers, but have not yet succeeded.

On November 5, she replied:

As you can imagine, we field hundreds of requests for interviews, and I am working as quickly as possible to answer your inquiry. Is it only Mr. Luter with whom you care to speak, or can someone else help you? Mr. Luter is based in Smithfield, Va., as you know.

I nagged her all the way up to New Year's Eve, until I heard again. "Please submit a list of questions that you would propose to ask Mr. Luter. As I have said, he is located in Smithfield, Va." I e-mailed her twenty-five questions. I mentioned I had a deadline. But I heard nothing further from her until April 7. "I understand that you have a deadline. I will be happy to have Mr. Luter answer questions you submit by email." I replied that I had e-mailed them to her three months before. She replied that "I am unable to open this attachment. Could you please cut and paste into an email and resend?" That was the attachment I had sent her three months earlier. I cut, pasted, and resent. Then I sent more e-mails. April 18, May 13, June 6. Nag, nag, nag. Mr. Luter was replaced by Mr. Schellpepper. On July 16, I sent my twentieth and final e-mail to Ms. Fitzpatrick.

> Your biography on the web states that you are an expert in public relations. I assume this expertise involves relating to the public in some appropriate way. This is my twentieth communication to you over nine months. I have patiently and persistently attempted to give Smithfield Packing a full and complete opportunity to discuss its operations with me. I complied with all your requests, even those you repeated. I have repeatedly asked for permission to visit the Tar Heel slaughterhouse and to interview first Mr. Luter, then Mr. Schellpepper. I have never even been given the courtesy of a "yes" or a "no." I sent numerous written questions. I have received no reply. Rereading your responses, I fail to detect any public relations whatsoever.

Matthew Scully had been correct. If I ran a place like that, I wouldn't let people in either.

THE HOG SQUEAL OF THE UNIVERSE

Wilbur's last day began before dawn. It was "harvest" time. He may have been hungry, for he might not have been fed the day before.[38] After being startled awake, he was herded, with about 250 others, onto a double-decker truck pulling a stainless-steel, triple-decker semi-tractor; I saw some with mud guards reading PORK TRAN.[39] This was happening all across Bladen, Sampson, and Duplin Counties and other nearby counties, perhaps in counties in Virginia and South Carolina too, for factory farms are often 50 miles from the slaughterhouse; one-third of the time the slaughterhouse is 100 to 500 miles away; 1 in 85 pigs travels an even greater distance to be killed.[40]

I can't tell you for certain what happened after Wilbur arrived at Tar Heel, for I wasn't there. But from my interviews with former Tar Heel slaughterhouse workers and some undercover sources, I can paint a likely picture. One *New York Times* undercover reporter wrote that

> kill-floor work is hot, quick and bloody. The hog is herded in from the stockyard, then stunned with an electric gun. It is lifted onto a conveyor belt, dazed but not dead, and passed to a waiting group of men wearing bloodstained smocks and blank faces. They slit the neck, shackle the hind legs and watch a machine lift the carcass into the air, letting its life flow out in a purple gush, into a steaming collection trough.
>
> The carcass is run through a scalding bath, trolleyed over the factory floor and then dumped onto a table with all the force of a quarter-ton water balloon. In the misty-red room, men slit along its hind tendons and skewer the beast with hooks. It is again lifted and shot across the room on a pulley and bar, where it hangs with hundreds of others as if in some kind of horrific dry-cleaning shop. It is then pulled through a wall of flames and met on the other side by more black men who, stripped to the waist beneath their smocks, scrape away any straggling bristles.[41]

As November 2007 neared and I had not received permission to enter the slaughterhouse, I put an ad in a few Bladen County newspapers saying that I was coming to Bladen County and wanted to interview past and present slaughterhouse workers for $25.[42]

"Steve" called me on October 24. He had worked several jobs at Tar Heel over eight years—in the scale room, where he weighed boxes and slapped on labels, and in quality control. Now he was working construction, for more money. I asked if we could speak when I came to Bladen County. He said he wanted to but would be working in the western mountains. He would be happy to speak on the phone. He was eager to give chapter and verse on the corruption of the slaughterhouse administrators with whom he had once worked and who had become some of the plant's most powerful administrators. I explained that I just wanted to know how the plant operated and how the pigs were treated. Disappointed, he said that he could enlighten me about that too, and I should call him the following evening.

A pig's 310-degree panoramic vision allows her to see what is happening all around.[43] At the slaughterhouse, a pig is often electrically stunned in order to induce an immediate epileptic seizure.[44] This isn't intended to kill but to drive her into unconsciousness. With this in mind, I asked Steve the next evening how the slaughter at Tar Heel was carried out. He said that, when the pigs arrive, they are moved down a ramp that is level with the truck into a V-shaped structure. After they are stunned, their bodies are placed on a conveyor belt with their back legs shackled about chest high, and they are hoisted upside down. A worker sticks them in the upper torso with a knife to sever the jugular vein. The purpose of "sticking" is to have the pig's beating heart push out all her blood and kill her before she regains consciousness. Husbandry scholar John Webster says that this traditional belief is false: there is no good reason not to have the pig's heart stopped by stunning.[45] Total exsanguination must be accomplished within forty seconds of stunning or the pig may regain consciousness.[46] Webster also claims that it is impossible to guarantee that a pig will be shackled, stuck, and bled out, all within forty seconds of stunning.[47]

Steve said the blood is drained into a trough cut into the floor to be collected so that it can be sold. Whatever remains of the pig is run through a 1,200-degree blue flame that burns away the hair without singeing the moving body. The carcasses are then dipped into a five-foot-by-five-foot vat of 140-degree solution. Except they are not always carcasses. Live and kicking pigs have been videotaped drowning in these scalding vats.[48]

Gail Eisnitz spoke about the killing process with a man named Price who claimed that he had worked as a Tar Heel pig sticker for two years. It's one of Tar Heel's highest-paid line jobs, for kill-floor workers set the pace for the entire plant.[49] Eisnitz asked Price if the hogs killed at Tar Heel are ever insufficiently stunned.

> "All the time," Price laughed. "Because if you're killing 16,000 hogs a shift, those guys aren't going to stun all them hogs all the time. Some hogs come out kicking and raising hell. . . . Most of the time those stunners are not getting the right charge to connect to the hog. Then, if a person can knock that hog down without stunning it and put a shackle around it, they're going to hang that hog up. If a hog ain't stunned correctly, then the shackler's supposed to let it hit the floor and somebody else is supposed to restun that hog and hang him up. . . . But the supervisors don't want the shacklers to do that. They want the shacklers to try to shackle the hog, hang it up, and keep on going. But, if the shackler drops too many hogs, they write that shackler up. A shackler out there don't have no choice but to hang hogs alive in order to keep his job."[50]

Eisnitz asked if the slaughterhouse workers ever beat the hogs.

> "That's all the time," Price laughed again. "You get a stubborn hog that doesn't want to go, they're going to beat that hog til he does. They use a shackle, a pipe, anything they can get their hand on. If the government's not around, which they're not, employees can get to beating that hog all they want to. The supervisor will not say nothing to the person. Because I have seen supervisors taking pipes and whatever they can to hit the hogs and knock them down."

Eisnitz asked Price if they ever stunned hogs by hitting them. "I've done it," he said. "Supervisors do it. But to do that, you've got to hit them across the head and knock them flat out."[51]

Steve told me that the females' vaginas are cut out and sent to Japan, where they're a culinary delicacy.[52] The blood is cooked and the plasma sold to hospitals. He emphasized that the Tar Heel slaughterhouse covers its costs entirely by selling the by-products of slaughter and that the meat is pure profit. He said the slaughter-house ran two shifts a day, one starting early in the morning, the other beginning midafternoon. The cutting floor starts up before the kill floor does, so the cutters can lug the half-frozen carcasses out of the blast cooler in which they were stored overnight and the slaughter can begin anew. He said that there's a rendering plant be-hind the slaughterhouse that manufactures dog food and such out of pig parts such as lard and bone meal. The plant's eight generators are huge, he said, able to power a city the size of Fayetteville.

Several other former slaughterhouse workers answered my news-paper advertisements. Steve was white. A Mexican worker spoke only Spanish. Another worker was a young black woman. In 2000, a *New York Times* reporter working undercover at the slaughterhouse revealed the racial tensions that simmer there.

> The few whites on the payroll tend to be mechanics or supervi-sors. As for the Indians, a handful are supervisors; others tend to get clean menial jobs like warehouse work. With few excep-tions, that leaves the blacks and Mexicans with the dirty jobs at the factory, one of the only places within a 50-mile radius in this muddy corner of North Carolina where a person might make more than $8 an hour. . . . It is money unimaginable in Mexico where the average wage is $4 a day.[53]

Gail and I drove to St. Paul's, population 2,300, eighteen miles from Tar Heel, just over the border into Robeson County. There we met Enrico, who said he had immigrated from Mexico. The Tar Heel slaughterhouse actively recruits workers from the immigrant dens of New York.[54] At one point its workforce was about 60 percent Hispanic.[55] According to anthropologist David Griffith, from East Carolina University in Greenville, there is a reason for that. "New immigrants make docile and more eager workers, willing to fill positions that native workers find repugnant. They serve as a constant reminder to native workers as well, reminding them of their vulnerability to being replaced by cultural 'others.' In this way they reduce the propensity among native workers to protest wages and working conditions."[56] But a series of federal raids on illegal immigrants at the slaughterhouse had ignited an exodus from the plant of more than 1,500 Hispanic workers which, as of December 2008, had boosted the percentage of black workers from 20 percent to 60 percent.[57]

We parked along St. Paul's main street in front of a business whose window had a sign that read: WE CASH CHECKS—PAYROLL, SOCIAL SECURITY, TAX REFUND, OR OTHER: CAMBIAMOS CHEQUES DE COMPANIES, SEGURO SOCIAL DECLARACION DE IMPUESTOS. Lots of signs on St. Paul's main street are in both English and Spanish. Restaurants lined the street: the El Rancho Mexican, the El Maguey Tienda Mexicana, and the Broad Street Café. Only the last was open. We ordered juice. It had no juice. It had no tea either. I settled for toast and water.

Then Enrico appeared. He was heavyset, in his midforties. He spoke no English, though he said he had been living in North Carolina for more than fifteen years. Now he lived nearby in "San Pablo's." Gail, who speaks fluent Spanish, translated for us. Enrico said he had come from Vera Cruz and worked in the slaughterhouse for three years. That had been some years ago. His job had been to separate the pigs' ribs from their meat. Now he was a labor organizer.

He said the pigs were offloaded in a long line, several trucks at a time. They were stunned with a gun to the head. Five or six were killed at the same time. Their bodies were placed upside down on a hook. An artery was cut, and the collected blood was used for dog food, among other things, and lipstick coloring. The pig carcasses were dunked into water so that the skin could more easily be removed, then passed single file through a flame. Workers wielding large knives sliced off the head, which fell into a container; two persons cut through the softer parts, and a machine whirred through the harder vertebrae. The head was sent to the "head room," where the tongue was cut out and the ears cut away. The skin was removed to be used to make pork rinds and cracklings. The intestinal sacks were pulled out and the legs cut off.

A black female former slaughterhouse worker was supposed to meet us in Elizabethtown, twenty-eight miles away, a route that took us past the slaughterhouse again. Melvin's Hamburgers and Hot Dogs was crowded with black females. Gail and I sat in a booth for half an hour, but no one approached. Finally, a woman who had been standing for a long time near the ladies' room came over and introduced herself. She said she had been watching to see whether I could be trusted. She now imagined I could be. She had two small wailing children in tow. Gail offered to take them for some food and drink and left us sitting across the table from one another. I opened my notebook. She didn't say anything. I asked her a question. She said she felt uncomfortable, a black woman speaking to a white man in public. I just raised my pen and waited for the answer.

She said she had worked on the line for nine months. She knew nothing about how the plant operated outside of her own job, having never been curious enough to look. Her job was helping to make chitlins. I said I didn't know what chitlins were. She didn't believe me. "Really," I said. "I don't." Then she realized I wasn't joking. "They're pigs' guts," she explained. "Intestines."

Somewhere in the vast Tar Heel slaughterhouse complex someone scoops out the intestinal sacks that hold the pigs' guts. She didn't know where they did it or how. She just knew that fatty sacks of guts thumped every fifteen seconds onto a long table from an overhead tube around which she and fifteen other women stood, eight to a side. She would reach for the sack and pry off as much fat as she could with her bare fingers. They make dog food out of that, she said. Then she would hook a long tube onto what she called a "pipe machine" to flush out the shit that remained in the intestines. That's what she did, she said, every fifteen seconds, for eight hours a day, interrupted only by a couple of fifteen-minute breaks. Someone down the line washed the intestines, then cut them into two-inch-long segments. "It is very important," she said, "that you don't break the intestinal sack when you pull the fat away. Else the shit leaks out." Sometimes she did break a sack or the pipe machine broke it, and sometimes it broke when it thudded onto the table. After nine months, the pain in her fingers from pulling off the fat got so bad she had to quit.

"Part of you must have been happy about that," I said. "The whole experience sounds awful." "Oh, no," she said. "I didn't want to leave. I'd go back now if I could. The money was damn good. Better than I've gotten since. I started at $6.80 an hour and worked my way to $8.30." She said she had received some workers' compensation, then enrolled in community college to become a nurse's aide. "I wish I could have kept my job."[58]

CHAPTER EIGHT

The World Pork Expo

Biological assets in the farrowing area include the sows
and piglets. Producers sometimes forget that these assets
are actually organisms with a nervous system that
have behavioral and physical needs.
—*John McGlone and Wilson Pond,* PIG PRODUCTION *(2003)*[1]

Hogs have traditionally been referred to as mortgage-lifters
on Iowa farms. They add value to grain produced on the
farm, make use of available labor and improve cash flow.
—*John D. Lawrence, "The State of Iowa's Pork Industry" (1998)*[2]

W HAT HAPPENED TO WILBUR and his mother—what
Mr. Nikita experienced, what both Matthew Scully and I
saw in eastern North Carolina, and what Gail Eisnitz wrote about,
is a new phenomenon. In the eight years following 1991, the number of hogs in North Carolina surged from 2.7 million to 10 million,
the number of factory hog farms jumped, while the total number of

hog farms steeply declined.[3] This trend would probably have continued had the North Carolina legislature not prohibited building more hog farms in 1997 in response to the severe environmental problems they created. North Carolina's trend is America's. The United States had more than 600,000 hog farms in 1970. In 1999, 7,125 factory farms produced nearly 70 percent of the nation's hogs.[4] In 2003, owners of 500,000 or more hogs accounted for 40 percent of all hogs slaughtered.[5] Yet, despite the rapid growth of hog production in North Carolina, its epicenter remains, as it has for a century, the state of Iowa, which raises 16 million hogs and produces one-fifth of America's grain, which are not unrelated.[6]

Des Moines is therefore a natural venue for the World Pork Expo. According to the National Pork Producers Council (NPPC), the "World Pork Expo is to agricultural events what Walt Disney's Epcot Center in Orlando, Florida, is to amusement parks of the [nineteenth] century. They are both a giant leap in the evolutionary process—educational, innovative and extraordinary."[7] World's Fairs held since the middle of the nineteenth century, were originally called "Universal Expositions"; an "exposition," subsequently shortened to "Expo" (as in Montreal Expo '67), was generalized to any large public exhibition or show, and *Expo* magazine is "directed to American convention and trade show professionals."[8] The eighteenth World Pork Expo's *Official Souvenir Program and Show Guide* for 2006 claimed title to "the world's largest pork-specific trade show." I had taken my kids to Epcot Center and expected the World Pork Expo to be equally "educational, innovative and extraordinary"—as well as international, thronged, and brimming with state-of-the-art demonstrations providing glimpses into novel and interesting ways the future may solve whatever pork problems vex the present.

A SLEEPING GIANT

In *The Pork Story: Legend and Legacy*, longtime NPPC executive vice president Orville K. Sweet recalled how overwhelmed he was when he attended his first American Pork Congress in 1979; it made him understand "that the pork industry was an aroused sleeping giant flexing his muscles, ready to challenge all competitors hoping to become the meat of choice."[9] He wasn't the only one aroused, for out of the Pork Congresses emerged the first World Pork Expo, intended as "the beginning of the quest to make pork the meat of choice by the year 2000." The NPPC was equally proud of pork's by-products: from the widest and most varied range of food products available from any animal to a host of pharmaceutical products, quality leather goods, beauty aids, brush bristles—the list goes on and on. Hogs stand uniquely highest among the animals in their extraordinary benefits to society, Sweet said.

As in most years, the 2006 World Pork Expo was held on the Iowa State Fairgrounds in early June. To prepare I trolled the Internet, visiting websites run by the NPPC, the National Pork Promotion and Research Board, and similar organizations; I also read *The National Hog Farmer, Feedstuff* ("the Weekly Newspaper for Agribusiness"), and other industry publications, as well as *Pig Production: Biological Principles and Applications.*

The fairgrounds were fabled. The adventures of the Frakes family chronicled in Phil Stong's 1932 book *State Fair* had occurred there. Abel Frakes' heart is set on his prize pig, Blue Boy, capturing the title of "Grand Champion" Iowa hog, while Abel's wife fantasizes that her mincemeat pie and sweet-and-sour pickles will win several state cooking titles. Stong knew of what he wrote. His grandfather had been superintendent of the fair's swine division, and Stong's job with the *Des Moines Register* included reporting on the fair's livestock shows. His novel became a film, then a musical—twice. In the movie, Will Rogers took a star turn as Abel, the family patriarch. After the film was in the can, the studio asked Rogers if he wanted Blue Boy the same way. But Rogers protested that he was uncomfortable eating a costar. *State Fair*, the musical, transformed the Frakeses into heartland troubadours singing through a crowd of farmers and their wives and children. I looked about. The sleepy, gray, wet fairground upon which I was gazing could never be mistaken for the flashy, sparkling Hollywood fairground of hillocks, big band swing, stomach-churning rides, cotton candy, and booths selling games of chance.

I rubbed circles into the fog condensing on the inside of my windshield and peered through the drizzle. A medium-sized stadium loomed hard to the right, a few large buildings stood in front, two short, intersecting roads led past the buildings, and tiny food booths hovered in the middle distance. I was preparing to sprint the quarter-mile into the Expo when a golf cart appeared. Then a spray of carts burst from the fairgrounds and began picking up soggy Expo visitors. The top of each cart bore a sign. One cart announced its NPPC sponsorship and inquired: WANT TO GET EXOTIC TONIGHT? WWW.THEOTHERWHITEMEAT.COM. Another trumpeted the National Pork Promotion and Research Board's newest tagline: DON'T BE BLAH.

The quest to make pork the meat of choice by the year 2000 had failed. Three weeks before, *The National Hog Farmer* ("the Pork Business Authority") had moaned that, despite forty years of industry promotions and the frequent introduction of new and improved pork products, per capita pork consumption in the United States "continues to languish around the 50-lb/person/year mark."[10] That was one-fifth of a pig a person a year.

"We are going to have to turn over every rock we can find to move pork through the marketplace," said Steve Murphy, chief executive officer of the NPPC.[11] "Don't Be Blah" and "Want to Get Exotic Tonight?" were parts of that rock-turning operation. According to *The Daily Pork* ("Exclusive Pork Coverage"), an online newspaper featured on the National Pork Promotion and Research Board's website, "Don't Be Blah" was a "clever campaign [that] pokes fun at the 'same old' recipe rotation featured nightly on so many American dinner tables, while enticing television, radio, print and online audiences with anything-but-boring pork meals."[12] Launched on Oscar night 2005, the "Don't Be Blah" campaign emerged from the National Pork Board's having "identified a segment of the population who aspire to be better cooks, but lack inspiration and confidence. According to the findings, this group of urban women 25–49 years old, many with children under 17 at home, doesn't often think about pork and how it fits within their hectic, family-focused lives."[13]

"As a special bonus for its readers," *The Daily Pork* offered a "written agreement between family members . . . a pledge to take dinner from blah to blissful, starring The Other White Meat." In this "dinner contract," made "by and among Mom and the Members of the Household," Mom certifies that she "will maintain adequate quantities of The Other White Meat in the refrigerator and freezer to keep meals from becoming humdrum, ho-hum, or just plain boring." In return, "the Members of the Household, agree to not stick peas, carrots, or green beans up our noses."[14]

"INDUSTRY WITHOUT ART IS BRUTALITY"[15]

There was a lot to see. The Expo program and guide announced that racing pigs would be "hoof[ing] round a sawdust track at blazing speeds . . . fun for the entire family" in the cavernous Cattle Barn. The Swine Show and Sale would take place there in a couple of days too. On the Expo's final day, I could go "Cruisin' with the Hogs"—as in watching one hundred Harley-Davidson motorcycles parade up the Grand Concourse.[16] Meanwhile, I could enter the World Pork Open Clay Target Championship, sign up for the World Pork Open Golf Outing, or lunch at the Great Pork Barbe-Qlossal on the Midway, where I could watch "the nation's best barb-quers . . . vie for cash prizes and national competition points." In the Swine Barn, the Junior National Swine Show was "fast becoming one of the top youth shows in the nation."

Free Spam was being dispensed from the eight-foot-wide, ten-foot-long SPAMMobile on the Midway. According to its website, www.spammobile.com, the SPAMMobile was designed to resemble the traditional blue-and-yellow Spam can. There I could join the Official Spam Fan Club.

Spam premiered the year the *Hindenburg* exploded. Today Spam not only is the name of a mammoth vehicle and a fan club but appears in the title of the smash Monty Python Broadway show *Spamalot* and is the word for a most irritating aspect of the Internet, the offers of pornography, marital aids, Nigerian get-rich schemes, and steaks. Spam is also the subject of fifteen times more haikus than the number of ships launched by Helen's face, including the classic:

> *Pink tender morsel*
> *Glistening with salty gel*
> *What the hell is it?*[17]

What Spam is is "SPiced hAM," made from chopped pig thighs and shoulders. According to the Webopedia Computer Dictionary, some claim that Internet spam was so named "because it has many of the same characteristics as the lunchmeat . . . :

- Nobody wants it or ever asks for it.
- No one ever eats it. . . .
- Sometimes it is actually tasty, like 1% of junk mail that is really useful to some people."[18]

Among the other enticements contained in the World Pork Expo program was that, in the evenings, I could "break out the long hair and taste for Seventies nostalgia, [and] take in the mellow sounds of Kentucky-bred songsters, Exile." If the seventies were insufficiently ancient, the sixties band, the Grass Roots, would be playing live on the MusicFest stage on the Grand Concourse. I could shop for Official World Pork Expo Merchandise at the Official World Pork Expo Merchandise Shop or at the World Pork Expo Farm Toy

Show and Sale. But the showpiece was the Trade Show taking place in the Cattle Barn and Varied Industries Building, which featured a wide array of pork industry products and services offered by more than five hundred exhibitors. But first there was the art exhibit.

Marcel Proust wrote that "only through art can we get outside ourselves and know another's view of the universe which is not the same as ours and see landscapes which would otherwise have remained unknown to us like the landscapes of the moon."[19] The journalist Alvin Sandars wrote in 1915 that "there is no higher form of art than that which deals with the intelligent manipulation of animal life;" and for the NPPC, this epigram "epitomizes the dreams that have inspired stockmen since the domestication of livestock."[20] If I wanted to understand pork producers, I needed to view their landscapes and witness their dreams.

The "PigCasso Art Show," being held in a corner of the Cattle Barn, was described in the program as an exhibition of "pig images in a variety of media." Warding off the rain with my program atop my head, I raced toward a young crew-cut fellow operating one of the golf carts with a sign asking if I wanted to "get exotic tonight" and asked him for a lift to the Cattle Barn. He told me to hop on, handed me a free Expo admissions ticket, and steered me through the puddles to the art show.

Most of the "PigCasso Art Show" consisted of a couple of dozen paintings mounted on temporary seven-foot walls. I was immediately drawn to *Pigolympia*, Jane Elgin's riff on Manet's scandalous submission to the 1865 Paris Salon. A young pink sow beckoned from the same brown bedspread and white satin bedsheet and pillow. Like Manet's courtesan, Elgin's pig gazed straight at the viewer. An attendant waited near a black cat with a suggestively erect tail. *Les chattes* was, in Manet's time, slang for both a prostitute and the female genitals.[21] Pigolympia's swinish attendant wore pink robes and offered colorful bouquets of flowers—probably gifts from the courtesan's admirers.

The inspiration for Elgin's work has been referred to as "the founding monument of modern art."[22] When it was first exhibited at the Paris Salon of 1865, a riot ensued—actually a series of them. Critics and correspondents claimed that art had finally reached its ugly, filthy, pornographic nadir.[23] The portrayal of a nude common woman as an object of beauty and sexual beckoning was an artistic bomb tossed toward an educated Parisian public uncertain whether Manet was parodying the classics, mocking their own love for gawking at nudes, or suggesting that the lower classes might be appropriate objects of their sexual desire. The Salon stationed armed guards nearby to prevent its defilement. Was Elgin now siding with the mob, for Pigolympia was . . . well, a "pig," slang for the lowest, lousiest, scummiest sort of prostitute, the sort that haunted Paris's Place Pigalle during World War II, leading GIs to name it "Pig Alley?"

The blue best-in-show ribbon was pinned to Colleen Collins's *Lunch Meet*, portraying rich babes of a certain age. Lunching at a posh and intimate café were three wealthy sows whose pert, upturned noses and appealingly thin and leggy bodies betrayed familiarity with the waiting rooms of plastic surgeons. One sow, her slim legs crossed, wore a gorgeous red dress and matching scarf. Across the small table sat a second sow stylishly attired in a cream-colored skirt and white blouse. The third, equally fetching in her large white hat, held up an "Ethanol List" as the other two looked eagerly on.

I wondered whether Iowa had an antibestiality statute. I checked on my computer. Iowa Code Annotated 717C.1 makes it a crime to "perform a sex act with an animal." That made me wonder how kind a view Iowa prosecutors might take of farmers masturbating boars, even for business purposes. I decided to check North Carolina law on the same subject. A Tar Heel State pig masturbator could be sent to jail for committing any common law "crime against nature," including bestiality, which, under the common law, included any sexual contact between human and animal.[24] I cast one last glance at Pigolympia, lingered for a long moment on the three babes, then moved on to *Pig Farmer's Dream*. This acrylic by Lilly Newkirk of Indianola, Iowa, demonstrated that there really is more to hog farming than sex. A farmer dressed in brown overalls and a broad-brimmed hat stood at the edge of a field near a wood. His head was tilted back, and he was staring into the sky. A white cloud billowed from his head and spread into the heavens. Inside were the smiling faces of three pigs, surrounded by five large "$" signs.

I heard a faint public-address announcement, then distant whooping. The pig races had begun. By the time I arrived on the other side of the Cattle Barn, the first contestants were being introduced. Four tiny starting gates emptied onto a sawdust-covered, semicircular track, ringed by temporary stands that brimmed with spectators. A clownish cowboy emcee was yelling into a microphone. The pigs, he said in a goofy voice, would be racing around the small track for an Oreo buried in sawdust at the finish line. There were to be several races.

The pigs were actually piglets, each wearing a different-colored T-shirt. Each race lasted fewer than ten seconds. The rest of the time was taken up by the goofy cowboy announcing the piglets' funny names.

> In gate number one, iiiit's Miiiiichael JACK-swine! Iiiiin gate number two, it's Sarah Jessica PORKER! Iiiin gate number three, it's Snoop HOGGY Hogg! Iiiin gate number four, it's Oprah SWIIINE-frey!

There was also Squealy NELSON! Britney SQUEAAAALS! IN-stink! And Rush LIM-hog! A bell sounded, the gates were yanked up, and the piglets were off, slipping and sliding through the sawdust, once around the three-quarter track. No one cared who won.

On the way out of the Cattle Barn, I paused to inspect items for sale by the Ohio Pork Council Women, which is a division of the

National Pork Council Women (NPCW). The NPCW was formed in 1963 as a women's auxiliary to the NPPC, at a time when women saw "the need to be part of the action—part of the pork-producing team!"[25] The NPCW went by the name of the National Porkettes until 1985, possibly, the NPPC noted, because "some of our urban friends . . . snicker at the name, not understanding its meaning or its connection with Pork."[26] Still, numerous state Porkettes chapters, now NPCW chapters, operated for many years, and they continue to operate today, even at the county level—for example, the Bremer County Pork Producers and Porkettes from Waverly, Iowa.[27]

One of the National Porkettes' initial projects involved setting up the pageants that led to the annual crowning of the National Pork Queen.[28] That title was eliminated in 1987, but for many years at least twenty states crowned their own Pork Queens; that number had shrunk to two, Iowa and Ohio, by 2005.[29] I expected that Amber Appleton, an Iowa State University freshman and reigning Iowa State Pork Queen, would be making the traditional appearance at the World Pork Expo to present ribbons and dish out pork. Two months before, she had been interviewed by the *Tribune* of Ames, Iowa, and asked, "What do you value most about the pork industry?" She had replied, "The pork industry has a huge impact on our economy by bringing in millions of dollars each year. It is also a great environment to raise children with fulfilled lives. Also, all the aspects for a successful hog operation are right here at home in Iowa: the feed, the land, the resources and technology."[30] But I could find no mention of her in the program.

Among the offerings were a pork wristband upon which was written, SHOW YOUR SUPPORT FOR BACON ($1.95), a GOOD LUCK PIG pin ($1.95), and pig dish towels ($2.95). Further down the row of booths was a display of HAWG ROCK CAFÉ T-shirts and T-shirts that asked, HAVE YOU HUGGED YOUR HOG TODAY? A pink pig hat was going for $15, a pair of pink pig socks for $10, and pink pig erasers for a quarter apiece.

The rain was slowing. I headed for the Grand Concourse, which was just a macadam roadway, took a left, and walked to the Varied Industries Building. Outside I picked up a map from the information booth. The pleasant, moonfaced, white-haired woman inside the booth thrust a petition in my hands and said she had a friend who had been baking pork and beans for the World Pork Expo for many years. This year the friend, suddenly and inexplicably, had decided against baking more beans. Would I sign a phony petition to encourage her to bake her beans next year? I would and I did. She was delighted.

"We Use Everything but the Squeal"[31]

According to McGlone and Pond, "The two most important elements to successful pork production are to have good pig people and good equipment. Good people understand, through intuition or training, that sows, boars, and growing pigs have behavioral needs. Good equipment is designed to accommodate the behavioral biology of the pig."[32]

I set about finding information about good pig people in the Varied Industries Building, but was distracted by a crowd that had gathered in a half-moon before the Pfizer Pharmaceutical Company booth, near the main entrance. There were men and boys dressed in overalls, T-shirts, and baseball caps with Harley, Peterbilt, John Deere, and Archer logos; some were tossing popcorn into their mouths from bags embossed with a farm logo. A Mennonite farmer wearing a starched white shirt, suspenders, a black broad-brimmed hat, and a long wispy beard was speaking intently into a cell phone. The women were attired in skirts or pants, the teenage girls in jeans. Some were laughing; everyone was smiling. They were watching a magician.

For twenty minutes, cheek by jowl with pork producers and their families, the magician launched a dizzying array of tricks—quarters disappeared then reappeared, steel balls ballooned to sizes impossible to hide yet he hid them, and he performed extraordinary feats of "mind-reading" and other legerdemain so smoothly that I was unable to discern, even from two feet away, how he pulled off a single trick. He encouraged folks to walk behind him, and they did. So did I. The entire time he directed a stream of invective at the cell phone–using Mennonite, the giggling teenage girls, and the pork producers in their overalls, all of whom absorbed his nonstop insults with great humor.

I thought he was one angry guy, the he meant everything he said, that he was asking himself, *What am I doing at the World Pork Expo, or whatever they call this thing?* and thinking that this audience of pork producers was beneath him, that Des Moines was in the middle of nowhere, that he was longing to return to Chicago or St. Louis. I would hear this tone the following night in the Wells Fargo Arena in Des Moines. Bruce Springsteen was playing with his Seeger Sessions Band. He was amused by the fact that, when he arrived and asked what events of note were transpiring in Des Moines, he was told about the World Pork Expo. He kept returning to it, joking that pork producers gathering in Des Moines was like the Mafia meeting in New Jersey, and ending his show around midnight with a wave of his hand, saying he was heading to the Expo and would see us all there.

It wasn't easy to find information in the Varied Industries Building on how the industry finds good pig people. I managed to come up with just three flyers. Murphy-Brown LLC was seeking a "Midwest wean to finish production manager" to be "responsible for 1,500,000 spaces of nurseries, finishers and wean to finish sites in IA, IL, MO, and SD with more than 500 contract growers." The company was also looking for a "maintenance manager" to be "responsible for maintenance and construction for 66,000 sows, nearly 200,000 nursery spaces and 150,000 finishing spaces in two locations in the OK panhandle," and two "2,500 sow farm managers."

Agricareers, Inc. was hunting for a swine herdsman to "assist on 3400 sow farrow to wean farm with two barns. Experience helpful but willing to train person if genuinely interested in swine production"; salary was $20,000 to $28,000. A third large swine company was searching for a director of operations for "35,000 sows, farrow to finish. . . . Good people skills needed . . . $85,000–$125,000 plus benefits." Finally, a swine assistant was needed to "oversee a 3 site confinement operation watching approximately 3600 head of nursery/finishing pigs—$28,000+." Slim pickings.

An essay I picked up by Dennis DiPietre, identified as a former economist for the Extension Service, helped explain why:

> One transformation happening through the meat chain, from production to retail, is the replacement of human labor with technology. . . . Agriculture may be one of the last vocations which is still typically thought of as a "hands-on" endeavor. However, that is changing quickly on several fronts, as the sheer complexity of tasks increase while the availability of skilled labor in agriculture is in decline. . . . As we lose more and more husbandry skill at the farm level, technology is slowly coming in to take up the slack. Some of the more recent examples include things like automatic sorting systems for finishing. Sort loss schemes by packers demand a fairly narrow range of weights for finished hogs to achieve optimal value. Finding someone who can consistently judge pig weight is very difficult. Barns are already filled with various electronic controllers that manage temperature, ventilation, fans and curtain drops in rather sophisticated ways. Automatic feeding systems in sow housing judge the animal's condition and proper dose feed. Sensors located in feed bins report the weight of feed remaining in the bins and even send it to the farmer over wireless Internet or radio transmissions. Record bureaus in India and Pakistan can't be very far behind. Driving trailers containing

pigs on their way to the wean-to-finish building through a
kind of vaccination garage where the vaccines are delivered by
atomization will likely be routine in a few years, all because the
labor involved is both tedious and subject to error.[33]

The National Pork Board's 2003 "National Pork Quality Audit"
concluded that pork producers often suffer heavy financial losses because the hogs they send to slaughter don't have uniform weights
and lie outside the core weight ranges demanded by meatpackers
who insist that the pigs they kill be neither too fat nor too lean. This
accounted for the wide array of automatic hog sorters that DiPietre
mentions. Hog sorters are stainless steel cages with scales weighing
250 pounds or more. Pigs learn to walk over these scales by themselves. Depending on their weights, the pigs are automatically fun-
neled toward the appropriate food. Ideally, every pig should weigh
the same when her throat is cut.

Companies hawking their wares in the Varied Industries Building boasted of how they could "raise your hogs automatically."
Sierens was selling the Sierens M-Sort, which combed hogs into
"this week's shipment and next week's shipment," and others that
sifted them into "high or low protein food courts and market pens."
Pork producers wanting to send a specific number of pigs to slaughter might have been interested in Farmweld's Fast II automatic hog
sorter, which programmed scales to identify the heaviest hogs or all
hogs above a certain weight ready for transport. The Sierens M-Sort
would spray hogs with different-colored dyes to identify them by
the weights they registered on the scales: green for hogs weighing
between 225 and 240 pounds, red for hogs between 195 and 210
pounds, and both green and red for hogs falling between 210 and
225 pounds. To avoid feeding hogs that had reached their desired
market weights, and to save producers a dollar or two per hog, pigs
could be fed two, even three, different diets, depending on their
weight. One automatic sorter, Phason's Auto-Sort Management

System, even estimated how long it would take a hog to reach a desired weight. The Sierens M-Sort locked the gates of the sorter to prevent hogs from walking through the scale without getting weighed and blasted air at any hog who fell asleep while standing on the scale or didn't exit fast enough. The "patented pig flow" of Schick Enterprises' SortAll Revolution 2 sorted hogs from one pen to another or straight into the holding pen from which they would be shipped to slaughter.

According to Bert Huftalin of Malta, Illinois, absentee producers using Phason's Auto-Sort Management System could check the weights of their hogs from anywhere in the world. PigWIN (Agrovision), Porcitec (Agritec), and PigCHAMP (FBS Systems) are Windows-based pig management programs that allow producers, anywhere, to view each pig's complete history at a mouse click, produce colorful charts that show performance indicators about an entire herd, track exactly how much feed is being used, and provide growth curves. The hand-held Sono-Grader uses ultrasound to test for pregnancy or the depth of a sow's back fat or loin muscle. Tiny transponders manufactured by Renco Corporation and EZid can be implanted into a hog's body; the information produced is then read, stored, and transferred to a computer.

Most packers pay based on a hog's "hot carcass" weight, the heft of what's left of the hog after every part of its body that can't be sold has been cut out or trimmed away. Lower hot carcass weights beget lower profits, and lower profits begin at the production facility. Dead hogs are gutted before their bodies are weighed; the heavier their virtually worthless guts are, the lower their hot carcass weight, and the less money the packer will pay. Feeding hogs high-fiber diets near slaughter time or letting them eat less than twelve hours before slaughter leads to lower hot carcass weights because at death their guts will contain undigested food or undiscarded feces. On the other hand, fasting hogs more than twenty-four hours before death will cause their bodies to burn away valuable tissue. This leads to lower profits too. On average, heavier hogs bring higher profit because the body parts cut out grow more slowly than the more valuable parts for which the producer is paid. Skin blemishes caused by mange or insect bites will be cut away, so it pays to prevent them. Bruising hogs' bodies after death leads to trimming too.[34] Stressing hogs by stocking them too densely in trucks, transporting them too far or for too long, subjecting them to extremes of hot or cold during transportation—all lead to lower hot carcass weights and lower profit.

"The Truth About Livestock Production"

The World Pork Expo program contained an interview with Neil Dierks, the NPPC's CEO. Asked about "the biggest threat facing the U.S. pork industry," Dierks responded, "Animal welfare issues." He did not mean that the NPPC was concerned about the welfare of hogs. Oh, no. He meant that the NPPC was concerned about the effect that those who do care about the welfare of hogs may have on the profit of factory farmers. The NPPC, he said, intended "to inform and educate public policy makers about current production practices that ensure high levels of animal welfare." And he promised the NPPC would "fight to protect producers' livelihoods."[35] Accordingly, the NPPC was intent on emphasizing how it had led the opposition "to successfully derail legislature that would have banned all 'downer livestock' . . . from entering the food supply."[36] "Downers" are animals so sick or so injured that they cannot walk to slaughter unaided and must be dragged. Thanks in part to the efforts of the NPPC, they still have to be dragged to their deaths. The NPPC also "committed early" to opposing an effort to prohibit sow stalls in Arizona and promised it would be "working to explain to Arizona citizens the truth about livestock production."[37]

Steel gestation and farrowing crates were crowding many of the aisles, and I needed help in understanding them. I settled into a comfortable chair provided by a pharmaceutical company and opened McGlone and Pond's *Pig Production*. According to this book, the two most common gestating and farrowing systems have long been the crate and the girth tether.[38] In 1991, the United Kingdom prohibited installation of either, because both were cruel; the European Union had banned girth tethers years before and the use of every kind of crate beginning in 2013.

Because crates are designed to maximize profit, they remain the most common American pork production system.[39] More gestation crate systems exist in the United States than anywhere in the world, and for an excellent reason: no law prevents American pork producers from using any system that will make them money.[40] Until 2002, there were no restrictions anywhere in the country. Then Florida amended its constitution by initiative petition to prohibit confining or tethering pregnant pigs to the degree that they couldn't turn around freely.[41] Five months after the 2006 World Pork Expo, Arizona voters would enact the initiative that the NPPC had been so determined to defeat by a margin of 65 to 35 percent. Beginning in 2013, it will be a crime in Arizona to tether or confine a pregnant pig during her pregnancy for the majority of a day so that she is prevented from lying down and fully extending her limbs or turning around freely. In 2007, Oregon prohibited the confinement of pigs in gestation crates. In 2008, Colorado enacted a phaseout of the crates, while Californians enacted Proposition 2 by the landslide referendum vote of 63 percent to 37 percent. Beginning in 2015, it will be a misdemeanor in California to house pregnant sows in crates too small for them to lie down, stand up, fully extend their limbs, and turn around freely.

The crates that manufacturers had erected in the aisles were formidable structures: 170 pounds of heavy-duty steel, seven feet long, two feet high, able to withstand incessant knocks by muscular pigs weighing hundreds of pounds. Their use would be nearly constant, as almost half a farm's sows are usually confined to crates at any one time. But their interiors were no more than twenty-four inches wide, and some, such as the ones made by EIP Manufacturing, were twenty-two inches.

I caught the eye of a young salesman standing near one of the crates. He came over and extended his hand. "What is this?" I pointed to the steel crate. "A gestation crate," he said. He had already started looking over my shoulder. "How long are the sows kept in them?" I asked. "About sixteen weeks," he said. Now he was edging away. "Then where do they go?" I asked. "To farrow, for about a week." He walked a few steps away from me. I followed. "Farrow?" I asked. "Give birth," he said. "Then what happens to them?" "Then it's back to the gestation crate," he said. "For how long?" "Sixteen weeks." "Then it all starts again?" He turned his back and left.

Central Confinement Service Ltd. was celebrating its twentieth year of designing "highly productive efficient and low maintenance systems for professional producers." It was giving away color brochures that featured whitewashed buildings as long as football fields, showing two or three of them built parallel to each other and connected by passageways at their midsections. Because these confinement buildings are so massive and often windowless, exhaust fans jut from their sides, ends, or tops to suck out the stale air that inevitably accumulates inside. Some of these fans are so gargantuan that they resemble jet engines getting ready to blast the building across the landscape; others are much smaller, but a building might need 150 of these.

Inside these buildings are pigs. Lots and lots of pigs. Sows by the hundreds may stand confined in steel crates lined up one against another. Each building may house 1,000 sows or 4,400 piglets; a complex may hold 8,000 sows. These pigs are forced to stand, not on earth, but on floors constructed from noncorrosive plastic, concrete, plastic with integrated rubber mat, cast iron, rust-resistant hot dip galvanized steel, stainless steel, or fiberglass. They need to rest on something solid and smooth or their rapidly growing feet and toes can become painfully inflamed and lame them. That is why some pork producers stand their pigs on floors made six-sevenths of concrete or three-quarters plastic-coated metal. Solid and smooth, these are better for pig feet. A pig marketed at a weight of 250 pounds has produced a ton and a half of waste.[42] Because waste can corrode a floor, many pigs are forced to stand on floors woven from 40 percent wire, so that their waste falls through the spaces.[43] Floors may deteriorate in other ways too. Producers often add large quantities of salt to pig feed so the pigs will eat more and grow faster. As pointed out by Slat Saver/Slot Lock, a division of Wahoo Concrete Products, these salts mix with water to create caustic chemicals that can burn even concrete and steel. To avoid this, producers may cover the damaged areas with sturdy plastic "slat savers" or apply an epoxy, as provided by, for instance, Vanberg Specialized Coatings.

I ran into another crowd at the end of an aisle in the Varied Industries Building. It was gathered around a continuous-loop video playing on a monitor mounted high above the floor. I had to push through to get a better look. It was playing a graphic demonstration of how a boar can be encouraged to ejaculate into a container while being held fast in something called a "minitube." Some people were watching it again and again.

Dead Sleds and Carcass Carts

The remaining exhibits in the Varied Industries Building were a bit of a letdown, as the purpose of the equipment changed from sex to death. Between 6 and 8 percent of pigs die before they are trucked from the factory farm to slaughter.[44] According to the U.S. Department of Agriculture, about 123 million pigs were slaughtered in 2006. That means 7 to 10 million died on their own before we could kill them. A producer can't just leave all those heavy bodies to rot where they fall.

Enter AgAlliance, Inc. ("Helping people build their dreams worldwide"). Using its products, a worker can load a 600-pound dead body onto the front or rear of its 33-pound Dead Sled Mover, the tapered sides of which form a "deep 'V' so [the] pig stays on."[45] Three graphic color photographs in one of its brochures demonstrated. A worker, having grasped the deceased by her snout with an instrument, yanks the body onto the dead sled and drags it out of its confinement pen. Alternatively, AgAlliance offers a Quick Load Dead Sled that comes with fixed casters on the rear and swivel casters on the front. Its V-shaped nose ensures that it will not snag gates.[46] A producer may also purchase two brands of Carcass Carts. The Solid Panel Markey Hog Cart comes with pneumatic tires, an optional third wheel, and a 900-pound winch, while its deluxe V-8 has a V-shaped center that cradles the carcass to lessen its chance of falling off.[47] All of this equipment would have been helpful on the Murphy Family Ventures Garland Sow Farm.

But removal is just the first step to disposal of the body. For the next step, one may utilize the products of Southern Breeze Fabricators, Inc. ("We blow no smoke!"). At the Expo, that company was handing out a CD-ROM showing a demonstration of four models of its incinerators. Larry Lewis ("Builder of fire-brick lined animal carcass incinerators") from Cedar, Iowa, was shown selling three livestock incinerator models, each individually built, and supervising the manufacturing process to ensure that all the fire-brick and top-loading doors fit correctly. Lewis's Livestock Incinerator Carcass Handler came with a 3,200-pound, two-speed hand winch that could easily be used to hoist a 650-pound sow. National Incinerator, Inc., sells the HD500 model specifically for swine disposal. With a 500-pound capacity, the HD500 could fit into a ten-foot-square space and left just 2 percent ash. Burn-Easy Refractory Block-Lined Crematories featured eight models capable of reducing 1,200 pounds of carcass to less than 12 gallons of ash.

I left the Varied Industries Building to pack for North Carolina. It was still soggy outside, and the sound system for the MusicFest stage was scratchy. But the Expo-goers didn't mind. A few were dancing to the music of the Grass Roots. Most were chatting and swaying to the two-score-year-old beat ("Sooner or later, love is gonna get you"), munching on roast pork, pulled pork, barbecued pork, baby back ribs, baked ham, pork roast, ham steak, pork chops, and sweet-and-sour pork. Roasted and baked and barbecued smells were wafting from the hospitality tents erected along the Grand Concourse.

I asked an official on the Grand Concourse when Amber Appleton was going to appear. He looked blank. "The Iowa Pork Queen," I prompted. He didn't know. When I returned home, I Googled "Amber Appleton" "World Pork Expo." There were no matches. I don't think she showed.

I had an hour's flight to O'Hare Airport, then a layover of almost two. Finally I was on the last leg, an hour and forty-five minutes to Raleigh-Durham. I so lost myself in reading and categorizing the hundreds of handouts I had picked up in the Varied Industries Building that it wasn't until I felt the plane begin to drop that I looked out the window. Parallel rows of great low whitewashed buildings, some as long as football fields, some connected by passageways at midsection, many sitting beside strange-colored lagoons, were passing six miles below. I was almost to the Cape Fear River.

CHAPTER NINE

A Pork Industry Visionary

We have to be able to process these things
and get them through the plant.
—*Ken Prusa*

The key to sustained profitability for pork producers
and the entire pork chain is increasing consumer
demand for pork.
—*Babcock Genetics, Inc.*

DESPITE ITS CEASELESS efforts to promote itself, the pork industry's major problem remains that people don't much like how its product tastes. "Over the past 40 years the Swine Industry has responded to consumer's [*sic*] requests for leaner pork by producing hogs with less fat. Though the majority of pork eaten today is much leaner than the pork from the 1960's, many consumers eat less pork because they feel it lacks overall flavor, tenderness, and juiciness. These mixed signals create challenges for pork producers, packers, and retailers who are attempting to satisfy consumer desires."[1] How does the pork industry induce consumers to purchase a tough, dry, flavorless meat? A challenge indeed, but one the pork industry is determined to meet.

In an attempt to make pork Americans' "meat of choice," the National Pork Board developed a set of criteria twenty-five years ago that was intended to identify the Ideal Market Hog (IMH).[2] This "symbol of excellence" came to be referred to as "Symbol"; the NPPC dubbed it "the symbol of the thinking of an industry."[3] Each NPPC president has thereafter received a fifty-pound bronze statue of Symbol upon his retirement.[4]

Symbol weighed 240 pounds. He had a feed conversion ratio of 2.5 and went to market in 150 days. He was slaughtered with the fat in his last rib 0.7 inches deep, and his loin muscle area totaled 5.8 square inches. His back-fat depth was 1.0 inch, and he carried 105 pounds of lean muscle on a 180-pound hot carcass, which he had accumulated at the rate of about three-quarters of a pound a day.[5] For the NPPC, the eponymous Symbol "symbolizes the sincere intent, efforts, and dedication of an industry to improve its product." For "the animal husbandry world," it symbolized "a high-yielding pig with the substance and stamina to endure the stress of controlled environment and to perform efficiently in feed conversion and reproduction."

By 1996, American pigs had been so drastically altered and defatted that the National Pork Board had to promulgate a new Symbol. This IMH, known as Symbol II, had a 195-pound hot carcass, minimum loin muscle of 6.5 square inches, appropriate color, water-holding capacity, and ultimate pH and an intramuscular fat level of at least 2.9 percent. It had to come from a maternal line capable of producing 25 pigs each year; be marketable at 156 days of age; possess a live-weight feed efficiency of 2.4, a fat-free lean gain efficiency of 6.4, and a fat-free lean gain of 0.78 pounds per day; and have a standard back-fat depth of 0.8 inches and a fat-free lean index of 49.8.[6]

The search for porcine perfection did not end there. The National Pork Board introduced Symbol III at the 2005 World Pork Expo. Symbol III described the IMH in the greatest detail so far. Symbol III was to utilize genomic technology to support maximum improvements in profitability and efficiency. It was to have certain *production* characteristics: a live-weight feed efficiency of 2.4, a fat-free lean gain efficiency of 5.9, and a fat-free lean gain of 0.95 pounds per day. It had to come from a maternal line that could wean more than 25 pigs a year, and it had to be ready to go to market at 156 days of age at a weight of 270 pounds. Symbol III was to be free of abscesses, injection-site blemishes, arthritis, bruises, and carcass trim, as well as structurally correct and sound. Its body and mind were to be entirely suited to living its entire life on an industrial farm. It had to be the product of a system that would ensure an opportunity for profitability for everyone at every stage in the production process, from producer to retailer, while providing a cost-competitive retail product.

This paragon among pigs was to have other desirable characteristics: a hot carcass weight of 205 pounds, a carcass yield of 76 percent, a loin muscle area of 6.5 square inches, a belly thickness of 1.0 inch, a tenth-rib back-fat depth of 0.7 inches, and a fat-free lean index of 53.0. Its meat was to have a muscle color score of 4.0, an ultimate pH of 5.9, a maximum drip loss of 2.5 percent, and an intramuscular fat level of 3.0 percent, with no intramuscular color variation or coarse muscle texture.[7] But this creature didn't exist. And so it would be up to the pork industry's scientists to create it.

The American Meat Science Association (AMSA) often lies at the center of these geneses. The AMSA is a member of the Federation of Animal Science Societies, which includes the American Dairy Science Association, the American Embryo Transfer Association, the American Registry of Professional Animal Scientists, the American Society of Animal Science, the Equine Science Society, Feed Analysis Consortium, Inc., the International Embryo Transfer Society, the National Coalition for Food and Agricultural Research

(NC-FAR), the Poultry Science Association, and the U.S. branch of the Poultry Science Association.[8] "Its unique role is to provide the forum for all interests in meat, commercial, academic, government, and consumer to come together in a reasoned, scientifically based atmosphere to address the needs of the processing and marketing segments of industry, the consuming public, its own members, and others in the biological and nutritional sciences."[9]

The AMSA's fifty-ninth annual Reciprocal Meat Conference was scheduled to be held at the University of Illinois two weeks after the 2006 World Pork Expo and to feature papers such as "The Hype from Hollywood: Tinseltown's Latest Assault on the Meat Industry," "The Swine Genome Sequencing Project," "Current Genetic Tools for Meat Quality Improvement," and "Trends Driving Consumer Meat Preferences." It also sponsored the Intercollegiate Meat Coaches Association (IMCA). For sixteen years, the IMCA had annually awarded the Intercollegiate Meat Judging Meritorious Service Award to meat scientists who had best served the Intercollegiate Meat Judging Program. Its 2005 award had gone to Auburn professor Bill Jones, whose "ability to produce all known specification defects from a single lamb carcass is legendary."[10]

After the unveiling of Symbol III, the Intercollegiate Meat Coaches quickly issued a "Policy Statement" in the area of "Pork Carcass Judging" in order to dispel any belief among its student pork producers that a leaner carcass was necessarily a better one.[11]

The National Pork Board has published live and carcass specifications for the Ideal Market Hog (Symbol III):

The ideal 10th rib fat thickness for market hogs is 0.70 inches. . . . Pork carcasses with less than 0.60 inches backfat have a higher incidence of bellies which are too thin for high quality bacon production and also tend to have unacceptably low marbling levels and less palatable pork. These problems are even greater when backfat is less than 0.50 inches and especially if backfat is less than 0.40. If last rib backfat thickness is less than or equal to [0.50 inches], *OR* if 10th rib backfat thickness is less than or equal to 0.30 [inches], then these carcasses are *TOO LEAN,* and the industry dictates that these carcasses should receive a deduction in carcass value due to inadequate belly yield/quality as well as being more apt to produce low quality pork. If this situation is presented in competition, students would be expected to evaluate the given carcass or carcasses against the contemporaries within the class and rank accordingly.[12]

ENGINEERING THE PERFECT CARCASS

As consumer desires shift, so does the IMH, and it has shifted twice. When a consumer need becomes manifest, as did the desire for lean pork, the meat scientists of the AMSA retreat to their laboratories to create new pigs. But they must have some idea of what sort of pig to build, and they realize that their creation of one positive carcass quality may have unforeseen negative impacts upon other desirable carcass qualities.

Back-fat depth is a prime example. A paper given at the 2004 twenty-ninth annual National Swine Improvement Federation in Ames, Iowa, rued that "the enhancement of carcass leanness over time has been at the expense of meat quality traits, namely intramuscular fat percentage, tenderness, and color, as well as eating quality traits such as flavor."[13] Intramuscular fat percentage is known to have a strong influence on consumer pork-buying decisions. But that's not the only influential fat. Prominent pork scientists have concluded that "by decreasing backfat depth over the last 15 years to conform to packer buying systems and the health conscience [*sic*] consumer, intramuscular fat and other meat quality traits have been negatively impacted."[14]

This nationwide cohort of meat scientists, often professors of animal science who work at state universities that belong to the American Meat Science Association, expend their entire careers attempting to determine, as precisely as possible, what pork consumers and packers want, how they can produce it, and what will advance the interests of pork producers in their ceaseless warfare with chicken producers, whose own scientists do the bidding of the Poultry Science Association, also a member of the Federation of Animal Science Societies.

Once meat scientists understand what will induce consumers to buy a piece of pork, meat geneticists swing into action to try to create it on the hoof, and the closer they come to reaching the mark, the more likely it is that factory farmers will produce and packers will kill the pigs they hope will make them the most money, and consumers will obtain the pork the industry hopes they want.

More than three hundred pig breeds exist, and meat geneticists are creating more. A breed of pig is usually selected for its uniformly distinctive appearance and some economically profitable characteristic: perhaps it has the capacity to produce a large number of live piglets each year or to express great quantities of milk, a body heavy with muscle or laden with fat, or nearly devoid of fat, muscles tending toward tenderness, juiciness, and flavorfulness, a high pH, reddish color, or low water-holding capacity, a strong sexual drive or the ability to conceive easily, the ability to gain a lot of weight each day, or docility when handled by people or when around other pigs.[15] The more lightly muscled a hog is, the comparatively heavier are its inedible (and therefore profitless) parts; the liver, heart, lungs, and guts are all relatively worthless, as are the head, feet, blood, and fat. The coarser, blacker, or redder the hair, the more likely it is that it will have to be trimmed, because the pork industry believes that consumers do not like coarse, black, or reddish hair on their pork. A pig with more muscle, less weighty inedible parts, and lighter hair is a good thing for the industry. Corporations, each claiming to have

manipulated genes and thereby transformed their pigs, fiercely compete to sell the products of their tinkerings. Today Durocs grow
quickly and require less feed to build muscle, while Yorkshires produce large litters and Landraces have a high weaning rate and high
post-weaning survival rate.[16]

An article in *Feed Management* emphasizes another desirable feature—a sow's capacity to wean piglets: "The number of piglets
weaned per sow per year is one of the most important indicators of
the herd's financial performance. Long-term survival of the operation therefore largely depends on the capability of the management
team to fully exploit the sow's inherent reproductive capacity."[17] A
publication from Albion Laboratories, Inc., that I picked up at the
World Pork Expo, featured the headache of a Minnesota couple who
fed their breeding sows the trace minerals bonded to amino acids
that are contained in Albion MAAC (Metal Amino Acid Chelates).
Their "problem" was that Albion MAAC increased the number of
pigs each of their sows produced each year by 19 percent, from 20.43
to 25.21. Where were the couple going to house all their additional
pigs?[18] Undoubtedly, Symbol IV will wean 30 PPSY. But as meat industry geneticists and producers drive to create that sow, independent scientists are warning of crippled bodies and exhausted spirits.[19]

Meanwhile, myriad corporations dedicated to the genetic manipulation of pigs in the service of production efficiency and profitability have sprung up. Premier Pork Systems LLC has created
G-MAX Durocs that arrive with "above average appetites and the
ability to grow extremely fast to heavy weights."[20] They boast of
progeny averaging an ultimate pH of 5.83, a Japanese Bar Color
Score of 3.65, a cooking loss of 21.2 percent, a purge loss of 0.97
percent, a score of 7 on the tenderness scale and a 6 on the juiciness
scale, an Instron rating of 5.36, and a Minolta rating of 44.9.[21] (I'll
explain what these strange numbers mean soon.)

PIC USA ("The better pork people") offer the PIC 280M ("The
industry's leading meat-quality boar"), which averages a daily

weight gain of 2.09 pounds, a finished weight of 275.41 pounds, a
hot carcass weight of 204.82 pounds, a carcass yield of 74.34 percent, 0.77 inches of back fat, and 2.38 inches of loin depth. It is
53.44 percent lean. Its loin Minolta L* rating averages 45.81. PIC
USA's PIC 327L ("The industry's leading lean production boar")
"has a strong reputation for: Excellent growth rate and feed efficiency, low backfat levels, and high lean content. The emphasis of
this boar is on reducing production costs and capturing value for the
highest lean content. . . . His progeny can be efficiently taken to very
heavy slaughter weights with low backfat levels."[22] Premier Pork
Systems claims that the New Premier LS-10 breed is descended
from a "hyper-prolific line developed . . . at the University of Nebraska. The extreme ovulation rate of the Nebraska line, resulting in
larger litter size, has been combined with the durability and milking
traits of Premier's current maternal GGP lines to create a phenome-
nal female (with a PPSY of 25.59)."[23]

Not to be outdone, Newsham Genetics has developed the Super-
Sire XM (Exceptional Meat), which promises growth, appetite, and
a lean carcass. Its SuperSire UL (Ultra Lean) brings producers excellent feed efficiency, daily weight gain, and a lean carcass, of
course.[24] But Newsham Genetics' proudest creation is the Super-
Mom. Her formal name is Newsham Line 37, and the company has
spent more than a decade researching and developing her.[25]

"SuperMom combines the unrivaled prolificacy of the Nebraska
Index Line along with the advanced carcass composition found in
the Newsham Line 7 genotype and the outstanding grow/finish and
superior carcass characteristics and maternal performance that producers have come to expect from the Newsham Line 3 genotype."[26]
That's not all. SuperMom was "designed to enter your breeding-
herd, yield large litters, support them through weaning, and remain
in your breeding herd for the long haul. Healthy and robust, Super-
Mom provides you with lower involuntary cull and death rates. Not
only does she produce more pigs, but SuperMom has the milk pro-

duction that allows her to wean vigorous pigs—giving them the edge they need for healthy daily gain and feed efficiency."[27] The offspring of SuperMom and SuperSire promise "maximum value due to their superior carcass quality." There is a lot of money to be made by using its superpigs, Newsham explains. "In a 2,000-sow operation, the Newsham Advantage could bring you as much as $186,000 per year in gross margin by reducing your deads, lights, and culls a typical 5 percentage points."[28]

Everything depends on "heritability," that rough measure of the extent to which genetic differences in a population lead to differences in individuals. If some genetic population difference never produces an individual trait, its heritability is "0." If a genetic difference always produces some trait, its heritability is "1." The more heritable a trait is, the more easily geneticists and producers can figure out how to create a pig that has it. Because most traits emerge from a complex, often poorly understood, interaction between genes and environment, they carry just a moderate or low heritability.

The rate of a herd's genetic improvement can be easily calculated. Producers or breeders look at a chart that geneticists produce that gives the heritability of a trait they want to produce. It will be a number between zero and one. They multiply that number by the "selection differential." That's the difference between how much of a desired trait the newly selected pig should have *minus* how much of that trait the average pig in the herd already has. Last, the producer or breeder divides this number by the herd's "generational interval": the period of time between the birth of one generation and the birth of the next generation.[29]

Because pork producers have long been obsessed with reducing back-fat depth, let's use a proposed reduction of back fat through genetic means as a sample calculation. According to the NPPC's 1995 Genetic Evaluation Program, the heritability of back-fat depth in pigs is 0.46. That means about 46 percent of the differences in back-fat depth among pigs is attributable to genetics. We're done with step one. Two to go. My *Pig Production* textbook helps solve the rest of this problem. Imagine that you're a pork producer whose herd averages 1.0 inch of back fat with a generational interval of 2.0 years. You buy replacement seedstock that averages 0.7 inches of back fat. Let's do the numbers. The difference between 0.7 and 1.0 is 0.3. Multiply that by 0.46. That gives us 0.138. Now divide by 2.0. The answer is 0.069. This means that the average thickness of back fat in the producer's herd will drop 0.069 inches the first year.

From this sort of training will emerge our future meat scientists. I was fortunate to meet one of today's meat superstars, a "master of the pork industry."

MASTER OF THE PORK INDUSTRY

At the World Pork Expo, I picked up the May 2007 edition of *The National Hog Farmer*, which featured certain "Pork Industry Visionaries" and "Masters of the Pork Industry." Among them were giant pork producers, upper-level meatpacking managers, a swine veterinarian, pig crowding and pig drinking researchers, and a pork market analyst. I first considered interviewing Professor Stan Curtis. *The National Hog Farmer* reported that he had switched from premed to animal science in college because he "longed for involvement with livestock." Curtis had "pioneered the study of the pig's mind while head of the Dairy and Animal Science Department at Pennsylvania State University during the 1990s. He and a student helped pigs learn how to play video games to get feed rewards—a first step in developing human-pig communication." That sounded interesting. "For all his accomplishments and awards over a 40-year career," the article concluded, "including the 2001 Pork Industry Distinguished Service Award from the NPPC, Curtis remains a humble servant of the industry." I was picking up the phone to call him at the University of Illinois when I saw the profile of Dr. Ken Prusa and decided to call Iowa State University instead.

Prusa earned his Ph.D. in Food and Nutrition at Kansas State University in 1983. He holds dual Iowa State University appointments as Professor of Food Science and Human Nutrition and Professor of Animal Science and teaches classes in experimental foods and sensory analysis. His official university biography touts his expertise in pork and his "special interest" in the "preharvest treatment of pigs for the improvement of pork quality and safety."[30] Because his primary research interest is on "factors that influence pork quality and sensory and instrumental analysis of meat and meat products, and new product development related to meat," his publications trend toward titles like "Influence of Lipid Content on Pork Sensory Quality Within pH Classification," "Correlation Among Selected Pork Quality Traits," and "A Molecular Genome Scan Analysis to Identify Chromosomal Regions Influencing Economic Traits in the Pig."[31] He has spent the past twenty years working with midwestern pork producers, pork packers, and pork grocers to deliver the pork products he believes consumers want.[32] His "close association with the packing and processing industries" is what enables him to help the pork industry attract consumers.[33]

Prusa received his first academic research grant from the NPPC to study the relationship of back fat to eating quality. For years he has applied the scientific method to the problem of increasing pork consumption by attempting to make the experience of eating pork more sensual, keeping in mind the admonition of a forty-year veteran of the meatpacker Swift & Company: "[he] reins us in and reminds us that we have to be able to process these things and get them through the plant."

When I got in touch with him, Prusa was Professor in Charge of the Sensory Evaluation Unit. I learned that this "provides facilities and expertise for the sensory evaluation of food products and/or ingredients. . . . Services include project design and management, panelist recruiting, screening, and training, computerized data collection (Compusense®), and statistical analysis. The following general kinds of sensory tests are conducted: discrimination tests, descriptive analysis tests with trained panelists, and consumer preference and acceptance tests."[34]

In a "Research Impact Statement" posted on the university website entitled "Identification of Superior Quality Pork for White Table Cloth Restaurants," Prusa wrote that his scientific work was aimed at redressing the following problem: "There is a lack of consistency in the quality of pork produced in this country . . . [that] makes it extremely difficult for pork to find its way onto the menus of the best restaurants." His major accomplishment has been the identification of "pH of the muscle as a major determinant of final pork eating quality. Pork with greater pH will be more tender, juicy and flavorful when compared with pork of lower pH."[35]

Having earned an undergraduate degree in chemistry, I understood that pH measures how acid or alkaline a solution is. In a 25-degree Celsius aqueous, or water-based, solution, a pH value of less than seven means that the solution is acidic; a solution with a pH greater than seven is basic or alkaline. I didn't see the connection between muscle pH and the sensuality of a pork-eating experience, but thought it would be interesting to learn about, and e-mailed Professor Prusa to ask if he would chat with me and show me around his Sensory Evaluation Unit.

I feared that he might respond like Smithfield Farms, which circled its wagons, then ran me around them for most of a year. But college professors don't generally have media relations departments and don't pay consultants to stonewall. Prusa immediately extended an invitation and off to Ames, Iowa, I flew. There I discovered that I was just the latest in a string of folks interested in what Prusa was doing, among them the History Channel's *American Experience* and the Public Broadcasting Service's *This American Life*. Prusa was a media veteran.

His directions to me warned: "Your mission, if you choose to accept it, is to get onto Central Campus at Iowa State University (others before you have failed)." Having spent days fruitlessly navigating the dusty back roads of Bladen County, I was wary. But I figured that the Central Campus of a major state university ought to be harder to miss than a factory hog farm in the middle of the boon-docks. With no trouble at all, I found my way to the Sensory Evalu-ation Unit (SEU) at Iowa State University's Center for Designing Foods to Improve Nutrition, located in McKay Hall.

Prusa greeted me with midwestern friendliness. He noticed that I was freezing, offered hot coffee or tea, suggested Earl Grey, intro-duced me to his colleague Christine Fedler, then led me through SEU's anteroom into a windowless inner room. It was spartan, holding just a single round table, six chairs, and a blackboard. I began stirring sugar into the tea he had poured into a MONSANTO CHOICE GENETICS mug.

Prusa said he had tested a wide variety of foods, the color of irra-diated ground beef, the viscosity of an energy drink for senior citi-zens, the flavor of walleye salmon fattened on flax oil, and numerous attributes of corn, soybeans, and granola bars.[36] But 90 percent of what his group does is to evaluate the quality of pork. He was con-vinced that big changes are coming to the pork industry. It was time, he said, to move away from pork as "the Other White Meat." This was news.

In a remarkably short time, he said, the pork industry had moved from churning out large fat pigs with heavily marbled muscles to producing very lean pigs. The "Other White Meat" campaign had succeeded in raising consumer consciousness. But the unfortunate truth, he said, is that lean modern white pork just doesn't taste very good. Today's meatpackers are rebelling at slaughtering ever leaner pigs, because pig fat is usually sliced from carcasses with automatic knives that cut away valuable muscle if the fat is less than about half an inch thick. There was another complication. Very lean carcasses don't produce good bacon, which requires at least a dollop of fat, and lean carcasses don't hold a cure. American bacon comes from pork bellies, the undersides of pigs. That is why pork bellies are the most valuable part of the carcass, so valuable they have been traded on the Chicago Mercantile Exchange in units of twenty tons, thirteen pounds to a belly, for nearly half a century.

Producers knew what to feed pigs—corn. Since the early eighteenth century, pigs had been considered a superb way to move corn to market. Then in 2005 the world upended. Huge quantities of corn were converted to ethanol and diverted for use as biofuel. The price of the remaining corn more than doubled between 2005 and 2007. Producers began to feed pigs Distillers Dried Grains with Solubles (DDGS), the leftovers from the process of distilling ethyl alcohol from fermented yeast obtained from condensed and dried grains.[37] DDGS is full of soft, long-chained polyunsaturated fats. After it's fermented to make ethanol, the by-product contains a little protein and fat in the form of corn oil.

Prusa explained that pigs convert about 1 percent of the corn they eat to fat but may convert 10 or 11 percent of corn oil. But their bodies don't metabolize a diet of greater than about 10 percent DDGS well, and it ends up being deposited as soft fat. And that makes lousy bacon. The fat of corn oil–fed pigs turns rancid faster than the fat of corn-fed pigs, and the shelf life of the resulting bacon, hams, and bratwurst is correspondingly shorter. Prusa said that producers have a similar problem with pigs fed soybeans: their back fat turns soft as jelly and doesn't produce the good lard needed for making pie crusts.

Pigs must eat starches to grow the two pounds a day that today's producers demand, he said. So producers began feeding them the glycerol derived from soy used in the baking industry. Any baked goods that fall to the bakery floor or don't meet standards—cookie dough, Pop-Tarts, potato chips, anything starchy, even ice cream bars—are blended, ground, and dried into a "baking meat." Then it's fed to pigs. They love it, Prusa said.

My tea was cold. Prusa asked if I wanted it warmed, then disappeared with my MONSANTO mug into the large kitchen off our room. When he reappeared, steaming mug in one hand, he was carrying two large pieces of meat wrapped in clear plastic bags in the other. I blew on the tea and eyed the meat. What are they? I asked. Boneless half-loins, he said. One was noticeably paler than the other, and more marbled. I touched it. It wasn't frozen, but it was cold. These are test samples, Prusa said. Producers and packers send him pieces of pig meat by Federal Express to test. When he's finished testing, he sends them the results. As if magically summoned, a Federal Express employee appeared at the door, and Prusa signed for a package. More pig meat, he said. Then he began to discuss "purge."

"Purge" involves two of the seventeen or so major measurements that Prusa's lab takes of pig meat: purge and chop purge, color reflectance, Japanese Color Bar, loin weight, ultimate pH, moisture concentration, fat concentration, protein concentration, marbling, cooking loss, juiciness, tenderness, chewiness, pork flavor, off-flavor, and instrumental tenderness. At least six minor measurements are taken as well: fatty acid profiles, iodine values, vitamin concentrations, mineral concentrations, and amino acid profiles.[38]

Purge is the water that seeps from dead pig muscle. About three-quarters of a pork loin's weight is water. Prusa wanted to ensure that enough water remains locked in the loin so the meat doesn't dry out. If that happens, the consumer may perceive the meat as being insufficiently juicy and tender. But excess purge concerns pork producers. Prusa explained that Americans ship an enormous amount of pork to Japan—743 million pounds in 2006.[39] It's first trucked in sealed containers in 30,000-pound lots to the West Coast, then loaded onto ships to sail fifteen days to Tokyo or Osaka. Three days later, it's sitting on a Japanese dinner table. Prusa thinks that an excellent pork loin has less than a 0.5 percent purge, with 1 to 3 percent purge being acceptable in the industry.[40] He has measured loins with a 5 percent purge. Even a 2 percent purge means that 600 pounds of excess water is shipped halfway round the world to Japan in each lot;

that's 14 million pounds of excess water shipped each year, and that's just to Japan.[41]

Ultimate pH

Prusa turned to his specialty, pH. The Japanese had sparked Prusa's interest in the objective measurement of the color of pork. That had catalyzed his breakthrough in understanding the importance of ultimate pH to pork taste. The Japanese shun lighter pork, he said. I had read about this in an Iowa State University press release that quoted Prusa as saying, "I was doing research in a meat packing plant and noticed that the Japanese buyers always chose the darker pork. I wanted to find out why, so I evaluated some darker products." Prusa realized that the Japanese were not selecting dark pork merely because they preferred a deeper color. No, it was because a darker color indicated a higher pH, and that meant the meat was more tender, flavorful, and juicy.[42] Producers who want to sell to the Japanese had better figure out how to create a darker product, Prusa said.

By August 2006, Iowa State was trumpeting Prusa as a pork pH pioneer, claiming that he "may have identified a characteristic that could prove to be as significant to the industry as leanness."[43] "Ultimate pH" measures how acid or basic pork loin muscle is twenty-four hours after death. Prusa's breakthrough idea was that pH, not fat, is "the driving factor influencing pork quality. It is much more important than intramuscular fat" because "high pH correlate[s] with the desirable characteristics of the other traits."[44] Pork, he said, should have an ultimate pH of between 5.6 and 5.9, perhaps higher; undesirable, extremely light, poor-quality pork carries a pH as low as 5.1.

Higher ultimate pH also correlates to an increased marinade-holding capacity, he said. It reduces "cooler shrink" and allows consumers to "enjoy a more consistently tasty, tender and juicy natural pork product. Therefore, selecting for pigs that produce a product having higher pH will satisfy the need to increase demand without putting back fat back into the product."[45] Prusa's ISU colleague Professor Tom J. Baas agrees: "Higher pH values are more desirable because they are associated with lower drip loss, darker color, more firmness, and increased tenderness of the loin chop."[46]

If a pig is stressed or moves about, Prusa said, its muscles use the glycogen they store to release energy. The by-products of heat and lactic acid lower muscle pH. Blood normally carries lactic acid to the liver to be metabolized. When pigs are slaughtered, the blood is removed from their bodies and whatever lactic acid has not been carried to the liver "tries to stay alive" in the muscle. The pH begins to drop. Prusa has measured the rate of that drop and investigated the degree to which chilling delays it.

Producers and packers care about how much acid dead pig muscle contains because the buildup of heat and lactic acid not only drops the muscle pH but denatures, or changes, the muscle proteins, just as egg whites are denatured, changed, by cooking. One muscle protein, myoglobin, the pigment responsible for coloring meat, is sensitive to heat. As the muscle protein, especially the myoglobin, is denatured, it releases water and the dead pig muscle gets paler and softer.

Prusa wants this stopped. Without enough water, pork doesn't taste good, so packers try to lock as much water into the muscles as possible. Prusa has also found that the higher the muscle pH, the higher the scores doled out by the testers on his sensory panels: meat with a higher pH has a nuttier, sweeter taste, they say. "Through sensory testing, we found pH to be a pretty strong driver of ultimate pork quality."[47]

Because so much depends on muscle pH, Prusa has spent much time figuring out how to keep that number as high as possible after a pig's death. He has arrived at dual solutions. First, chill the carcasses faster than they are being chilled now. Removing heat keeps the muscles in their native state longer, slows the denaturing of muscle protein, and impedes the rate of pH decline. Second, reduce the stress a pig experiences just before she is killed. "Stress causes a high metabolism rate, which creates a lot of adrenaline. When that happens right before slaughter, it causes a really rapid pH decline. If there's a rapid pH decline in the hot carcass, it's even worse. At that point, there's not much you can do for quality."[48]

Professor Prusa placed a large blank sheet of white chart paper on the table, took up a blue Sharpie, and sketched two perpendicular axes. He labeled the y-axis "pH" and the x-axis "Time After Death." Then he sketched a curve that fit measurements he had taken. This line showed that, at 90 degrees Fahrenheit, which is the approximate temperature of a muscle's interior after death, even during refrigeration pH falls from about 7.0, which is neutral (neither acid nor base), to 5.8 by the third hour after death. He hadn't taken earlier measurements because the outside of the carcasses were too frozen for him to penetrate with his instruments. By twenty-four hours, pH had stabilized at about 5.7. Many packing plants freeze the carcass at about minus-40 degrees Fahrenheit, which drops the internal muscle temperature to about 60 degrees Fahrenheit. Blowing wind over the carcasses drops the windchill temperature to minus-60 or minus-65 degrees Fahrenheit.

Prusa sketched a second curve, above the first one and shallower. It showed that a deep chill causes muscle pH to fall to 6.2 in three hours, before leveling off at 5.7 in twenty-four hours. Better for pH, but not good enough. Prusa wants carcasses chilled faster. His third curve, drawn above the second and shallower still, showed that, if chilled at a low enough temperature—what Prusa called "slow chill"—at three hours the pH of pork is about 6.6 and stabilizes at 6.0 in twenty-four hours. But to achieve this higher pH, he said, packers are going to have to change the way they do business.

Slaughterhouses may choose to electrocute pigs into unconsciousness, perhaps by placing one probe behind an ear and another over the heart. Once blackness descends, the jugular vein is sliced and the pig bleeds to death. Prusa said that the electrical stunning of pigs, which occurs at the rate of nineteen a minute, hastens the carcass's undesirable pH decline because it suddenly stimulates the muscles and causes them to contract. This devours energy. Exciting or stressing pigs just before slaughter produces a lactic acid buildup. Optimally, pigs should be delivered to the slaughterhouse two to four hours before death, then lowered into a chamber precharged with a 60 percent or greater concentration of carbon dioxide. The pigs would then be asphyxiated and silently keel over, with little waste of energy. No capillaries would be burst. And it would be a more humane method of slaughter than electrical stunning, he said.[49] Prusa said that killing with carbon dioxide is a new trend, but not a new idea.

But carbon dioxide stunning takes more time—about nineteen seconds a pig—than electrical stunning. Also, their carcasses must be chilled within forty-five minutes of death, but that forty-five minutes is hectic, as workers strip the dead pig to its hot carcass weight of about 180 pounds. A little cleanup and into the chill the remnants must go, all in forty-five minutes. It "buffers them out," so that muscle pH might be 6.4 when the hot carcass enters the chill, as opposed to 6.2 after electrical stunning. Prusa is looking for a chill that ends with a pH of 6.0.

Think of glycogen as a gas tank for muscles, Prusa said. You want to kill the pig when its tank is as low as possible. We can't entirely empty its tank or the pig will die before we can kill it. But we might withdraw feed earlier than we do now, so that the food doesn't have the chance to be transformed into glycogen. Or we might alter their genetic code to produce pigs that require, or store, less glycogen. Or we might exploit some existing genetic variation. There are many possible variations. Some slaughterhouse carcasses that Prusa has tested have a pH of 5.3; others have a pH of 7.0. How is it, he wonders, that a pig carcass can have a pH of 7.0?

Perhaps they have a genetic defect. But by the time he measures those carcasses in the slaughterhouse, the variables have multiplied. He doesn't know where the pigs came from, how they were fed and maintained, over what distance they were transported, what the weather was like during their raising and transporting, what the humidity and barometric pressure were on the day of slaughter, how the pigs were loaded on and unloaded from the trucks that took them to the slaughterhouse, and which of myriad other possible stresses they might have been exposed to. Then there is the matter of how long the pigs waited to die. Trucks typically carry 180 to 250 pigs to the slaughterhouse. If nineteen pigs are stunned every minute, the last pig is dead ten to twelve minutes after the first. Packers try to time arrivals so that they don't have to wait too long in line. But they don't want the production line shut down for lack of carcasses. The same pig, Prusa said, might come to slaughter on two consecutive days and emerge as two very different products. That's why he prefers to have pork producers send him meat from pigs about which he has a lot of information.

I mentioned that Smithfield had been giving me the jolly runaround for months over visiting its Tar Heel slaughterhouse. Prusa said it had taken him five years to obtain permission for his students to enter the Swift & Company pig slaughterhouse in Marshalltown, forty miles east. Since the attacks of September 11, 2001, Swift requires that his foreign students be in the United States at least a year before entering the slaughterhouse. Prusa said that what slaughterhouses were really doing, he said, was trying to protect the confidentiality of some small technological advance; perhaps they had begun using a piece of pig in a new way, similar to the way in which the riblet—that boneless meat from the end of a pig's rib that has nothing to do with actual ribs—once began to be used. That's why students are not permitted to bring cameras or cell phones.

THE HUMAN SENSORY PANEL

Prusa said in an interview that "if an animal health company develops a new feed additive for pigs, for example, they want to know if it has an impact on pork quality, . . . they come to us. . . . One of the most important instruments that we use is the trained human sensory panel. We train undergraduate and graduate students, staff and other faculty to objectively evaluate pork for texture profiles (tenderness, juiciness, chewiness, mealiness), taste profiles (sweet, sour, salty, bitter) and flavor notes (roasted, nutty, meaty, browned)."[50] He told me that he runs sensory panel sessions two or three times a week. I asked whether panelists could really be trained to evaluate pork objectively. He said they could and pressed down a second large piece of chart paper onto the table, labeled it "Sensory," and drew a blue line down the center. On the left, he wrote "Objective," on the right "Subjective." Under "Objective," he scribbled: "Trained Panelists."

Prospective sensory panelists learn how each of their five senses is involved in the experience of eating and drinking. Prusa gives them cups covered with aluminum foil. Inside is food. They shake the cups to hear what the food sounds like as it crashes against the sides, poke holes in the foil to permit them to inhale the aroma, gaze at the food to determine color and size, and touch it to gauge its texture. Finally they taste it. He teaches them to rate the intensity of the pork's toughness, tenderness, juiciness, chewiness, dryness, and rancidness.

He switched off the overhead lights and bathed us in an eerie red glow, then placed a tray holding half a dozen articles on the table and asked me to tell him what color they were. I couldn't. He flicked off the red light, and the objects blazed forth in primary colors. On went the red light. He handed me a card with a rectangle drawn on it. I couldn't see anything else. He turned off the red light, and a pink "X" suddenly connected the opposite angles. He used the red light, he said, to show sensory panelists how light affects their perceptions. We judge dark things, like pork, to be flavored more intensely. He wants sensory panelists to learn to judge flavors independently of what they see and to focus on the taste of the pork, not on what it looks like.

For each sensory panel, Prusa trains six to ten people over a period of several weeks, for a minimum of six hours, to evaluate foods objectively. He prefers freshmen, who will be on campus for four years, and pays them up to $10 an hour. "We'll give them samples of pork that we know are extremely tough, extremely tender, extremely juicy, flavorful or not flavorful. Then we actually calibrate them on those extremes. It's just like calibrating any type of instrument. . . . It's amazing how good they can be. We use them as calibrated instruments."[51] With enough practice, he assured me, they can learn to rate foods in an objective and consistent manner.

Prusa handed me the paper that sensory panel members use during training to evaluate the qualities of broiled pork loin, which is the cut from near the top of the rib cage. Attributes are evaluated on a ten-point scale. The first pork loin attribute to be evaluated is juiciness. Prusa defines juiciness as "the amount of liquid that is released in the mouth during chewing."[52] A juiciness score of one means the pork loin is dry, and a ten means it's juicy. Routine juiciness scores for broiled pork loin generally fall, Prusa said, between six and eight, with mealy or dry pork scoring just a one or two. Tenderness is "the amount of force needed to chew the pork sample during the first two chews." The higher the score, the more tender the meat. A score of one means the pork loin is tough; ten is tender. Tenderness ratings generally fall between six and eight, though pork tenderloin, a particularly lean part of the pork loin, often scores a ten. Chewiness is "the total number of chews needed to sufficiently break up the sample before swallowing."[53] Because panelists consistently score most pork as a one or two on the chewiness scale, Prusa has concluded that pork "is not exceptionally chewy."[54]

The panelists also evaluate a slew of undesirable pork off-flavors: acid, ammonia, beany, bitter, boarlike (tastes relating to boar taint), cardboard, chemical, earthy, fishy, grassy, liver, metallic, milky, putrid, salty, serumy or bloody, and sour.[55] Prusa's sensory panelists consistently determine that there isn't much flavor locked in pork, for scores are "usually low." This led Prusa to conclude that "broiled, grilled, or roasted, unseasoned traditional pork does not have an abundance of flavor."[56]

He led me into an adjoining room to see where the panelists do their tasting. It was long enough to contain ten booths, ten chairs, ten tables, and ten foot-and-a-half pass-through windows that had been cut into a false wall from which Prusa's assistants offered the panelists their test samples. I felt a breeze. Prusa explained that the room is positively pressured to ensure that extraneous smells don't seep in and confuse the panelists. The lights can be reddened so that the panelists can't see the color of what they are eating. Each panelist sits in a booth. No panelist can see any other. They are forbidden to eat anything in the forty-five minutes before they begin tasting. Prusa's staff pushes samples through the windows in numbered cups, with everyone getting his or her sample at the same time. Each panelist then tastes the sample, evaluates it on a computer, cleanses the palate with unsalted crackers and water, and waits for the next sample to emerge from the window.

Several times a year, Prusa invites untrained consumers, in panels of one hundred, to evaluate foods. "We like to look at the whole sensory experience, the whole experience of vision, touch, hearing, smell, to bring everything together so when the consumer is out there buying that product we make sure we cover all the bases."[57] He wants to know whether consumers like something or don't and whether they agree with the opinions given by the trained panelists. Or don't.

Finally, he walked me into the huge adjoining kitchen. George Foreman Clamshell Cookers were everywhere, a dozen, perhaps fifteen. Prusa likes them because they heat evenly on both sides. He places a "thermocouple" inside every pork chop and pork roast to ensure that each is cooked to the same temperature, for he has learned that panelists distinguish between samples that were cooked at different temperatures. He uses only disposable plastic or glass petri dishes for washing, since glass dishes may leave a perfumy smell.

Several expensive instruments he uses to measure pork quality sat along a far wall: scales, a pH meter, a Chroma meter, and an Instron Universal Testing Machine.[58] As we walked over, he said that boneless pork loins generally weigh between seven and ten pounds. But the pork industry is looking for consistency in weight to ensure consumer-pleasing package uniformity. "Slices from a seven-pound loin in the same package with slices from a ten-pound loin will not project a uniform in-package appearance."[59] He uses the "star-probe Instron" to measure tenderness by determining the amount of force needed to puncture or compress a cooked pork loin chop. The lower the value, the less force needed, and the more tender is the chop. A typical broiled chop gives way at four to five kilograms of force, while the typical tenderloin requires only about two and a half kilograms. He sometimes attaches a "Warner-Bratzer shear" to the Instron; this measures the force required to shear a core of pork.[60] It also tests fracturability, hardness, stringiness, springiness, and adhesive force; the last is most useful when testing something with the consistency of peanut butter. The Instron Universal Testing Machine is especially valuable for testing something new that hasn't been approved for human consumption, not even for freshmen.

He measures cooking loss by weighing meat before and after cooking. Excellent cooking loss values fall below 20 percent but may range higher than 30 percent.[61] He said that loin fat should fall in the 2 percent range to bolster the low-fat claims that modern pork producers make on supermarket labels. His colleague Tom Baas believes that marbling "is necessary for a juicy and flavorful cooked product. On the other hand, pork with large amounts of marbling supplies excess calories and is visually objectionable to some consumers."[62] Both Prusa and Baas rate visual marbling on a ten-point scale, matching the meat to increasingly marbled pictures of pork loins; each point corresponds to a percentage of intramuscular lipid, with scores between two and four most desirable. Other cards, produced by the National Pork Producers Council, show photographs of pork chops on a six-point scale. Prusa also correlates the degree of marbling with the percentage of intramuscular fat revealed through chemical analysis.[63] Because this analysis requires that the fat in a raw pork loin be extracted with flammable ether, he sends the sample to a commercial lab.

The problem of unattractive muscle color is serious for producers and packers. If consumers don't like the color of a piece of meat, they won't buy it. Baas has concluded that consumers think the ideal color for fresh pork is reddish pink and that they reject grayish or pale pork, on one extreme, and purplish pork, on the other.[64] Minolta Chroma Meter in hand, Prusa can establish a muscle's Hunter L* values by shooting a flash of light onto the meat, then measuring its wavelength. A Hunter L* value is the amount of light that is reflected from a muscle's surface, zero being pure black, and one hundred pure white. The lighter the pork, the higher the Hunter L* value, with forty to sixty being typical. A value between forty-three and forty-seven is acceptable in the pork industry, and the closer to forty-three the better.[65] Prusa also measures pork's a* values, which indicate the degree of redness, and b* values, which measure yellowness as well as lightness or darkness on a rough, but important, six-point Japanese Color Bar, which he showed me. A score of one means the pork is very light, and a score of six means the meat is very dark. Both are undesirable. Values of three to four are best.[66] Pork color must trend toward the reddish if producers wish to sell their product in Japan. Prusa walked me out of the laboratory and kindly agreed to answer any questions I might come up with.

A few months later, I learned that People for the Ethical Treatment of Animals (PETA) had placed another undercover stock worker in a farm near Bayard, Iowa, located sixty-five miles southwest of the Sensory Evaluation Unit. Owned by National Pork Producer II LLP, it had been sold to MowMar LLP. The farm supplies Hormel

Foods in Minnesota. I called PETA attorney Dan Paden, and asked if he would pass on my phone number to this now undercover worker, along with my request to speak to him. As with Mr. Nikita, I wasn't permitted to use his name. I'll call him Mr. Hale.

Mr. Hale said that he worked at a sow-breeding farm for seven weeks after a whistle-blower told PETA about cruelty that was going on there. It was a huge farm, with six or seven thousand sows and nearly twenty employees. After he wrote on his application that he had no experience working with hogs, Mr. Hale was assigned to the farm's farrowing department. He was never trained. Instead, he was required to learn his job by observing two colleagues. They turned out to be the farm's worst abusers. Mr. Hale said he had been startled by the ignorance of many of his coworkers, some of whom were unable to subtract sixty-five crates from seventy-five crates, or add eleven to twenty. Some were felons too, or druggies. His supervisor was arrested at work and charged with domestic violence.

Paden sent me a video that showed clips of some of what Mr. Hale had seen and heard. I watched a man pound the backs of sows with a gate rod. As he struck again and again, he was chatting with Mr. Hale.

> "When I get pissed or get hurt or the fuckin' bitch won't move, I grab one of these rods and shove it in her asshole."
>
> "You take the . . . rods and shove it in their asshole?" Mr. Hale asked.
>
> "Yeah. Fuck 'em."

The man also had a thick, three-foot-long herding cane that he shoved up the asses and vaginas of sows whenever he felt like doing it, said Mr. Hale.

> "Hurt 'em," a worker advised Mr. Hale. "There's nobody who works for PETA out here. . . . These motherfuckers deserve to

be hurt. Hurt! Hurt! Hurt! Hurt! If you gotta hurt 'em, hurt 'em! Take out your frustration on them!"

As I mentioned in the Prologue, I watched a worker casually, repeatedly smash the heads of baby piglets, scarcely larger than his hand, against a cement floor, then laugh when blood spattered his forearm. The camera focused on a wriggling mass of bloody babies who had been tossed onto a large pile. Some were obviously dead. Some were obviously not. Other screaming, upside-down babies were filmed being castrated and having their tails cut off without anesthesia. One worker kicked the belly of a sow twelve times with his steel-toed shoes to encourage her to move. I counted each thud. A badly injured sow, capable only of dragging her rear legs, was prodded up an aisle inside the barn until a worker pushed a captive bolt pistol to her head and pulled the trigger. Mr. Hale said this brutality happened every day and was inflicted by many workers. "They would joke about it," he said. "It was all lighthearted. They enjoyed it." On October 22, 2008, the Greene County Attorney's office charged the twenty-six-year-old former manager and five present and former employees, ranging from eighteen to sixty years of age, with livestock abuse, aiding and abetting livestock abuse, and livestock neglect.[67]

CHAPTER TEN

The Genesis Disaster for Animals

There is no country in the world where the Christian
religion retains a greater influence over the souls of
men than in America . . . [and] Christianity therefore
reigns without obstacle, by universal consent; the
consequence is . . . that every principle of the
moral world is fixed and determinate.

—*Alexis de Tocqueville*, DEMOCRACY IN AMERICA *(1835)*[1]

Religion is the single most important factor that drives
American belief attitudes and behaviors. It is a powerful
indicator of where Americans will end up on politics,
culture, family life. If you want to understand America,
you have to understand religion in America.

—*Michael Lindsay, assistant director of the
Rice University Center on Race, Religion, and Urban Life (2008)*[2]

Nature . . . will be forever deaf and dumb in the presence
of Judeo-Christian societies.

—*Calvin Martin, "The War Between Indians and Animals" (1981)*[3]

W E H A V E S E E N H O W religious certainties justified the Europeans' extermination of the Native Americans and the enslavement of black Africans in Bladen County, and elsewhere. These certainties depended on the ability of us humans to create fundamental distinctions between "Us" and "Them." We create them because these certainties make our worlds work for us, fulfill our desires and goals, affirm our beliefs. Some "kinds" are benign (Red Sox fans versus Yankee fans, Geminis versus Sagittarians, Manchester United versus Liverpool), and some are malignant (Puritan versus Indian, Christian versus infidel, white versus black, human versus nonhuman animal). Some "kinds" may persist over the spans of many lives.

Culture cements, sustains, and perpetuates our "kinds." As cultures evolve, "kinds" change. Sociobiologist Edward O. Wilson has written that "human beings are consistent in their codes of honor but endlessly fickle with reference to whom the codes apply. . . . The important distinction . . . is between the ingroup and the outgroup, but the precise location of the dividing line is shifted back and forth with ease."[4] George Orwell understood how effortlessly those shifts can be manipulated. In *1984*, Winston Smith's Oceania is perpetually at war, just not always with the same foe. But when Eurasia is the enemy, it has always been the enemy. And when Eastasia is the enemy, it has always been the enemy.

"Kinds" that don't shift when culture does may linger, but they will finally wither and die. We may fight to ward off new culture and preserve the old: witness the Amish, who have cabined themselves as best they can from the modern world, following the admonition of 2 Corinthians 6:14: "Be ye not unequally yoked together with unbelievers: for what fellowship hath righteousness with unrighteousness? And what communion hath light with darkness?"[5] Yet culture captures us with varying force and longevity. My eleven-year-old stepdaughter Mariana is presently transfixed by a sixteen-year-old Disney Channel singer named Miley Cyrus, who plays an ordinary girl named Miley Stewart who secretly transforms into the rock star Hannah Montana. Mariana wants to be Hannah Montana. Her bedroom is festooned with Hannah Montana posters, a clock, a blond wig. If you have a daughter between the ages of six and fourteen, you know what I'm talking about. Or perhaps you did. By the time you read this, you may not remember who Hannah Montana was, and neither may Mariana. Cultural change mercilessly prunes. Abraham Lincoln and Charles Darwin remain powerful cultural forces. But few of their contemporaries retain a cultural grip, and they are but a century and a half gone. Nearly half the world believes God is monotheistic: Allah has been capturing minds for fourteen hundred years and counts more than a billion adherents today. Two-thousand-year-old Jesus has more than two billion followers alive.

Few cultural forces rival that of God. Theodicies, which include religious sanctions of beliefs and actions, are "more potent and effective than any other."[6] They work so remarkably well because they make it appear that some Transcendent Being, whom we'll call God, has blessed some cultural arrangement, which allows the adherent never to doubt its moral rightness.[7] To question the arrangement is to question God's judgment.[8] But, Edward O. Wilson and George Orwell assert, religious certainties may change as culture shifts, and cultures can shift with religious certainties. As competing religious claims arise or strengthen, they may challenge the "plausibility" of the prevailing certainties, undermine, and eventually supplant them.[9]

The Old Testament's Book of Genesis is "supremely a book about relationships," mostly human relationships.[10] Unlike Americans of the sixteenth, seventeenth, eighteenth, and nineteenth centuries, modern Americans have generally rejected the beliefs that killing Native Americans and enslaving blacks were moral acts grounded on correct interpretations of Genesis. According to the evangelical Nelson Study Bible, "Some once believed that [a Genesis] verse justified the slavery of African peoples (who, it was alleged, were descended from Canaan), but those people misinterpreted the verse. Canaan was under the curse of his father."[11] Today's Zondervan's King James Study Bible agrees: "Noah's prophecy cannot be used to justify the enslavement of blacks, since those cursed here were Canaanites, who were Caucasians."[12]

THE DIVINE RIGHT TO EXPLOIT

Genesis also contains some exceedingly influential statements about the proper relationships between humans and nonhuman animals. William Tyndale translated Genesis 1:26–28 from the Hebrew:

> And God sayd: let us make man in oure symilitude ad. after oure lycknesse: that he may have *rule over* the fysh of the see and over the foules of the ayre and over catell and over all the erth and over all wormes that crepe on the erth. And God created man after hys lycknesse after the lycknesse of God created he him: male and female created he them. And God blessed them and God sayd unto them. Growe and multiplye and fyll the erth and subdue it and have *domynyon* over the fysh of the see and over the foules of the ayre and over all the beastes that move on the erth.[13]

The Geneva Bible said:

> Furthermore God said, Let us make man in our image according to our likeness, and let them *rule over* the fish of the sea, and over the fowl of the heaven, and over the beasts, and over all the earth, and over everything that creepeth and moveth on the earth. Thus God created the man in his image, in the image of God created he him; he created them male and female. And God blessed them, and God said to them, Bring forth fruit, and multiply, and fill the earth, and subdue it, and *rule over* the fish

of the sea, and over the fowl of the heaven, and over every beast that moveth upon the earth. (emphasis added)

King James I's committee produced this version:

And God said, Let us make man in our image, after our likeness: and let them have *dominion* over the fish of the sea, and over the fowl of the air, and over the cattle, and over all the earth, and over every creeping thing that creepeth upon the earth. So God created man in his own image, in the image of God created he him; male and female created he them. And God blessed them, and God said unto them, Be fruitful, and multiply, and replenish the earth, and subdue it; and have *dominion* over the fish of the sea, and over the fowl of the air, and over every living thing that moveth upon the earth. (emphasis added)

What did "rule" mean to Tyndale and the Geneva translators, and what did "dominion" mean to King James's committee? "Dominion" certainly carried a strong sense of power, the right to govern and control, to own, dominate, in early seventeenth-century minds. Thomas Hobbes defined it as "the right of possession."[14]

These words, "rule" and "dominion," were used elsewhere in the Bible. In Genesis 37:8, Joseph's older brothers are displeased when he relates a dream in which the brothers are binding sheaves in the field, Joseph's sheaf stands up, and the brothers' sheaves bow to it. "Shalt thou indeed reign over us? Or shalt thou indeed have *dominion* over us?" ask the brothers in the King James Version. "What, shalt thou reign over us, and *rule* us? Or shalt thou have altogether *dominion* over us?" asks the Geneva Bible.

In the King James Version, Psalm 72 says that a king's son "shall have *dominion* also from sea to sea, And from the river unto the ends of the earth,"[15] meaning that God's kingdom shall extend to all the world.[16] The Hebrews sing in Isaiah 26:13 of the King James Version: "O Lord our God, Other lords besides thee have had *dominion* over us," while the Geneva Bible says, "O Lord our God, other Lords besides thee, have *ruled* us."

Debate over the proper interpretation of these verses continues, and will continue. But there can be no dispute about the power of the "folk dominion" they inspired.[17] For centuries, the Genesis verses were popularly interpreted as providing license freely to exploit creation and only occasionally a solemn duty to steward it.[18] Historian Keith Thomas tells of "the breathtaking anthropocentric spirit in which Tudor and Stuart preachers interpreted [Genesis]."[19] He considers it unnecessary to determine whether Christianity is "intrinsically anthropocentric." His point is that a "reader who came fresh to the moral and theological writings of the sixteenth and seventeenth centuries"—written in large part by those preachers and other commentators who were the leading exponents of the settlement of North Carolina—"could be forgiven for inferring that their main purpose was to define the special status of man and to justify his rule over other creatures."[20] It wasn't just man who was said to recognize his divine right to exploit creation. The English thought that creation recognized it too, as these four poems suggest.

. . .

The pheasant, partridge, and the lark
Flew to thy house, as to the Ark.
The willing ox of himself came
Home to the slaughter with the lamb,
And every beast did thither bring
Himself, to be an offering. . . .
— FROM "TO SAXHAM" (1640)
BY THOMAS CAREW[21]

. . .

The painted partridge lies in ev'ry field,
And for thy mess is willing to be kill'd.

And if the high-swoln Medway fail thy dish,
Thou hast thy ponds, that pay thee tribute fish,
Fat aged carps that run into thy net,
And pikes, now weary their own kind to eat,
As loth the second draught or cast to stay,
Officiously at first themselves betray.
Bright eels that emulate them, and leap on land,
Before the fisher, or into his hand. . . .

—FROM "THE FOREST" (1612)
BY BEN JONSON[22]

. . .

The brute creation are his property,
Subservient to his will and for him made.
As hurtful these he kills, as useful those
Preserves; their sole and arbitrary king. . . .

—FROM "THE CHACE" (1735)
BY WILLIAM SOMERVILLE[23]

George Herbert put it most bluntly, if least poetically, in his 1633 poem "Providence": "The beasts say, Eat me."[24]

Unlike America's Indians, who recognized reciprocity in the relationship between human and nonhuman animals, the English saw only domination, with many having little regard for the suffering of any animal.

I once saw a gentleman, recalled William Hinde in 1641, "being about to feed his hawk, pull a live pigeon out of his falconer's bag, and taking her first by both wings, rent them with great violence from her body, and then taking hold of both legs, plucked them asunder in like manner, the body of the poor creature trembling in his hand, while his hawk was tiring upon the other parts, to his great contentment and delight upon his fist." The *Gentleman's Recreation* (1674) recommended catching a hart in nets, cutting off one of his feet and letting him go to be pursued by young bloodhounds.[25]

The Geneva Bible claimed that Genesis 9:4, in which God prohibited Noah from consuming "flesh with the life thereof, I *mean* with the blood thereof," is an admonition against cruelty.[26] The first, albeit toothless, anticruelty statutes were enacted by the Puritans of the Massachusetts Bay Colony in 1641. Britain finally followed in 1821, and the American states after that. Pulling the wings off pigeons in the park might get one sent to jail in Elizabethtown today, but industrial hog farming probably won't, for North Carolina's anticruelty statute exempts "lawful activities conducted for purposes of production of livestock" and "lawful activities conducted for the primary purpose of providing food for human or animal consumption."[27] I might be wrong. As I write, the Sampson County district attorney is prosecuting one of Mr. Nikita's former colleagues for cruelty to hogs. I expect his defense attorney to argue that his client is exempt. In 1967, the prominent medieval historian Lynn White Jr. attacked what he claimed were the Judeo-Christian roots of our present ecological crisis in the prestigious journal *Science*. White pulled no punches. So far as the Bible was concerned, "no item in the physical creation had any purpose save to serve man's purposes"; "man shares, in great measure, God's transcendence of nature"; and "it is God's will that man exploit nature for his proper ends." If human actions toward animals and the rest of Creation are "out of control," White concluded, "Christianity bears a huge burden of guilt."[28] White was called right, wrong, and worse.[29]

If White was right that the traditional reading of Genesis permits Christians brutally to raise and brutally to slaughter Bladen County's hogs, as it once permitted them to kill the county's Native Americans and enslave its blacks, then important theological responsibility rests with two Christian giants. Saint Augustine and Saint Thomas Aquinas promoted a biblically based hierarchical division of Creation into a human "Us" and a rest-of-Creation "Them." These two were not alone in what they advocated. But they stand alone in their influence. Augustine was elevated to sainthood by acclamation; he was a talented, amusing, and prolific writer and an innovative religious thinker; the reader shuts his *Confessions* wishing he could invite the man to dinner. With Saints Ambrose, Jerome, and Gregory the Great, Augustine was named one of the original "Four Great Doctors of the Western Church" in 1298. He has been called "the chief authority of the mediaeval Latin writers on creation."[30] Aquinas, also a saint and a Church Doctor, is often proclaimed Catholicism's leading theologian and philosopher.

In *The City of God*, Augustine discussed the Commandment "Thou shalt not kill."

> Must we . . . reckon it a breaking of the commandment, "Thou shalt not kill," to pull a flower. . . . When we say, Thou shalt not kill, we do not understand this of the plants, since they have no sensation, nor of the irrational animals that fly, swim, walk, or creep, since they are dissociated from us by their want of reason, and are therefore by the just appointment of the Creator subjected us to kill or keep alive for our own uses; if so, then it remains that we understand the commandment simply of man.[31]

Christ, Augustine claimed, "judged we had no community in justice with beasts and trees."[32] Nor community in law.[33] Aquinas would emphasize and expand this hierarchy:

> For just as in the generation of things we perceive a certain order of procession of the perfect from the imperfect (thus matter is for the sake of form, and the imperfect form for the sake of the perfect), so also is there order in the use of natural things. For the imperfect are for the use of the perfect; plants

make use of the earth for their nourishment, animals make use
of plants, and man makes use of both plants and animals.[34]

As intellectual beings, humans are ruled by God "as though he
cared for them for their own sake, while other creatures are ruled as
being directed [to human beings] . . . every other creature is naturally under slavery," Aquinas wrote.[35] They exist merely "for the sake
of" mankind, as lungs exist for the sake of the whole animal.[36] He
implied that their irrationality means that nonhuman animals lack
immortal souls.[37] One should treat animals with kindness, Aquinas
said, not for their own sakes, but so that humans don't get in the
habit of being cruel to other men.

> Hereby is refuted the error of those who said it was sinful for a
> man to kill brute animals; for by the divine providence they are
> intended for man's use according to the order of nature. Hence
> it is not wrong for man to make use of them, either by killing
> them or in any other way. For this reason the Lord said to Noe
> (Gen. ix.3): *As the green herbs I have delivered all flesh to you.*
>
> And if any passages of Holy Scripture seem to forbid us to
> be cruel to brute animals, for instance to kill a bird with its
> young (Deut. xxii.6), this is either to remove man's thoughts
> from being cruel to other men, lest through being cruel to ani-
> mals one become cruel to human beings; or because injury to
> an animal leads to the temporal hurt of man, either of the doer
> of the deed, or of another.[38]

Aquinas demanded that humans withhold any love they might
feel for nonhuman animals, even as a matter of charity, for charity

> is a kind of friendship. Now the love of friendship is twofold:
> first, there is the love for the friend to whom our friendship is
> given, secondly, the love for those good things which we desire

for our friend. With regard to the first, no irrational creature can be loved out of charity; and for three reasons. Two of these reasons refer in a general way to friendship, which cannot have an irrational creature for its object: first because friendship is towards one to whom we wish good things, while, properly speaking, we cannot wish good things to an irrational creature, because it is not competent, properly speaking, to possess good, this being proper to the rational creature which, through its free-will, is the master of its disposal of the good it possesses. Hence the Philosopher [Aristotle] says (Phys. ii.6) that we do not speak of good or evil befalling such like things, except metaphorically. Secondly, because all friendship is based on some fellowship in life; since "nothing is so proper to friendship as to live together," as the Philosopher [Aristotle] proves (Ethic. viii.5). Now irrational creatures can have no fellowship in human life which is regulated by reason. Hence friendship with irrational creatures is impossible, except metaphorically speaking. The third reason is proper to charity, for charity is based on the fellowship of everlasting happiness, to which the irrational creature cannot attain. Therefore we cannot have the friendship of charity towards an irrational creature.[39]

A Christian Misunderstanding

Dominion. Rule. Reign. All seem interwoven through an Old Testament in which humans stand as kings to animals, exercising dominion over them the way a king exercises dominion over his subjects and ruling them as a king rules his subjects. But what was the relationship of Middle East Bronze Age kings to their subjects? At the time, "shepherd" was a "widely used metaphor for 'king' in the ancient Near East."[40] Ancient kings often assumed the title of "Shepherd," which "is used most often in the context in which the king provides for his flock and protects his flock from those who would harm it."[41] "The Lord is my *shepherd*," said David in the Twenty-Third Psalm of both the Geneva Bible and the King James Version. "I shall not want."[42] The Geneva Bible explained that this means that God "hath care over me and ministereth unto me all things."[43] David acknowledged "that the Lord is his Shepherd-King."[44] When he said that God "leadeth me in the paths of righteousness,"[45] David meant that "as a shepherd leads his sheep in paths that offer safety and well-being, so David's Shepherd-King guides him in ways that cause him to be secure and prosperous."[46]

The King James Study Bible is a typical conservative example of modern evangelical Protestant Genesis interpretation that assists twenty-first-century evangelicals in making sense of these critical Genesis verses. It says that, "since man was created in the image of the divine King, the delegated sovereignty [kingship] was bestowed on him." But "as God's representative in the creaturely realm, he is steward of God's creatures. He is not to exploit, waste, or despoil them, but to care for them and use them in the service of God and man."[47]

All this should have been very good for nonhuman animals. But it hasn't been, and the question is: "why not?" For one thing, there is more in Genesis about the proper relationship between human and nonhuman animals. Tyndale's reader learned that, after the Flood, God told Noah, in Genesis 9:2–3, that "the feare also and drede of yow be vppon all beastes of the erth and vppon all foules of the ayre ad vppon all that crepeth on the erth and vppon all fyshes of the see which are geven vnto youre handes. And all that moveth vppon the erth havynge lyfe shall be youre meate: Euen as ye grene herbes so geue I yow all thing."[48] "By this permission," says the Geneva Bible, "man may with a good conscience use the creatures of God for his necessity."[49]

The Flood caused problems in my household. For months I read *The Children's Bible in 365 Stories* to nine-year-olds Siena, Christopher, and Mariana. Noah's story really made them sit up. This wasn't just snakes and apples and Adam and Eve, but the near-destruction of the entire earth. Cool. Siena got it that God punished all the wicked humans by drowning them in the Flood. But why, she asked, would He have also drowned millions of innocent animals? Why didn't He just kill the bad humans? And why would He let humans kill animals after the Flood when he hadn't let them do that before?

Where to begin, Siena? A Jewish scholar from France named Rashi, who lived one thousand years after Jesus, wrote that, "since animals exist just for the sake of man, their survival without man would be pointless." Siena didn't buy that. Okay, there was another man, John Calvin, also French. He lived in the sixteenth century and said that God killed the animals in the Flood because they served humans.

> For GOD not being contented with the punishement of men, proceeded in taking vengeaunce vppon beastes, vpon fowles, and vpon all kinde of liuing creatures that are vppon the earth, Wherein he seemeth to punishe beyond all measure . . . those things which were created for man's sake, & which liued not to his vse perished with him: and no meruell. The Asses and the Oxen with other beastes and in nothing offended: but because they were subjects vnto man, they were drawen also into the same destruction.[50]

Siena thought that made no sense either. So I tried again. An English minister, Henry Vesey, explained that "the creatures were not made for themselues, but for the seruice and vse of man: and therefore the euill that is not come vpon them, is not their punishment properly, but a part of ours."[51] "You mean," Siena asked, "that God killed the *animals* to punish *us?*" "That's what the minister wrote." She just shook her head.

The Protestant Reformation did animals little good. Commenting on God's Genesis grant of dominion over the animals to "them," Calvin noted: "The use of the plural number intimates that this authority was not given to Adam only, but to all his posterity as well as to him. And hence we infer what was the end for which all things were created; namely that none of the conveniences and necessaries of life might be wanting to men."[52] In short, in seventeenth-century England, "to be kind to animals because they deserve kindness in and of themselves is almost unthinkable."[53]

Richard Land is the conservative president of the Southern Baptist Convention's Ethics and Religious Liberty Commission. In 2002, he authored "the Land Letter," which encouraged President Bush to invade Iraq, on theological grounds that were premised on "facts" long since disproven.[54] Three years later, *Time* magazine declared Land one of the country's "twenty-five most influential evangelicals." Land, said *Time,* is a longtime friend of former President George W. Bush and "helped engineer the 16-million-member convention's 1979 shift from moderacy to hard-line conservatism." He hosts a weekly radio talk show on the Salem Radio Network ("Christian Radio's #1 News Network—with its cutting-edge interactive format, Richard Land Live! is the future of Christian talk radio").[55] Land thinks Lynn White was wrong when he ascribed the present environmental crisis to the Judeo-Christian Bible, but only "because Christians themselves have misunderstood and/or misapplied the message."[56]

> Certainly Christianity in its historical expressions has had its blind spots, even in its brightest moments, even in the midst of the Reformation. . . . "At certain points the people in the stream of the Reformation were inconsistent with the biblical teaching they claimed to follow. Many areas existed in which people did not follow the Bible as they should have, but two are outstanding: first, a twisted view of race, and second, a noncompassionate use of accumulated wealth." I believe we should

add as a third area or category of a major blind spot a failure adequately to understand and/or bear witness to a truly biblical view of creation and humanity's relation to it and to the God who created them both. Far too often what its critics such as White have rejected is not true Christianity, not even [C. S.] Lewis' "mere Christianity," but a "sub-Christian" theory and/or practice in a post-Christian era.[57]

This view is not confined to Protestants. In 1990, Pope John Paul II wrote:

> In his desire to have and to enjoy rather than to be and to grow, man consumes the resources of the earth and his own life in an excessive and disordered way. At the root of the senseless destruction of the natural environment lies an anthropological error, which unfortunately is widespread in our day. Man, who discovers his capacity to transform and in a certain sense create the world through his own work, forgets that this is always based on God's prior and original gift of the things that are. Man thinks that he can make arbitrary use of the earth, subjecting it without restraint to his will, as though it did not have its own requisites and a prior God-given purpose, which man can indeed develop but must not betray. Instead of carrying out his role as a co-operator with God in the work of creation, man sets himself up in place of God and thus ends up provoking a rebellion on the part of nature, which is more tyrannized than governed by him.[58]

If Lynn White erred in his understanding of Judeo-Christian guilt, he had company. "For centuries," wrote the conservative philosopher John Passmore in 1974, "it came to be standard Christian teaching that men could do what they liked with animals, that their behaviour towards them need not be governed by any moral considerations whatsoever."[59] Matthew Scully explains that "domin-ion" has often been understood by Christians to mean "license," in the sense of the unlimited power to exploit Creation. As a result of this "folk dominion" (again, my term), says Scully, "we assume that our interests always come first, and if it's profitable or expedient that is all we need to know. We assume that all these other creatures with whom we share the earth are here for us, and only for us. We as-sume, in effect, that we are everything and they are nothing."[60]

"Animals, Too, Are God's Creatures"

Francis of Assisi's life challenged Augustine's view of "dominion." "Before him," writes the historian Adrian House, "Christians inter-preted *Genesis* as entitling them to treat all other forms of life as their slaves; he, in contrast, believed that as works of God they should be respected and loved no differently from men."[61] Francis was no radical nature-worshiper; he accepted Creation as being ver-tical, hierarchical: "Every creature says and proclaims 'God made me for thee O man!'"[62] Yet Francis took the first medieval steps toward restoring some degree of horizontality, reciprocity, and mutuality of love and respect between Christians and the rest of Creation.[63]

Brother Leo, Francis's oldest companion, wrote that Francis "had so much love and sympathy for [animals] that he was disturbed when they were treated without respect. He spoke to them with a great inner and exterior joy, as if they had been endowed by God with feelings, intelligence, and speech."[64] Failure to treat animals ap-propriately "greatly offends the Creator," Francis said.[65] He "called all creatures *brother*."[66] By calling animals "Brother" and "Sister," Francis emphasized their kinship; "it was a step toward balancing a perceived 'I-it' relationship with an 'I-Thou' relationship of respect and affection between humans and creatures."[67] He was not anthro-pomorphizing Creation, but trying to "link humankind with crea-tures in a positive emotional manner, aiding people to identify with them and feel their kinship with them."[68]

His "regard for creation in matters relating to food included a new attempt to return to Biblical standards and a forbearance of unnecessary violence to creatures out of love for them."[69] Though he sometimes ate meat when it was offered, Francis released a trapped rabbit and tossed fish back into lakes, then admonished them to be wary of future hooks. He refused to kill animals and famously tried to prevent the slaughter of two lambs headed for market: "'God forbid,' replied the saint, 'this must not happen. Take the mantle I am wearing and give them to me.'"[70] He removed worms from the road so they would not be trampled, and made a companion, instead of a meal, of a pheasant sent him to eat when he was ill. He gave bees honey or wine in the winter so they would not perish from the cold.[71]

Saint Bonaventure, elected Minister General of Francis's Friars Minor thirty years after his death, saw Francis's relationship with animals as evidence of his partial return—a complete return was impossible until the Second Coming—to the relationship that humans once had with the creatures of Eden before the Fall.[72] Thus, "Francis' accomplishment culminated in 'restoring man's harmony with the whole of creation'" in which "all creatures . . . are bound together in a harmonious interdependence ensured and presided over by the just and benevolent eye of God."[73]

Francis's regard did not stop at other animals. The Catholic theologian and philosopher C. K. Chesterton explains that Francis "was a man who did not want to see the wood for the trees. He wanted to see each tree as a separate and almost a sacred thing, being a child of God and therefore a brother or sister of man."[74] And so the sun, wind, air, and fire he called "Brother," and the moon and water he called "Sister."[75] That is why Lynn White proposed naming Francis patron saint of ecologists. In 1979, Pope John Paul II did that. Today Pope Benedict XVI might name Francis patron saint of "Creation Care," as environmentalism is becoming known in Christendom. As Cardinal Ratzinger, Pope Benedict was asked about the horrors of industrial farming: "Are we allowed to make use of animals, and even to eat them?" He replied:

This is a very serious question. At any rate we can see that they are given into our care, that we cannot just do whatever we want with them. Animals, too, are God's creatures . . . creatures we must respect as companions in creation and as important elements in the creation. . . . Man should always maintain his respect for these creatures. But he knows that at the same time he is not forbidden to take food from them. Certainly a sort of industrial use of creatures, so that geese are fed in such a way as to produce as large a liver as possible, or hens live so packed together that they become just caricatures of birds, this degrading of living creatures to a commodity seems to me in fact to contradict the relationship of mutuality that comes across in the Bible.[76]

I wrote the Pope to inquire whether Cardinal Ratzinger's opinion was Pope Benedict's. Monsignor Gabriele Caccia, assessor at the Vatican's Secretariat of State, replied that the Pope was too busy to respond. But His Holiness had asked Caccia to direct me to *The Catechism of the Catholic Church*, numbers 2415–18 and 2456–57.[77] I suspect that the Holy Father never saw my letter, for Benedict appears thoroughly modern on the issue of Creation Care in a way that the more conservative Catechism of the Catholic Church does not—and understandably so, since it was written before climate change was fully appreciated.

The result of what is essentially the conflict between Augustine and Aquinas, on the one hand, and Francis, on the other, writes Matthew Scully, is

two worlds often bearing no relation at all to one another—as in a place . . . in North Carolina, where you can find a factory farm, a captive hunting ranch, and a Baptist church literally neighboring one another (an obvious reference to Tar Heel). For many Christians, there is this one world in which man made in the image of God affirms the inherent goodness of animals, feeling himself the just and benevolent master. And then there is this other world, the world of reality in which people and industries are left free to do as they will without moral restraint or condemnation, without reproach or even much in the way of self-reproach. There is the stirring world of "All Creatures of Our God and King," the lyrics written by Saint Francis himself and often sung by Catholics filing out of Mass. And then there is the world of the Easter feast of lamb or ham or veal, to be enjoyed without the slightest thought of the privation and misery the lamb or pig or calf endured at human hands.[78]

According to John Passmore, for the next eight centuries, Francis's views had "little or no influence."[79] Anyone visiting Bladen County's industrial hog farms or its Tar Heel abattoir would have to agree. Today thirty-eight thousand intelligent, feeling pigs, raised in appalling industrial conditions, by Christians, will be brutally slaughtered at Tar Heel, by Christians, and produce enormous profits, for Christians, and it will happen again tomorrow and then the day after that. And hardly anyone has cared for decades.

And so it might have continued for centuries, little noticed, unhindered—a powerful, gigantic, profitable, and blood-soaked industry roaring on. Except for one thing. The "folk dominion" alleged to provide carte blanche to exploit animals also rationalized the untrammeled exploitation of non-animal nature. A series of twentieth-century environmental catastrophes than began that, by the turn of the twenty-first century, would include massive global climate change. Unlike helpless pigs, the rest of nature could fight back.

CHAPTER ELEVEN

"A Newfound Passion" [1]

To wrap our prejudice in the Scripture
is a sinful thing to do.
—*Southern Baptist Convention spokesperson (1999)* [2]

Both our present science and our present technology
are so tinctured with orthodox Christian arrogance
toward nature that no solution to our ecologic crisis
can be expected from them alone. Since the roots of
our trouble are so largely religious, the remedy must
also be essentially religious.
—*Lynn White Jr.* [3]

Was it permitted to believe that there was nowhere upon
the earth, or above the earth, a heaven for pigs, where they
were requited for all this suffering? . . . And now was one
to believe that there was nowhere a god of pigs, to whom
this pig personality was precious, to whom these pig-
squeals and agonies had a meaning? Who would take

> this pig into his arms and comfort him, reward him
> for his work well done, and show him the
> meaning of his sacrifice?
> —*Upton Sinclair*[4]

MORE THAN THREE-QUARTERS of Americans are Christians. Over half of American Christians are Protestants. More than half the Protestants are evangelicals. Over two-thirds of evangelical Baptists and more than three-quarters of Southern Baptists live in the American South. More than 40 percent of North Carolinians are evangelical Protestants.[5] Almost half of American Protestants are Baptists. The largest Baptist denomination, with over 16 million members, is the Southern Baptist Convention (SBC). Bladen County is overwhelmingly evangelical Protestant, and most of them are Southern Baptists.[6] Thirty-seven church and study group members belong to the Bladen Baptist Association.[7]

The SBC is the second-largest American religious denomination, after Catholicism's 66 million, although you wouldn't know that from Bladen County, where there are about 100 more Catholics than there are Baha'is. You can't find a Jew.[8] What Southern Baptists believe, and think about, and do influences what happens in Bladen County. Fortunately, it is from the ranks of these evangelical Southern Baptists that a most serious challenge to the belief in the paradigm of "dominion as license" is being mounted. The reason is pragmatic. The Bible hasn't changed, but the earth has. Humans have been altering its climate since the beginning of the Industrial Revolution, the impact of those changes has become clear, and a worldwide consensus has emerged that something must be done about it immediately. Many religious are reevaluating their responsibilities to God's Creation, and not just God's climate-related Creation. All of it.

The struggle is well under way. "Creation as Wal-Mart" has reigned so successfully for so long because it accords nicely with human selfishness.⁹ "Creation as ward" will be less attractive because it carries more responsibility than it bestows privilege. In the short run, it will not give many Christians what they want, what they have long had, and what they feel entitled to. But if we stay the course, irreversible environmental catastrophe will be upon us and Christians, like everyone else, may end up with very little indeed.

THE CARE OF CREATION

The conservative evangelical Southern Baptist leader and radio host Richard Land wrote in 1992 that all Creation belongs to God. Humans come first and possess a Divine authority to rule, but only as vice regents who must carefully manage God's land and animals, wild and domestic.[10]

> All life deserves respect. We have the right to use animals and plants for human food. We do not have the right to disregard living things or to treat them as inanimate objects. We have the right to domesticate and to raise cattle and to use them for human food. We do not have the right to act in a callous, cruel, or cavalier manner toward any living creature. We have a right as painlessly as possible to use animals in research to better human health. I don't believe we have the right to use animals or to cause them discomfort merely to improve cosmetics.[11]

"Creation Care" books have begun piling up.[12] J. Matthew Sleeth's *Serve God, Save the Planet: A Christian Call to Action* is just one prominent example. It was published in 2006 by Zondervan, the Bible publisher that describes itself as "an international Christian communications company with a heart for helping people find and follow Jesus Christ by inspiring them with relevant biblical and spiritual resources."[13] Sleeth is "convinced that when the church becomes fully engaged in the problems of creation care, we will overcome seemingly insurmountable odds. As the thirty million evangelical Christians—and all those who consider themselves people of faith—grow in their understanding that God holds us accountable for his creation, we will begin to see positive changes on an unprecedented scale."[14]

When those changes begin to be felt, fair credit will go to Richard Cizik. Vice president of government affairs for the 30 million–strong National Association of Evangelicals (NAE) until December 2008, Cizik has been described as "a pro-Bush Bible-brandishing reverend zealously opposed to abortion, gay marriage, and embryonic stem-cell research"; he has also been called Washington's most effective evangelical lobbyist and was recently named one of *Time* magazine's "World's 100 Most Influential People."[15] Cizik was converted to "Creation Care" in a university lecture hall; it was, he said, "not unlike my conversion to Christ." He explained: "I was at a conference in Oxford where Sir John Houghton, an evangelical scientist, was presenting evidence of shrinking ice caps, temperatures tracked for millennia through ice-core data, increasing hurricane intensity, drought patterns, and so on. I realized all at once, with sudden awe, that climate change is a phenomenon of truly biblical proportions."[16]

Cizik was transformed into a fierce advocate for Creation Care, which he sees as

> simply our articulation of a biblical doctrine, which is that we are commissioned by God the Almighty to be stewards of the earth. It is rooted not in politics or ideology, but in the scriptures. Genesis 2:15 specifically calls us "to watch over and care for" the bounty of the earth and its creatures. Scripture not only affirms this role, but warns that the earth is not ours to abuse, own, or dominate. The Bible clearly says in Revelation 11:18 that "God will destroy those who destroy the earth. . . . It was by and for Christ that this earth was made, which means it is

sinfully wrong—it is a tragedy of enormous proportions—to destroy, degrade, or despoil it. He who has ears, let him hear."

Cizik criticizes the claim that the Bible's grant of dominion over Creation amounts to a license to exploit.

That is a deeply flawed interpretation. Dominion does not mean domination. It implies responsibility—to cultivate and care for the earth, not to sully it with bad environmental practices. The Bible also teaches us that Jesus Christ is not only redeeming his people, but also restoring God's creation. Obviously, since the fall of man and entrance of sin into the world, all of creation has yearned for its redemption from sin and death and destruction. That will occur with the Second Coming of Christ. But in the meantime we show our love for Jesus Christ by reaching out to and healing the spiritually lost and by conserving and renewing Creation. Christ's call to love nature is as simple as his call to love our neighbors as ourselves.[17]

"I believe the very reputation of the gospel is at stake," Cizik says. Notoriously, evangelicals did not act aggressively against racism during the twentieth-century civil rights movement. Cizik is determined that they not repeat that mistake.[18]

He acknowledges that most evangelicals have still thought little about Creation Care. "I would say that this newfound passion, this concern for Creation Care as we call it, . . . comes straight from God and the Holy Spirit who is regenerating people's hearts to realize the imperative of the scriptures to care for God's world in new ways. It comes from God Himself. . . . The climate change crisis that we believe is occurring is not something we can wait ten years, five years, even a year, to address. Climate change is real and human induced. It calls for action soon. And we are saying action based upon a biblical view of the world as God's world. . . . If we are to be obedient to the Scriptures, there is no time to wait, no time to stall, no time to deliberate."[19]

In 2004, the NAE issued "For the Health of the Nation: An Evangelical Call to Civic Responsibility."

> God gave us the care of his earth and its species to our first parents. That responsibility has passed into our hands. We affirm that God-given dominion is a sacred responsibility to steward the earth and not a license to abuse the creation of which we are a part. We are not the owners of creation, but its stewards. Summoned by God to "watch over and care for it" (Gen. 2:15). . . . We believe we show our love for the Creator by caring for his creations.

Two years later, more than eighty evangelical leaders produced the Evangelical Climate Initiative.

> Over the last several years many of us have engaged in study, reflection, and prayer related to the issue of climate change (often called "global warming"). . . . For most of us, until recently this has not been treated as a pressing issue or major priority. Indeed, many of us have required considerable convincing before becoming persuaded that climate change is a real problem and that it ought to matter to us as Christians. But now we have seen and heard enough to offer the following moral argument related to the matter of human-induced climate change. . . .
>
> Christians must care about climate change because we love God the Creator and Jesus our Lord, through whom and for whom the creation was made. This is God's world, and any damage that we do to God's world is an offense against God Himself (Gen. 1; Ps. 24; Col. 1:16). . . .

Christians, noting the fact that most of the climate change problem is human induced, are reminded that when God made humanity he commissioned us to exercise stewardship over the earth and its creatures. Climate change is the latest evidence of our failure to exercise proper stewardship, and constitutes a critical opportunity for us to do better (Gen. 1:26–28).[20]

There was foot-dragging. In January 2006, the Prison Fellowship's Charles Colson, Focus on the Family's James Dobson, chair of the American Family Association Donald Wildmon, Richard Land, and eighteen others drafted an "appeal letter" to the NAE: "The existence of global warming and its implications for mankind is a subject of heated controversy throughout the world," they wrote, without irony. They asked the NAE to "not adopt any official position on the issue of global climate change. Global warming is not a consensus issue, and our love for the Creator and respect for His creation does not require us to take a position."

The NAE's president responded:

In 2003, the NAE General Council unanimously approved the document "For the Health of the Nation: An Evangelical Call to Civic Responsibility." This landmark statement included a section concerning the environment. We stand by that document as the overarching principle that should guide our discussion. God created the earth and we are to steward that creation. Earlier this month the NAE Executive Committee re-affirmed our commitment to that principle and passed the following motion: "Recognizing the ongoing debate concerning the causes and origins of global warming, and understanding the lack of consensus among the evangelical community on this issue, the NAE Executive Committee, while affirming our love for the Creator and his Creation, directs the NAE staff to stand by and not exceed in any fashion our approved and adopted statements concerning the environment contained within the Evangelical Call to Civic Responsibility."[21]

The following year, Wildmon, Dobson, and twenty-three other evangelicals demanded that the NAE silence or dismiss Richard Cizik: "We have observed that Cizik and others are using global warming to shift the emphasis away from the great moral issues of our time, notably the sanctity of human life, the integrity of marriage and the teaching of sexual abstinence and morality to our children. In their place has come a preoccupation with climate concerns." They failed.[22] "To be biblically consistent means you have to, at times, be politically inconsistent," Cizik wryly observed.[23]

Charles Colson recently coauthored a book with a professional Creationist in which he displays dreadful ignorance about science in general and evolutionary theory specifically. He also seeks to rewrite history by claiming that most Christians have always been slavery abolitionists.[24] Colson signed "the Land Letter" encouraging George Bush to invade Iraq and demanding that the NAE cease working on climate change, which he thinks is as real as evolution. Along with Donald Wildmon and James C. Dobson, Colson also signed the so-called Cornwall Declaration in 2000, a document that lists global warming, overpopulation, and rampant species loss among concerns the signers considered unfounded or greatly exaggerated.[25] By November 2007, he was promoting the climate change equivalent of "be kind to animals": "Can you think of one instance where scripture praises excessive consumption or waste? I can't."

Colson thinks that climate change is a minor itch that can be scratched by turning lights off. He claims, wrongly, that "most Americans—liberal and conservative—remain divided on the basic questions: 'How serious is [climate change], what causes it, and [what] should [hu]mankind do about it?'"[26] But the point is that even Colson emphasizes "the importance of good stewardship toward the rest of creation," and he signed the NAE's "For the Health of the Nation: An Evangelical Call to Civic Responsibility."[27]

On March 10, 2008, I opened the *New York Times* and encountered "The Southern Baptist Declaration on the Environment and Climate Change." Neela Banerjee reported that:

> signaling a significant departure from the Southern Baptist Convention's official stance on global warming, 44 Southern Baptist leaders have decided to back a declaration calling for more action on climate change.... "We believe our current denominational engagement with these issues has often been too timid, failing to produce a unified moral voice," the church leaders wrote in their new declaration. . . .
>
> Jonathan Merritt, the spokesman for the Southern Baptist Environment and Climate Initiative and a seminarian at Southeastern Baptist Theological Seminary in Wake Forest, N.C., said the declaration was a call to Christians to return to a biblical mandate to guard the world God created.
>
> The Southern Baptist signatories join a growing community of evangelicals pushing for more action among believers, industry and politicians. Experts on the Southern Baptist Convention noted the initiative marked the growing influence of younger leaders on the discussions in the Southern Baptist Convention.
>
> While those younger Baptists remain committed to fight abortion, for instance, the environment is now a top priority, too.[28]

Baptists tend to be democratic, decentralized, and nonhierarchical. The SBC is a voluntary association of tens of thousands of independent local churches, large and small. It has long been a repository of biblical certainty; in a 1980s poll, the vast majority of Southern Baptist pastors and lay church leaders agreed that the Bible contains the "inerrant Word of God, accurate in every detail."[29] They still agree: the SBC's 2000 Southern Baptist "Statement of Faith," harmonious with prior Statements of Faith, declares: "The Holy Bible was written by men divinely inspired and is God's revelation of Himself to man. It is a perfect treasure of divine instruction. It has God for its author, salvation for its end, and truth, without any mixture of error, for its matter. Therefore, all Scripture is totally true and trustworthy."[30]

They believe the Bible is fixed, but disagree on which Bible that is. Presently Southern Baptist ministers prefer, in almost equal numbers, the traditional King James Bible, the New King James Bible, the New International Version, and the New American Standard Bible.[31] These bibles don't all say the same thing. Example: the King James Versions, new and old, grant humans "dominion" over Creation, while the New International Version allows humans to "rule."

REPENTANCE

Southern Baptist positions on other important issues have evolved, even as the Bible has stayed the same. The SBC's 1989 "Resolution on Racism" conceded that "Southern Baptists have not always clearly stood for racial justice and equality." Neither did the cabinet of the Confederate States of America. In fact, the SBC was conceived expressly to protect the institution of Southern slavery. In 1845, the General Missionary Convention of the Baptist Denomination in the United States, then controlled by Northerners, refused to appoint Southern slaveholders as missionaries, and its Acting Board proclaimed that "we can never be a party to any arrangement which would imply approbation of slavery."[32] That catalyzed the sectional schism. One Baptist minister, Thornton Stringfellow, who became a powerful voice in support of slavery and who found support for it throughout the Bible, enthusiastically embraced his new role as a *Southern* Baptist minister.[33]

Southern Baptists weren't the only racist Christians. When former vice president John Calhoun, from South Carolina, complained on the floor of the U.S. Senate that "three great evangelical churches" had been "torn asunder" by the conflict over slavery, he was referring to the Baptists, but also to the Methodists and Presbyterians.[34] In 1864, the General Assembly of the Presbyterian Church in the Confederate States of America proclaimed that "we hesitate not to affirm that it is the peculiar mission of the Southern Church to conserve the institution of slavery."[35]

After slavery was abolished, Southern Baptists retreated to the next trench line, where they wholeheartedly supported a century of racial segregation and inequalities on the same biblical grounds to which they had appealed to justify slavery. They emphasized the Curse of Ham and added the story of the Tower of Babel, in which God scattered the races intending that they be kept separate forever.

It was only in 1995 that the SBC conceded that its "relationship to African-Americans has been hindered from the beginning by the role that slavery played in the formation of the Southern Baptist Convention. . . . Many of our Southern Baptists forbears [*sic*] defended the right to own slaves, and either participated in, supported, or acquiesced in the particularly inhumane nature of American slavery"; moreover, "in later years Southern Baptists failed, in many cases, to support, and in some cases opposed, legitimate initiatives to secure the civil rights of African-Americans." Implicitly acknowledging the Hammite Curse, the SBC recognized that "racism profoundly distorts our understanding of Christian morality, leading some Southern Baptists to believe that racial prejudice and discrimination are compatible with the Gospel."[36] Two examples from the 1950s will suffice: *the Alabama Baptist* editorialized: "We think it deplorable in the sight of God that there should be any change in the difference and variety in his creation and he certainly would desire to keep our races pure," while *The Christian Index*, the newspaper of the Georgia Baptist Convention, declared,

"The Lord at Babel gave them their languages and the bounds of their habitation. The White race in Europe, the copper colored races in Asia and the Black or Negro race in Africa. If the Lord had wanted us to all live together in a social way, why did he separate us in the beginning[?]"[37]

This "folk segregationist theology" was more the property of church deacons and auxiliaries, of laymen's associations and laypeople, than of the denominational leaders, theologians, and ethicists, who often acknowledged that these biblical stories were irrelevant to racism.[38] Such Baptist theologians were among the SBC's "progressive elite" on race relations and included faculty members from Southern Baptist seminaries, the SBC's Social Service and Christian Life Commissions, and Southern Baptist state conventions. Southern Baptists recognized them as among their best educated and most knowledgeable in biblical interpretation and could see that they represented the entire range of Baptist theologies.[39]

But this Southern Baptist progressive elite did not start as integrationists. From the end of World War II to the eve of the U.S. Supreme Court's 1954 decision in *Brown v. Board of Education*, they were content to demand that "separate" truly be "equal." And that was all. After *Brown*, they began to urge Southerners not to resist court decisions on desegregation. Only after 1960 did they begin demanding complete racial integration.[40] Pointing to Genesis verses saying God made humans in His image and to verses in Paul's Letter to the Hebrews declaring that Jesus died for all our sins, they argued that human equality, not racism, had been divinely ordained.[41] The Curse of Ham was bogus: Noah, not God, cursed Ham, and the curse was directed at the Palestinian Canaan, not the African Ham. And the Tower of Babel story condemned the worship of false idols and languages, not racial differences.[42]

Some leaders began to pirouette, the most prominent example being the hugely popular fundamentalist Texas pastor, and future SBC president, W. A. Criswell. In 1956, Criswell had raged before a joint session of the South Carolina legislature that racial desegregation was un-Christian. In 1968, he said that those seeking biblical support for segregation simply "don't read the Bible right," and he publicly repudiated his support for racial segregation as biblical truth.[43] The plausibility crisis that these Baptist progressive elites created in folk segregationist theology did not lead to a rapid end to Baptist support for racial inequities. But they undermined its divinity. If racial segregation was to survive, it would be on its secular merits, not on any sacred grounds. That meant that segregation was suddenly amenable to contradiction by fact.

According to historian Mark Newman, these progressive elites "helped influence the vast majority of Southern Baptist institutions to adopt nondiscriminatory policies in the late 1960s and 1970s," and though they achieved only minimal integration within the SBC, "by condemning racial discrimination and denying that the Bible endorsed segregation, the progressive elite created a crisis in the plausibility structure of the segregationist Southern Baptist majority . . . [and] helped to make flagrant segregation and discrimination unacceptable among most Southern Baptists."[44]

The Southern Baptist "Declaration on the Environment and Climate Change" was evidence that the Creation Care position of the progressive elites was changing. Here, perhaps, was the beginning of the end of the third dark chapter of Bladen County's history.

A Declaration of Stewardship

Jonathan Merritt's declaration about the Baptist position on climate change used the word "timid" twice to describe the SBC's Creation Care inactions. Admittedly, the SBC has not been entirely silent. Its "messengers"—the representatives who attend the annual meetings—had passed five environmental resolutions in thirty-eight years. A 1970 "Resolution on the Environment" acknowledged that "man has created a crisis by polluting the air, poisoning the streams, and ravaging the soil." It had added that churches should "help remedy this environmental mismanagement by practicing and proclaiming a positive awareness that 'the earth is the Lord's,'" and it "urge[d] Christians everywhere to practice stewardship of environment" and to work "to correct the ravaging of the earth."

Four years later, the SBC's "Resolution on Stewardship of God's Creation" stated that "God, who is the author of the universe, views his creation as being very good. And the Scriptures confront us with our responsibility to God as stewards." It asked God to forgive mankind "for the selfish use of God's creation" and urged aggressive conservation measures. The "Resolution on Environmental Stewardship" in 1990 reminded Southern Baptists that "the earth is the Lord's, and ... the sinfulness of the human race has led to the destruction of the created order ... as evidenced by the endangerment of the earth by pollution, human extravagance and wastefulness, soil depletion and erosion, and general misuse of creation."

In 2006, the resolution "On Environmentalism and Evangelicals" reiterated that, while God had created men and women in His image and likeness and commanded them "to exercise caring stewardship and dominion over the earth and environment ... mankind as free moral agents willfully disobeyed God, plunging the whole creation into corruption because of our sin ... from which the fallen creation awaits restoration. ... Since the fall into sin, humans have often ignored the Creation, shirked their stewardship of the environment, and further defiled the good creation. ... [T]he messengers renew[ed] our commitment to God's command to exercise caring stewardship and wise dominion over the creation." But they complained that "environmentalism is threatening to become a wedge issue to divide the evangelical community and further distract its members from the priority of the Great Commission." (The Great Commission is what many Christians see as the divinely appointed duty to spread the word of Jesus throughout the world.)

The messengers voted down a proposal to encourage government funding of global warming research and oil energy alternatives. "Some in our culture have completely rejected God the Father in favor of deifying 'Mother Earth,'" transformed environmentalism into a neopagan religion, and "elevated animal and plant life to the place of equal—or greater—value with human life," the resolution said. The SBC would "resist alliances with extreme environmental groups whose positions contradict biblical principles and . . . oppose solutions based on questionable science." Finally, the 2007 messengers passed the resolution "On Global Warming." Among its twenty-two provisions was this: " . . . Christians are called by God to exercise caring stewardship and dominion over the earth and environment." Wiley S. Drake, the SBC's fundamentalist second vice president, summarized the other twenty-one provisions as, "We don't believe in global warming."[45] The resolution "urge[d] Southern Baptists to proceed cautiously."

This was the last straw for Merritt and the 2008 Declaration's signatories. Thirty-eight years of "be kind to Creation" resolutions repudiated Christian responsibilities. So these Creation Care progressive elites acted. Like their forebears opposed to racial segregation half a century earlier, they spanned the spectrum of Southern Baptist theology. The original signatories included not just the SBC's then-current president, Frank S. Page, but James Merritt and Jack Graham, former SBC presidents, the president of Southeastern Baptist Theological Seminary at Wake Forest, the director of the Center for Great Commission Studies, two professors of church history, a professor of systematic theology, a professor of missions, a professor of historical theology and patristics, and a professor of evangelism, the director of church plantings of the New Orleans Baptist Theological Seminary, the presidents of Palm Beach Atlantic University, Union University, California Baptist University, Beeson Divinity School, and Southwest Baptist University, the regional director for Southeast Asia of the SBC's International Mission Board, the director of LifeWay Research, the research arm of LifeWay Christian Resources of the Southern Baptist Convention, the executive director or officer of the West Virginia, Kentucky, Colorado, and Oklahoma Conventions of Southern Baptists, and a member of the SBC's Executive Committee. Hundreds of new signatories have been added and more keep coming.

The Declaration said in part:

> We have recently engaged in study, reflection and prayer related to the challenges presented by environmental and climate change issues. These things have not always been treated with pressing concern as major issues. Indeed, some of us have required considerable convincing before becoming persuaded that these are real problems that deserve our attention. But now we have seen and heard enough to be persuaded that these issues are among the current era's challenges that require a unified moral voice.[46]
>
> . . . There is undeniable evidence that the earth—wildlife, water, land and air—can be damaged by human activity, and that people suffer as a result. When this happens, it is especially egregious because creation serves as revelation of God's presence, majesty and provision. . . . We humbly take responsibility for the damage that we have done to God's cosmic revelation and pledge to take an unwavering stand to preserve and protect the creation over which we have been given responsibility by Almighty God Himself.
>
> . . . In the face of intense concern and guided by the biblical principle of creation stewardship, we resolve to engage [the issue of global warming] without any further lingering over the basic reality of the problem. . . .
>
> While we cannot here review the full range of relevant Christian convictions and Baptist doctrines related to care of the creation, we emphasize the following points:

We must care about environmental and climate issues because of our love for God—"the Creator, Redeemer, Preserver and Ruler of the Universe . . . "—through whom and for whom the creation was made. This is not our world, it is God's. Therefore any damage we do to this world is an offense against God Himself. . . . We share God's concern for the abuse of His creation.

We must care about environmental issues because of our commitment to God's Holy and Inerrant Word, which is "the supreme standard by which all human conduct, creeds and religious opinions should be tried. . . ." Within these Scriptures we are reminded that when God made mankind, He commissioned us to exercise stewardship over the earth and its creatures. . . . Therefore our motivation for facing failures to exercise proper stewardship is not primarily political, social or economic—it is biblical.[47]

"Right Now I Would Be Ashamed to Have Christ Return"

Three weeks after the Declaration was issued, I landed again at the Raleigh-Durham International Airport. This time I drove to Carver's Creek Restaurant on Raleigh's Capital Boulevard. The sign over the entrance read Fresh Rib and Fresh Steak. Having Googled each other, Jonathan Merritt and I were able to walk right up and shake hands. He was moonfaced and fresh, intelligent and serious, sounding as I imagined a Southern Baptist from Snellville, Georgia, would sound. Jonathan said he had graduated on a full scholarship from Jerry Falwell's Liberty University in 2006, with a bachelor's degree in biology. His professors had taught him Creationist Biology as truth and just enough Evolutionary Biology so that he would know what he was fighting against; they had warned that "you can't believe that leftist propaganda" about environmental concerns.

Jonathan's family is socially and theologically conservative. Falwell had been a close longtime family friend. Jonathan is the son of Declaration signatory James Merritt, a recent two-term SBC president and the holder of master of divinity and doctorate of philosophy degrees from the Southern Baptist Theological Seminary in Louisville, Kentucky. Merritt Sr. is a trustee of Liberty University in Lynchburg, Virginia, the pastor of Cross Pointe, the Church at Gwinnett Center near Atlanta, and host of the international broadcast ministry *Touching Lives*, broadcast on Trinity Broadcasting Network, the Church Channel, and Liberty Channel.[48] The Touching Lives Ministry says it

> believes the Bible is God's Holy Word. We believe that all 66 books of the Old and New Testaments were divinely inspired by God. Even though given through human personalities, the Bible is the perfect treasure of God. We believe the scriptures are inerrant and infallible in their original manuscript. The Bible is our full and final authority on all matters of faith and practice. The Bible has God as its author, salvation for its end, and truth, without any mixture of error, for its subject matter.[49]

James Merritt would tell *The Christian Index*, "I'm just a little to the right of Ronald Reagan."[50]

If you ask Jonathan if he is a political conservative, he will say he is, and if you ask him if he respects Dr. Falwell, he will say he does (though not Falwell's archaic Creation Care views), and greatly so. Recently Jonathan wrote: "I long for Ronald Reagan. Don't you . . . ?"[51] If he has broken with family tradition, it is because he decided that, while one may vote Republican, it's not one's Christian duty to do so.[52] He remains solidly pro-life and anti–gay marriage: the Southern Baptist "Declaration on the Environment and Climate Change" insists that "we are proud of our deep and lasting commitments to moral issues like the sanctity of human life and biblical definitions of marriage. We will never compromise our con-

victions nor attenuate our advocacy on these matters, which consti-
tute the most pressing moral issues of our day."

Merritt admitted he was once an "enemy of the environment," an
inveterate litterbug who, when criticized, would smirk and reply, "I'll
vote Republican." "Harming the environment was a joke," he said,
"egotistical and funny." Then, like Cizik, Merritt had a conversion
experience. His occurred in the fall of 2006 during his systematic
theology class at the Southeastern Baptist Theological Seminary. His
professor, Dr. John Hammett, said that "when we destroy God's creation it is very similar to tearing a page out of the Bible." At that moment, Merritt says, "God began to work in my heart."

Also like Cizik, Jonathan Merritt changed his life. He stopped
drinking bottled water because few plastic bottles are recycled and
their manufacture and transport require huge expenditures of energy,
and because $15 billion a year is spent on bottled water while one
and a half billion humans lack clean water. Once he would have ordered steak for lunch at Carver's Creek; no more. I asked him why
not. He said he had watched videos of industrialized farming cruelties and concluded that the animals were not being treated in a
Christian way. "You know, a lot of Christians don't know that after
the Flood God made a Covenant not just with Noah and his descendants but with 'every living creature.' That means the animals too.
God felt remorse that he had to destroy so much of his Creation. We
Christians kill animals in worse ways than God did, but we don't feel
remorse."[53]

Jonathan meditated on his Christian duties to Creation for a year,
waiting for God to warm his heart and tell him how to be both "salt
and light." That phrase had made its way into the Declaration. ("We
can do better. To abandon these issues to the secular world is to
shirk from our responsibility to be salt and light. The time for
timidity regarding God's creation is no more.") It comes from
Matthew 5:13–16, in which Jesus told his disciples: "Ye are the salt
of the earth. . . . Ye are the light of the world. A city that I set on a
hill cannot be hid. Neither do men light a candle, and put it under a

bushel, but on a candlestick, and it giveth light unto all that are in the house. Let your light so shine before men, that they may see your good works."[54]

Once God spoke to him, Jonathan acted without delay. By the fall of 2007, he was convinced that a Christian could be pro-life, pro-marriage, pro-family . . . and pro–Creation Care. He persuaded five intelligent, highly respected Southern Baptists, who represented a range of theological positions, to form a Declaration drafting committee. He hoped they would produce a centrist, broadly acceptable document that could claim the middle between what Jonathan saw as a reactionary, Republican, Falwell-like, "environmentalism-is-the-devil," "dominion-means-license" position and an "Al Gore," "Chicken Little," Kyoto Treaty–supporting, "the-sky-is-falling" stance; he wanted the Declaration to embody a "biblical expression of a broad environmentalism."

Merritt's father, James, was one of the five committee members. A month after the Declaration was issued, James would tell *The Christian Index* that he

> believes the Church too often has brought up the end of life's parade rather than leading it. That's why he feels his son's document on the environment is a step toward taking back what rightly belongs to believers. "For example," he says, "we do not have a good track record on the Civil Rights Movement and ending segregation. In some ways protecting the environment has the same polarization factor that keeps us away from having a voice. We have been so alienated by the efforts of the Left that we don't want to get involved for fear of associating with them. Christians should have a place at the table when it comes to shaping public opinion; instead we have abdicated our role in this discussion," he says. Creation care, he maintains, is one of the foundational tenets of Scripture, "going back to the first three chapters of Genesis."

Dr. Daniel Akin was another member. President of the Southeastern Baptist Theological Seminary, Akin helped engineer the conservative takeover of the Southern Baptist Convention. That had been necessitated, he said, by the fact that "Southern Baptists were not just drifting, but plunging headlong into theological liberalism."[55] Timothy George, president of Beeson Divinity School in Birmingham, Alabama, and senior editor of *Christianity Today*, was a third member. Charles Colson recently dedicated a book to "the saints who over the past 2,000 years have courageously defended . . . Christian orthodoxy [including] . . . Timothy George, whom God has raised up for this time to defend the faith given once for all time." A fourth, David Clark, was president of Palm Beach Atlantic University and a former CEO of the National Religious Broadcasters. The fifth, David Dockery, was a professor of New Testament and president of Union University in Jackson, Tennessee.[56] By drafting the Southern Baptist Declaration, these men established themselves as part of the "progressive elite" spearheading the Creation Care movement, even if they might not be—and might not want to be—characterized as "progressive" in any other sense.

"Dominion" means to Jonathan that we must be faithful stewards, carers for all of Creation—air, water, climate, natural resources, wildlife, domesticated animals. In a Salem Radio interview, he said that teachers have dominion over their students and we should be glad they don't treat their students the way we treat Creation. "We Christians laud the sanctity of life, but we don't fight against capital punishment or for animal rights or against deforestation," he said. "Right now I would be ashamed to have Christ return and see this. God created the world and we don't value it."

Unlike Falwell, who was determined to withdraw from the secular world and erect parallel Christian institutions, Jonathan says that he and a generation of young Southern Baptists believe that their "salt and light" duties lie in being "a positive redemptive force in culture," working to change it for the better. He intended for the

Declaration to be the latest in a line of "special words" that Southern Baptists issue in crises: "As the dawning of new ages has produced substantial changes requiring a special word, Southern Baptist churches, associations, and general bodies have often found it necessary to make declarations in order to define, express, and defend beliefs." He wanted the Declaration grounded in "God's inerrant word—the Holy Bible," situated within the mainstream of Southern Baptist belief, with appeals to biblical authorities, Southern Baptist Resolutions, and Statements of Faith that demand that Christians be nature's stewards. That is just what the drafters did.

In the media release that accompanied the Declaration's release, Timothy George said, "As evangelical, Bible-believing Christians, Southern Baptists want to take seriously the stewardship that God has granted us to care for his creation." Daniel Akin heralded the Declaration as "a call to be informed and get involved in caring for creation, what John Calvin called 'the theater of God's glory.'" James Merritt urged "Southern Baptists [to] lead the way in modeling proper care of the environment in both practice and precept because this is a God-created world that deserves the very best of our ecological stewardship."

I asked Jonathan how Southern Baptists were responding to the Declaration. He said that depended. "On what?" I asked. On how old the person is, he replied. Akin has received substantial criticism from older Southern Baptists, some complaining that a focus on Creation Care diverts attention from the Great Commission. "We can't be so concerned with evangelization that we let a vital issue such as our responsibility toward Creation fall into a secondary place," Jonathan said. "We're supposed to be preaching the whole Bible, not just the parts about abortion and marriage. I haven't received a single negative comment from anyone under the age of forty." LifeWay Research has found that younger Protestants generally are falling away from their churches in large numbers.[57] "There is no young leadership in the Southern Baptist Convention," Jonathan said. "Young leaders will return only if we start having relevant conversations with them. We're not so much interested in a national voice as we are in living the right ways in our communities. God gave us the power to be instruments of good. For us, it's no longer enough to say the right words. Those words must be accompanied by visible expressions of transformative power. We're supposed to be little Christs," he said. "Christ in Christ's absence."

The November 2008 presidential election seemed to bear Jonathan out. Barack Obama doubled John Kerry's percentage of votes received from evangelicals ages eighteen to forty-four. "There is definitely a generational division," said David Gushee, professor of Christian Ethics at Mercer University. As Merritt claims, Gushee says that younger evangelicals "are attracted to a broader agenda beyond abortion and homosexuality that includes the environment, poverty, human rights and torture."[58]

It was one thing for a twenty-five-year-old seminary student to try to kick-start a revolution, but something else for a pastor deeply experienced in religious politics to sign on. Merritt's father agreed with his son in his *Christian Index* interview, but added he had signed the Declaration "not as a father but as a concerned follower of Jesus Christ."

> If we don't reach out and embrace the younger generation of conservatives who are coming out of our seminaries we are going to see an even faster graying of our denomination. We must shift our thinking in the way we pro-actively and positively engage with the next generation of leaders or we will continue to get what has been documented with recent studies—a saturation of their absence in our convention. In a conversation with Danny Akin the other day he told me that he did not have one negative response from anyone under the age of 40. There is a new world of younger, conservative evangelicals out there and if there is not room for a healthy debate of

this nature they will simply leave. They will see the Southern Baptist Convention as irrelevant.[59]

"Maybe You Can Be a Fundamentalist Without Being an Idiot"

I wanted to know why Frank S. Page, then the SBC president, had signed the Declaration. Page holds a Master of Divinity degree and a Ph.D. in Christian Ethics from the Southwestern Baptist Theological Seminary in Fort Worth, Texas. On Falwell's death, he issued a statement that Falwell had been "delighted to witness the conservative direction of the Southern Baptist Convention in the last decades."[60] He agreed to meet. I flew to Charlotte, North Carolina, rented a car, and turned onto the Billy Graham Parkway. On the hundred-mile drive south to the First Baptist Church of Taylors, South Carolina—Page's church—I listened to conservative talk show host Mike Gallagher inveigh against bogus climate change concerns.[61]

Friendly, gracious, his open face framed by wire-rimmed spectacles and sandy hair, Page greeted me from behind his office desk, beckoned me to sit, and immediately asked my religion. He said he wanted to speak to me in the way I could best understand. I had to admit that I was an atheist, then added that I had just celebrated Passover, in a secular Jewish kind of way. He warned me that he is foremost an evangelical Christian and that he would attempt to convert me. "My relationship with Christ is the most important relationship I have in the world," he said. I said that was okay if he tried to convert me and, if he didn't mind, might I take notes. He didn't mind.

I could see why Page had upset the establishment candidate to win the SBC presidency two years before. "I'm not trying to undo a conservative movement that I have supported all these years," Page said after his election. He promised to appoint SBC leaders who be-

lieve the Bible is inerrant, yet have "a sweet spirit." "I'm an inerran-
tist," he said. "I believe in the word of God. I'm just not mad about
it."[62] He smiled a lot.

He held up a letter from Al Gore and read me a paragraph in a
tone I guessed passed for peevishness in Frank Page. "Gore irritates
you?" I asked. "Yes," Page replied, smiling. "Why did you sign the
Southern Baptist 'Declaration on the Environment and Climate
Change'?" I asked. "I knew it was going to be a political hot potato,"
he said. "But it was right. There are times when you have to do the
right thing."

The blowback, however, has been more unpleasant than he ever
imagined. "I have been called things I have never been called before.
'Anti-Christ,'" he said. "In the Bible, enemies are sometimes called
'dogs.' I was called a dog. I've been accused of becoming part of the
'Al Gore crowd.' Some extreme right-wing SBC leaders are concerned that we're adopting a left-wing liberal agenda. Bob Jones
University in Greenville, not far from here, won't even let its students attend my church. One Alabama church sent me a nasty letter.
I could tell they hadn't even read the document, and I told them not
to bother me until they had. A lot of people who criticized me have
come back and said, 'I didn't read the document.' Rush Limbaugh
crucified me. Crucified me! He said Southern Baptists should stick
to winning souls and leave everything else alone. He has no idea
what we're about. We're a teaching ministry as well as a reaching
ministry, and Creation Care is just one of the thousands of areas
about which we are supposed to teach."

I read him the Declaration paragraph that said, "Some of us have
required considerable convincing before becoming persuaded that
these are real problems that deserve our attention." "Did you require
'considerable convincing'?" I asked. He shook his head. "No. I was
on the SBC's Resolutions Committee a few years back. I became fa-
miliar with the issues when we were preparing the 2006 'Resolution
on the Environment.'" He paused. "There was another reason I

signed. The younger generation is falling away. If we are going to have a vibrant voice in the future, we can't ignore them. We have been cutting off a huge number of people."

I told him that Jonathan Merritt had said the same thing just a couple weeks before in Raleigh. "Jonathan and I haven't discussed that," Page said. "But he is correct, though I'd put the line at about thirty-five instead of forty. It's strong in his 'Bridger Generation,' the generation after 'Generation X,' those between eighteen and twenty-nine. We need to say to them, 'We hear you. We agree with you.' Paul always tried to connect with the culture of wherever he was preaching without compromising the message. Look at how he spoke to the people of Athens. It's not that we're going to agree on everything. But if we happen to agree, we should say so. We're saying, 'We care. We're aware of you. We're with you. We haven't gone far enough. Too long we have been silent.' We'll never compromise the message. But we as evangelicals have been silent for too long. No longer. I will not be silent. I spoke a few weeks back at Furman, a very liberal university not far from here. I was told that many more people attended than usual because they knew I had signed the Declaration. For the first time they were thinking that maybe you can be a fundamentalist without being an idiot."

I said, "But after the Declaration was released, you issued a statement that said that, although some of God's people have been too timid about responsible environmental care, 'I don't believe this to be true of the Southern Baptist Convention in an official capacity. . . . I stand totally behind the resolutions that have been passed in recent years.' I think that you *do* believe that the SBC has been too timid. Don't you?" He nodded. "Yes. We have not gone far enough. 'Dominion' is not license to abuse the earth. God gave us the capacity for rational thought and the responsibility to guard over the beautiful earth that He gave us. We have a large responsibility to exercise environmental stewardship, or Creation Care, which is a new phrase that means the same thing."

"Why the sudden shift?" I asked. "There's been no sudden shift," he replied. "We've always believed that we must exercise responsible biblical stewardship, which is the same thing as dominion. I gave a talk recently to some scientists along the coast of South Carolina, atheists, who kept mentioning this article written thirty years ago by that college professor. What was his name?" "Lynn White?" I suggested. "That's him," Page said. "He got it wrong."

"What about factory farming?" I asked. "Is there is a difference in the responsibility that God gave us toward air and water and the climate and what we owe domesticated animals?" I explained what was being done to hogs in Bladen County. Page grew up in Robbins, North Carolina, a one-square-mile city of one thousand people fewer than eighty miles northwest of Tar Heel. It had been part of Bladen County long ago. He said that he knew something about factory farming, but wasn't aware of how large the industry had grown in southeastern North Carolina. He didn't know there was a slaughterhouse in Tar Heel. He said he had been strongly affected by watching a widely circulated video, taken by an undercover agent for the Humane Society of the United States, of a cow being abused at a California slaughterhouse earlier in the year.[63] I told of my fruitless attempts to gain access to the Tar Heel slaughterhouse and how I had been trying to get permission to ask Joseph Luter IV some questions, but had been frustrated by Smithfield's media relations folks. "Aren't these animals part of the Creation we are supposed to care for?" I asked.

"Yes, they are," he said. "Right now Christians are mostly talking about Creation Care in the context of climate change, but it definitely includes animals. Many younger evangelicals are big into animal rights," he said. "My twenty-two-year-old daughter can watch a man's head get cut off on television, but doesn't get nearly as upset as when Benji [the film dog] hurts his toe.[64] Creation Care is in its ascendancy in evangelical circles, especially among our younger people. Animals don't have souls. But they're like our babies at four to six weeks. They're sensitive to pain and suffering. They have feelings. We have to protect them."

"I read Dr. Land's press release," I said. Richard Land hadn't signed the Declaration. Instead, his press release stated that the Southern Baptist Convention's Ethics and Religious Liberty Commission disagreed that Southern Baptists have been "too timid" in addressing the issues of environmental stewardship.[65] "I'm a lawyer, and his struck me as a procedural objection. He never said he opposed the Declaration. He just said that it's not up to individual Southern Baptists to set SBC policy. That's for the Convention." "Richard is a very smart man," Page said. "Oxford graduate. Went to Princeton. He's sympathetic to Creation Care. But Richard has a pretty big ego. And this idea wasn't his." I asked him about the SBC position on biological evolution. In 1982, the messengers had adopted a "Resolution on Scientific Creationism" that began, "Whereas the theory of evolution has never been proven. . . . "[66] "Do you believe that the theory of evolution has never been proven?" I asked. "I waver," he said. His problem with Darwinian evolution was that he didn't see any place in it for God. Then there's the problem of one species evolving into another. Genesis says that plants and animals spring into being, "each according to its kind."[67] But there are "multitudes of Christians who believe in intraspecies evolution," he said. "Even James Dobson, who's a member of the very small Nazarene Church, does. But why does it matter? I don't think evolution has anything to do with Creation Care. It's a non-issue."

I had a last question, the one I had discussed with Siena. "Human wickedness made God bring the Flood to destroy nearly every living creature. Before it, humans were vegetarians. Why, after the Flood, did God permit humans to eat animals?" "I don't know," Page replied. "I guess sin affects others around you. If you commit a sin, your family is affected. The Fall affected everything. Everything Christ did was to bring us back to Eden, to return us to where we were before the Fall." "So when Christ returns, we'll all be vegetarians again?" I asked. "I guess," he said. "Then again, Adam and Eve didn't wear clothes. But let's not even go there." He grinned.

Two months later, I rang Jonathan Merritt. He was upbeat. The Declaration, he said, was doing as well as he could have hoped. He had taken out an advertisement about the Declaration in *World Magazine,* which is distributed to every messenger at the annual SBC convention, and looked forward to attending the annual SBC convention. "Abortion and marriage remain the two most important issues for us," he said. "But this generation is not a two-issue generation. We care about Darfur. We care about the environment and we care about the animals." He said that Richard Land spearheaded an effort in April by the Institute on Religion and Democracy to obtain one million signatures on a very watered-down version of the Declaration called "We Get It!" "They had a press conference at the National Press Club in April," he said. "Just five religious newspapers showed. It's the same old crowd saying the same old thing. Dobson, Perkins, Land. It just wasn't news!" he said gleefully.[68] "The SBC changed once. Now it's changing again. We're changing it," Jonathan said. "We have the perfect model. They showed us how to do it."

While the road to changing the minds of Southern Baptists is becoming more clear, the way to ending Bladen County's war on pigs remains obstructed. If Lynn White and Matthew Scully are correct, this war can be ended at the ballot box and in Raleigh's legislative halls and courtrooms by those who may share the common view, secular or religious, that it is wrong to abuse animals in industrial farming.

How wide our common ground actually is remains to be seen. Richard Land has written:

> For those outside the Christian faith who have been environmentally involved, I have good news and bad news. The good news is that we repent of past insensitivity and neglect. The

bad news is that: "There is . . . a distinctively Christian response to ecological concerns. The Christian doctrine of creation approaches the study from a different perspective,
reaches conclusions from different assumptions, proposes solutions from this different assumption and works at ecology
for different reasons." We sometimes will agree with the secular environmentalists. We will often disagree, however, because
we have a different approach and a different attitude.[69]

The influential environmentalist Aldo Leopold believed that his
famous "land ethic" "simply enlarges the boundaries of the community to include soils, waters, plants, and animals, or collectively, the
land . . . [and] changes the role of *Homo sapiens* from conqueror of
the land-community to plain member and citizen of it. It implies respect for its fellow-members and also respect for the community as
such."[70] Leopold's and Land's views of the human's place in nature
conflict. But they demonstrate that a common respect for Creation
can unite both the religious and the secular. The powerful message
of the Declaration is this: "Time has nearly run out. Cultural and religious values are going to change or life is going to become very
hard." When evangelicals begin to consider the problem, most will
renew their commitment to stewarding all of God's Creation, from
the *alpha* to the *omega*, and not merely act to forestall climate change.

Hogs are part of Creation, and Christians are starting to recall it.
In 2006, the United Nations Food and Agricultural Organization
(UNFAO) issued a report in which it concluded that raising food
animals "emerges as one of the top two or three most significant
contributions to the [world's] most serious environmental problems,
at every scale from local to global . . . [including] land degradation,
climate change and air pollution, water shortage and water pollution
and loss of diversity."[71] The livestock sector is "responsible for 18
percent of greenhouse gas emissions measured in CO_2 equivalent.

This is a higher share than transport."[72] In a September 2008 presentation, the chair of the Nobel-winning Intergovernmental Panel on Climate Change (IPCC) asserted that "a reduction in the size of the livestock industry through reduced consumption is the most effective way of cutting [greenhouse gases] from animal production. Anyone who lives 70 years as a vegan will prevent over 100 tons of CO_2 equivalent."[73] Creation Care charges Christians with stopping the industrial raising and slaughtering of animals, not just because its victims are part of the Creation we are bound to steward, but also because it is responsible for a significant portion of climate change.

Some animal rights activists are demanding vegetarianism, even veganism now, or nothing. But since only 4 or 5 percent of Americans claim to be vegetarians, "nothing" is far the more likely outcome.[74] I ask these activists to weigh the horrors of Bladen County's industrial farms and the Tar Heel slaughterhouse against the consequences of doing nothing to alleviate the hour-to-hour sufferings of its victims. Is not a life lived off the factory farm and a death humanely inflicted superior to the terrible lives we know they lead and the horrible deaths we know they suffer in Bladen County today?

After I published *Rattling the Cage: Toward Legal Rights for Animals,* Harvard Law School professor Laurence H. Tribe agreed publicly to discuss it with me at Boston's Faneuil Hall. Later he published his talk. At one point, he said, "Speaking of religion,"

> . . . I have in mind the lesson that crusades to protect new values, or to attach old values to new beings and new entities, must take great care to avoid religious intolerance or antagonism. Here I tread on sensitive ground, and I may have misread some things in Steve's book, but at times arguing for animal rights appears to rest on a condemnation of religion, at least of Western religion, as the real culprit in helping people

to rationalize self-serving subordination of the rest of the animal kingdom. True, religion and its crusades have been guilty of many things. But I think it is a mistake to tie the protection of nonhuman animals so tightly to anything that might be understood as antireligious or antispiritual. Making that link can alienate scores of potential allies.[75]

Jonathan Merritt and Frank Page help illuminate what Tribe meant. The condemnation Tribe rightly detected was not of Genesis, but of a "folk dominion theology" that helps people rationalize their subordination of the rest of the animal kingdom, just as a "folk racist theology" once helped people rationalize black chattel slavery and racial segregation and the extermination of Native Americans.

Ending the industrial farming and slaughter of hogs does not contradict a single biblical verse. Instead, the Bible demands that we end them: "the earth is the Lord's," and we are its steward, not its enemy. But we are also sinners. Once we sinned against Native Americans. Now we repent that past. But the Indians are nearly gone. Once we sinned against black slaves. Now we repent that past. But slavery ended 150 years ago, racial segregation half a century ago. Today we sin against much of God's Creation and grievously against the hogs of Bladen County. We have an opportunity, not to repent a past, but to repent the present, to become salt and light and end our sinning when it can do some good. Recognizing our sins may require the destruction of industrialized farming and slaughter, and it may even require that the animals themselves be granted legal rights sufficient to allow them to be properly defended.

This last idea may sound extreme. Yet what you believe about God's intentions for Bladen County's hogs is subject to the same plausibility crises that once undermined Native American genocide, black slavery, and racial segregation. The possibilities of biblical interpretation are enormous. The difficulties inherent in interpreting even a document as brief as the U.S. Constitution are notorious. Imagine if it were 175 times longer and drafted over a period of 1,500 years by scribes from different cultures in different places, with the English translated partly from the Hebrew, partly from the Greek. There are at least two dozen competing English versions of the Bible; Protestant battles over which translation is most accurate are pitched.[76] A professor of American religious history and the history of Christianity explains that "below the surface-level dispute[s] . . . lurk troubling questions. . . . Who has the authority to translate scripture? How authoritative is the Bible in translation? Can translation be divorced from interpretation?"[77] At least arguments over the meaning of the Constitution don't begin with disputes over which Hebrew or Greek translation is the more accurate.

There is no "right" way to interpret the Constitution.[78] There is no right way to interpret the Bible. The conservative evangelical theologian Millard J. Erickson believes that Genesis 9:4 means that while animals may exist to nurture and sustain humans, that is not the only reason they live. "Nothing is wrong . . . when humans utilize the rest of the creation to sustain their own lives and to meet their legitimate needs. They must, of course, be certain they do this in a way which does not violate or compromise any other of God's commands or principles."[79] "Dominion," says Erickson, is "not for the sake of the one having dominion, but for the sake of the one or ones being ruled over. . . . This means that animals, plants, and minerals are not merely means to ends. They are ends in themselves. They are not merely to be utilized and exploited, but to be cared for."[80]

Modern translators agree that Genesis 9:4 means something like, "I give you, Noah and your descendants, everything alive on earth to eat as food." One reasonable interpretation is that God was referring to everything that existed. If so, God may never have intended for humans to tamper with His animals and create new creatures. The SBC's 1995 "Resolution on the Patenting of Animal and Human Genes" says that "the scriptures of both the Old and

New Testaments plainly teach that God alone is creator and owner of all he has made (Genesis 1:1; Colossians 1:15–16). . . . Humans are given the mandate to be stewards of the earth and of animal life, not usurpers of God's prerogatives and not co-creators (Genesis 1:28)." Every one of Bladen County's hogs, every modern domesticated animal, has been thoroughly re-created by humans through genetic and traditional breeding techniques to the point that they scarcely resemble their wild ancestors. Perhaps God never intended to give *these* artificial products of technology to humans.

Richard Land, Frank Page, Richard Cizik, and Jonathan Merritt may not yet be ready to end the horrors of industrial hog farming and slaughter in Bladen County by granting basic legal rights to hogs. But they may be ready to stop their industrialized abuse on biblical grounds. That would change the way these animals live and die. It would be a first step. In the *Federalist Papers*, Madison or Hamilton wrote:

> If men were angels, no government would be necessary. If angels were to govern men, neither external nor internal controls on government would be necessary. In framing a government which is to be administered by men over men, the great difficulty lies in this: you must first enable the government to control the governed; and in the next place oblige it to control itself. A dependence on the people is, no doubt, the primary control on the government; but experience has taught mankind the necessity of auxiliary precautions.[81]

No one knows better than evangelicals that men are not angels. Power corrupts us and absolute power corrupts us absolutely. Bladen County demonstrates how thoroughly our absolute power over hogs has corrupted us. Experience has taught us that only fundamental rights can stand between any of us and cruel despotism. The day may come when Christians recognize that the only way they can fulfill their duty as Creation's stewards is to robe some animals with the legal rights necessary to protect them from our unangelic, thoroughly corrupted selves. Then perhaps men and animals can begin talking with one another on this continent again.

ACKNOWLEDGMENTS

I hated writing this book. Thomas Clarkson, the person most responsible for ending the slave trade, wrote that what he saw the first time he boarded a slaver "filled me with melancholy and horror. I found soon afterwards a fire of indignation kindling within me." I have often been filled with melancholy and horror. I became melancholy by speaking to the friendly folks at the World Pork Expo who sell the torture instruments to salt-of-the-earth factory farmers who use them to torment intelligent pigs for gain, by reading the trade magazines that advise factory farmers how to wring one more piglet from the tired bodies of used-up sows or manipulate the genes of these unfortunate creatures to produce pained bodies that might make them a few more dollars, and by dealing with corporate public relations flacks who see their job as keeping me and you from knowing what is happening inside the slaughterhouse.

Though I know they occupy the bottom rungs of society, and their lives are ceaseless struggles, still I was filled with horror interviewing slaughterhouse workers who cared only about whether they were being paid enough to disassemble these magnificent creatures and whether they were sharing enough of the wealth being accumulated by managers (who I could not interview) who enrich themselves on the agonies of their fellow beings, and watching videos of uneducated, ignorant, and sometimes vicious stockpeople inflicting agonies upon sensitive souls, because government has never cared enough to tell them they can't do that.

I wrote this book because the plight of factory farmed animals kindled a fire of indignation within me. It became my duty to tell the story of how Americans came to feel entitled to exploit these most helpless among us and to complete that story, and make sense of it, by connecting it to past stories in which we did the same things, for similar reasons.

I finished the book because I was also inspired by people as determined as Clarkson to bring this exploitation to a halt, once and for all, by my hero, Mr. Nikita, who works for low wages and no recognition—I couldn't even use his name—and attorney Dan Paden and Bruce Friedrich of People for the Ethical Treatment of Animals, former Republican presidential speechwriter Matthew Scully, John Coetzee, Southern Baptist seminarian Jonathan Merritt, who is helping to rally the Christian faithful to a truer understanding of how God intends us to relate to the rest of His Creation, and Prissy Carpender, who grasped the connection between how her ancestral land were once the site of human, and were now the locus of nonhuman, oppression.

I was helped by people who had no idea why I wanted to know what I wanted to know, but who were just doing their jobs well, the staff of the Bladen County Superior Court and the Registry of Deeds, the librarians of the Elizabethtown Public Library and of the Wilson Library at the University of North Carolina at Chapel Hill, Jaya Joshi of the Aquifer Protection Department of the North Carolina Division of Water Quality, and Teresa Rodriguez of the North Carolina Division of Water Quality.

Others were just plain helpful, Southern Baptist Convention president Frank S. Page, Emily Averitte, the owner of Walnut Grove, the anonymous Bladen County factory farmer and his wife, Professor Ken Prusa of Iowa State University, and Kenneth Robinson, Director of Archeology Laboratories at Wake Forest University in Winston-Salem.

I thank numerous law students who are dedicated to protecting nonhuman animals and who worked hard on research, Jalila Assisi, Valli Brandt, Stacey Francese, Christina Fullington, Camille Kancio, Megan Lewis, Sarah Lawrence, Keith Lynch, Nicole Roth, May Saetang, Michael Saetang, Lindsey Sundberg, Sara Terravova, Rob Troncoso, and Rachel Wechsler.

A thank you to scientific experts from around the world for their help, Dr. Francoise Wemelsfelder, Professor Per Jensen, Professor Joy Mench, Dr. James K. Kirkwood, Professor Lesley Rogers, Professor Samuel D. Gosling, and Professor Christine Nicol.

Thanks to Brad Goldberg and the Animal Welfare Trust for its support.

Thank you, Merloyd Lawrence, my long-time editor at Da Capo Press. No writer ever had a better friend and advocate that do I in Merloyd. All the other praise I typically heap she deletes. Thanks also to John Radziewicz, Da Capo's publisher, for believing in my books, and to Lissa Warren, publicist for a decade, and Kevin Hanover, Da Capo's marketing director, for ensuring that the world hears about them.

Finally, I could not have immersed myself in the sufferings of pigs for years were it not for the love and support of my family. Helping my children, Christopher, Siena, and Mariana, intellectually and emotionally mature, traveling with them, coaching their sports teams, helping them progress in school, learning from them how the latest technologies work, and sharing their ever-more-complex lives, and watching their sister, Roma, progress to her college graduation, and head perhaps to law school, is much of what gives my life meaning. Thank you.

Then there is Gail, who provides nearly everything else. At age 50 I hit the jackpot.

Notes

Chapter 1: Tar Heel Foundations

1. David Berreby, *Us And Them: Understanding Your Tribal Mind* 12 (Little, Brown, and Co. 2005).

2. Colin Kidd, *The Forging of Races: Race and Scripture in the Protestant Atlantic World, 1600–2000* 1 (Cambridge University Press, 2006).

3. http://www.city-data.com/township/hollow-bladen-nc.html (last visited April 8, 2008).

4. http://www.agr.state.nc.us/stats/2007agstat/countyestimateshogspigs.pdf (last visited August 23, 2008).

5. The carving of Bladen County commenced in 1750, when Anson County, which borders South Carolina, was created. In 1752, another section far to the north was sliced away to form part of Orange County, where the University of North Carolina at Chapel Hill is today. Two years later, Cumberland County, where Fayetteville is, came into existence. By the turn of the eighteenth century, Rowan (1753), Mecklenburg (1762), Brunswick (1764), Surrey (1770), Burke (1777), Wilkes (1777), Rutherford (1779), Moore (1784), Rockingham (1785), Robeson (1787), Iredell (1788), Stokes (1789), Ashe (1789), Buncombe (1791), Cabarrus (1792), Lincoln (1799), Richmond (1799), and Montgomery (1799) Counties had all been carved to some degree from Bladen County. The nineteenth century added Columbus (1808), Haywood (1808), Davidson (1822), Macon (1828), Yancey (1833), Davie (1836), Henderson (1838), Cherokee (1839), Caldwell (1841), Cleveland (1841), Stanly (1841), Mcdowell (1842), Catawba (1842), Union (1842), Gaston (1846), Alexander (1847), Watauga (1849), Forsyth (1849), Yadkin (1850), Jackson (1851), Madison (1851), Harnett (1855), Polk (1855), Alleghany (1859), Mitchell (1861), Clay (1861), Transylvania (1861), Swain (1871), Graham (1872), and Scotland (1899) Counties, which amounted essentially to the entire western half of the state. These dissections continued into the early twentieth century, when Lee (1907), Avery (1911), and Hoke (1911) Counties came into existence.

6. http://www.secretary.state.nc.us/kidspg/history.htm (last visited September 17, 2007).

7. Douglas L. Rights, *The American Indian in North Carolina* 36 (2nd ed., John F. Blair, 1957). Another source says that Durant was attorney general and speaker of the North Carolina House of Burgesses and that on August 4, 1661, he purchased, "in the second oldest recorded deed of the area, land from Cisketando, King of the Yeopin Indians. By 1662 Durant was living on his property in Virginia on the Albemarle Sound which became North Carolina in 1665. Today that land is known as Durants Neck, in Perquimans County, North Carolina." http://www.lucas-family.org/gd/ (last visited September 17, 2007). See also http:/gen.culpepper.com/historical/rebellion/durant.htm (last visited September 17, 2007), which calls Durant's Deed the first.

8. "All That Territory Or Tract Of Ground, Situate, Lying, And Being Within Our Dominions In America, Extending From The North End Of The Island Called Luck Island, Which Lies In The Southern Virginia Seas And Within Six And Thirty Degrees Of The Northern Latitude, And To The West As Far As The South Seas; And So Southerly As Far As The River Saint Mathias, Which Borders Upon The Coast Of Florida, And Within One And Thirty Degrees Of Northern Latitude, And West In A Direct Line As Far As The South Seas Aforesaid. . . . "http://statelibrary.dcr.state .nc.us/nc/history/history.htm (last visited September 15, 2007).

9. See note 8.

10. Telephone conversation with Kenneth Robinson, Director of Archaeology Laboratories, Wake Forest University, Winston-Salem, North Carolina, August 25, 2008.

11. *Ibid.*

12. "A Historical and Genealogical Account of Andrew Robeson of Scotland, New Jersey, and Pennsylvania and of His Descendants from 1653 to 1916, Begun by Susan Stroud Robeson, Assisted by Caroline Franciscus Stroud, Compiled, Edited and Published by Kate Hamilton Osborne Press of J. B. Lippinscott Company, Philadelphia 1916, Updated by Suzanne Olivia Sanborn Rushing from 1992 to 1998, Assisted by Mary Doris Lyon Sanborn." From the Robeson Family Papers (#5130) in the Southern Historical Collection, Manuscripts Department, Wilson Library, the University of North Carolina at Chapel Hill.

13. http://www.hpo.dcr.state.nc.us/nrlist.htm (last visited April 8, 2008).

14. Jeffrey J. Crow et al., *A History of African Americans in North Carolina* 1 (rev. ed., Office of Archives and History, North Carolina Department of Cultural Resources, 2002).

15. *African Americans in Early North Carolina: A Documentary History* xi (Alan D. Watson, ed., Office of Archives and History, North Carolina Department of Cultural Resources, 2005).

16. Alan D. Watson, "Arrivals in the East: Settlement of the Coastal Plain 1650 to 1775," *Tar Heel Junior Historian* 34, 34 (Spring 1995).

17. Jeffrey J. Crow, *supra*, note 15, at 2.

18. http://www.yale.edu/lawweb/avalon/states/nc05.htm (sec. 110) (last visited April 9, 2008).

19. Hugh Thomas, *The Slave Trade* 203 (Simon & Schuster, 1997).

20. *Ibid.*

21. *African Americans in Early North Carolina: A Documentary History, supra,* note 16, at xi.

22. Hugh Thomas, *supra,* note 20, at 264.

23. *African Americans in Early North Carolina: A Documentary History, supra,* note 16, at xi–xii; Jeffrey J. Crow, *supra,* note 15, at 3, 4; Marvin L. Michael Kay and Lorin Lee Cary, *Slavery in North Carolina 1748–1775* 2, 229 (University of North Carolina Press, 1995); http://www.digitalhistory.uh.edu/black_voices/voices_display.cfm?id=10 (last visited November 2, 2007).

24. Jeffrey J. Crow, *supra,* note 15, at 4.

25. *Ibid.,* at 11.

26. John Hope Franklin, *The Free Negro in North Carolina 1790–1860* 18, table II (University of North Carolina Press, 1995).

27. Marvin L. Michael Kay and Lorin Lee Cary, *supra,* note 24, at 221, table 1.1.

28. 1763 Tax List of Bladen County, North Carolina (in possession of author).

29. Marvin L. Michael Kay and Lorin Lee Cary, *supra,* note 24, at 221, table 1.1.

30. *The Projectile Point Classification Project: A Classification of Projectile Points in Existing Archaeological Collections from North Carolina (Phase II)* by I. Randolph Daniel Jr. and R. P. Stephen Davis Jr., 1996, http://www.rla.unc.edu/publications/pdf/techrep/techrep26.pdf, at A-4 and A-5 (last visited September 3, 2008).

31. Telephone conversation with Kenneth Robinson, Director of Archaeology Laboratories, Wake Forest University, Winston-Salem, North Carolina, August 25, 2008.

32. Patricia Barker Lerch, *Waccamaw Legacy: Contemporary Indians Fight for Survival* 4 (University of Alabama Press, 2004).

33. Thomas E. Ross, *American Indians in North Carolina: A Geographic Interpretation* 137 (Karo Hollow Press, 1999). No documentation connects the modern Waccamaw to the early Waccamaw and Cape Fear Tribes; *id.* at 139.

34. Patricia Barker Lerch, *supra,* note 33, at 3.

35. Charles Hudson, *The Southeastern Indians* 122 (University of Tennessee Press, 1976).

36. Thomas E. Ross, *supra,* note 34, at 15; Douglas L. Rights, *supra,* note 7, at 4–5, 259; Ruth Y. Wetmore, *First on the Land: The North Carolina Indians* 25–29, 48–49, 115 (John F. Blair, 1975).

37. Patricia Barker Lerch, *supra,* note 33, at 2; Thomas E. Ross, *supra,* note 34, at 9, 16; Ruth Y. Wetmore, *supra,* note 37, at 48–73.

38. Charles C. Mann, *1491: New Revelations of the Americas Before Columbus* 93–96 (Alfred A. Knopf, 2006); Shepherd Krech III, *The Ecological Indian: Myth and History* 95–97 (W. W. Norton & Co., 1999); Russell Thornton, *American Indian Holocaust and Survival: A Population History Since 1492* 23 (University of Oklahoma Press, 1987).

39. Thomas E. Ross, *supra,* note 34, at xi, 13.

40. Patricia Barker Lerch, *supra,* note 33, at 4.

41. Telephone conversation with Kenneth Robinson, Director of Archaeology Laboratories, Wake Forest University, Winston-Salem, North Carolina, August 25, 2008.

42. Patricia Barker Lerch, *supra*, note 33, at 4.

43. *Ibid.*, at 11, 140.

44. Theda Purdue, *Native Carolinians: The Indians of North Carolina* 15 (North Carolina Division of Archives and History, 1985).

Chapter 2: Carolina Magic

1. Calvin Martin, *Keepers of the Game: Indian-Animal Relationships and the Fur Trade* 156 (University of California Press, 1978).

2. P. Marion Simms, *The Bible in America: Versions That Have Played Their Part in the Making of the Republic* 14 (Wilson-Erickson, 1936).

3. James Axtell, *The European and the Indian: Essays in the Ethnohistory of Colonial North America* 275 (Oxford University Press, 1981).

4. Virginia DeJohn Anderson, *Creatures of Empire: How Domestic Animals Transformed Early America* 19 (Oxford University Press, 2004).

5. Charles M. Segal and David C. Stineback, *Puritans, Indians, and Manifest Destiny* 35 (G. P. Putnam's Sons, 1977).

6. Calvin Martin, *supra*, note 1, at 186. The idea that the human/nonhuman animal relationship and that special and that animals have "masters" or "keepers" is widespread throughout Eurasia and is also found in Africa. Lydia T. Black, "The Nature of Evil: Of Whales and Sea Otters," in *Indians, Animals, and the Fur Trade* 109, 113 (Shepherd Krech III, ed., University of Georgia Press, 1981).

7. Calvin Martin, *supra*, note 1, at 70, note b, 188.

8. Virginia DeJohn Anderson, *supra*, note 4, at 19–20.

9. Calvin Martin, *supra*, note 1, at 34. Do not confuse the Algonquon Indians, who lived west of Montreal, with the Indians who speak an Algonquian language. James Axtell, *Beyond 1492: Encounters in Colonial North America* 202 (Oxford University Press, 1992).

10. James Axtell, *supra*, note 10, at 33; James Axtell, *supra*, note 3, at 73; Calvin Martin, *supra*, note 1, at 71; James Axtell, *The Invasion Within: The Contest of Cultures in Colonial North America* 15 (Oxford University Press, 1985). "Scholars today believe that the natives respected the 'souls' or animating 'spirits' only of living things, not rocks or land *per se*, and normally supplicated and thanked not individual plants and animals, but rather the 'boss-spirits' or representatives of species." James Axtell, *supra*, note 10, at 203.

11. Virginia DeJohn Anderson, *supra*, note 4, at 20; Charles Hudson, *The Southeastern Indians* 340 (University of Tennessee Press, 1976).

12. Antonia Mills, "Reincarnation Belief Among North American Indians and Inuit: Context, Distribution, and Variation," in *Amerindian Rebirth: Reincarnation Belief Among North American Indians and Inuit* 15, 34 (Antonia Mills and Richard Slobodin, eds., University of Toronto Press, 1994).

13. John Witthoft, *The American Indian as Hunter* 6 (Pennsylvania Historical and Museum Commission, 1967). See Edith Turner, "Behind Inupiaq Reincarnation: Cosmological Cycling," in Antonia Mills and Richard Slobodin, eds., *supra*, note 13, at 67, 76; Jean-Guy A. Goulet, "Reincarnation as a Fact of Life Among Contemporary

Dene Tha," in Antonia Mills and Richard Slobodin, eds., *supra*, note 13, at 156, 159; Robert Brightman, *Grateful Prey: Rock Cree Human-Animal Relationships* 2, 161 (University of California Press, 1993); Calvin Martin, "Introduction," in *The American Indian and the Problem of History* 10 (Calvin Martin, ed., Oxford University Press, 1987); Adrian Tanner, "Bringing Home Animals: Religious Ideology and Mode of Production of the Mistassini Cree Hunters" 260–61 (Ph.D. dissertation, University of Toronto, 1976) (emphasis added); Alanson Buck Skinner, "Notes on the Eastern Cree and Northern Saulteaux," 9(1) *Anthropological Papers of the American Museum of Natural History* 76 (American Museum of Natural History, 1911).

14. Robert Brightman, *supra*, note 14, at 2.

15. Shepherd Krech III, *The Ecological Indian: Myth and History* 120 (W. W. Norton & Co., 1999); Calvin Martin, *supra*, note 1, at 186; Virginia DeJohn Anderson, *supra*, note 4, at 29.

16. Calvin Martin, *supra*, note 1, at 11, 15.

17. Thomas W. Overholt and J. Baird Calicott, *Clothed-in-Fur and Other Tales: An Introduction to an Ojibwa World View* 143 (University Press of America, 1982).

18. Calvin Martin, *supra*, note 1, at 186–87.

19. Shepherd Krech III, *supra*, note 16, at 146.

20. *Ibid.*, at 147.

21. Calvin Martin, *supra*, note 1, at 35–36.

22. Ruth Y. Wetmore, *First on the Land: The North Carolina Indians* 135 (John F. Blair, 1975).

23. Virginia DeJohn Anderson, *supra*, note 4, at 38; Colin Galloway, *New Worlds for All: Indians, Europeans, and the Making of Early America* 74 (Johns Hopkins University Press, 1997); Calvin Martin, "The War Between Indians and Animals," in Shepherd Krech III, ed., *supra*, note 7, at 11, 15.

24. Christopher Vecsey, "Envision Ourselves Darkly, Imagine Ourselves Richly," in Calvin Martin, ed., *supra*, note 14, at 120, 124–25; Thomas W. Overholt and J. Baird Calicott, *supra*, note 18, at 155 (emphasis in the original); Calvin Martin, *supra*, note 1, at 74.

25. Thomas W. Overholt and J. Baird Calicott, *supra*, note 18, at 146, quoting from "The Woman Who Married a Beaver," *id.*, at 74, 75.

26. Calvin Martin, *supra*, note 1, at 33.

27. *Ibid.*, at 35, 116.

28. Ruth Y. Wetmore, *supra*, note 23, at 135.

29. Charles Hudson, *supra*, note 12, at 340.

30. Shepherd Krech III, *supra*, note 16, at 165.

31. Thomas W. Overholt and J. Baird Calicott, *supra*, note 18, at 141.

32. Charles Hudson, *supra*, note 12, at 157–58; Douglas L. Rights, *The North American Indian in North Carolina* 212, 213 (2nd ed., John F. Blair, 1988) (1957).

33. Shepherd Krech III, "'Throwing Bad Medicine: Sorcery, Disease, and the Fur Trade Among the Kutchen and Other Northern Arthapaskans," in Shepherd Krech III, ed., *supra*, note 7, at 83, 95.

34. *Ibid.*, at 83, 88–89; Annette McFayden Clark, "Koyukon Athabascan Ceremonialism," 2 *Western Canadian Journal of Anthropology* 80, 80–84, 85–86 (1970).

35. Antonia Mills, "Reincarnation Belief Among North American Indians and Inuit: Context, Distribution, and Variation," in Antonia Mills and Richard Slobodin, eds., *supra*, note 13, at 15, 17.

36. John Witthoft, *supra*, note 14, at 6.

37. Thomas W. Overholt and J. Baird Calicott, *supra*, note 18, at 146.

38. Calvin Martin, *supra*, note 1, at 35, 74, 116; Edith Turner, "Behind Inupiaq Reincarnation: Cosmological Cycling," in Antonia Mills and Richard Slobodin, eds., *supra*, note 13, at 67, 71 (emphasis in the original); Robert Brightman, *supra*, note 14, at 118, 119.

39. Antonia Mills, "Reincarnation Belief Among North American Indians and Inuit: Context, Distribution, and Variation," in Antonia Mills and Richard Slobodin, eds., *supra*, note 13, at 15, 20. See Shepherd Krech III, *supra*, note 16, at 206; Edith Turner, "Behind Inupiaq Reincarnation: Cosmological Cycling," in Antonia Mills and Richard Slobodin, eds., *supra*, note 13, at 67, 75, 76; Robert Brightman, *supra*, note 14, at 165; Thomas W. Overholt and J. Baird Calicott, *supra*, note 18, at 141; Stanley Walens, *Feasting with Cannibals: An Essay on Kwakiutl Cosmology* 163 (Princeton University Press, 1981); Frank G. Speck, "Penobscot Tales and Religious Beliefs," 48 *Journal of American Folklore* 22–23 (January–March 1935).

40. John Lawson, *A New Voyage to Carolina* 58 (Hugh Talmage Lefler, ed., University of North Carolina Press, 1967) (1709).

41. Thomas W. Overholt and J. Baird Calicott, *supra*, note 18, at 147.

42. Robert Brightman, *supra*, note 14, at 119.

43. Frank G. Speck, Leonard Broom, and Will West Long, *Cherokee Dance and Drama* 84 (University of Oklahoma Press, 1983). "The numbers four and seven occur repeatedly in Cherokee myths and rituals. As such, they are not really magic numbers but expressive of the Southeastern belief system." Charles Hudson, *supra*, note 12, at 134.

44. James Mooney, "Myths of the Cherokee," *Bureau of American Ethnology: Nineteenth Annual Report for 1897–1898* 261–62 (U.S. Government Printing Office, 1900).

45. Shepherd Krech III, *supra*, note 16, at 159–61.

46. *Ibid.*, at 174–77.

47. Calvin Martin, *supra*, note 1, at 165–66.

48. See generally Shepherd Krech III, ed., *supra*, note 7, at 178, 180.

49. Ruth Y. Wetmore, *supra*, note 23, at 136.

50. Robert Brightman, *supra*, note 14, at 288.

51. David Wilcox, "Skin, Rum, and Ruin," 13 *Southern Exposure* 57, 60 (1985).

52. Calvin Martin, *supra*, note 1, at 51, 57, 60–61 ("despiritualization"), 106–9, 144, 145–46, 148–49; James Axtell, *supra*, note 3, at 251.

53. Chrestian Le Clerq, *New Relation of Gaspesia, with the Customs and Religions of the Gaspesia Indians* 277 (William F. Ganong, ed., Champlain Society, 1910).

54. Calvin Martin, "The War Between Indians and Animal," in Shepherd Krech III, ed., *supra*, note 7, at 11, 16.

55. John McDougall, *Saddle, Sled, and Snowshoe* 282 (William Briggs, 1896).

56. Chrestian Le Clerq, *First Establishment of the Faith in New France* 269 (John G. Shea, 1881) (1691).

57. Robert Brightman, *supra*, note 14, at 290.

58. *Ibid.*

59. See, for example, Chris Brown, "Beyond the 'Invented Indian': Acknowledging Original Conservation," http://72.14.209.104/search?q=cache:2ym7dvimwtij:www.terralingua.org/discpapers/discpaper6.htm+keepers+of+the+game&hl=en&ct=clnk&cd=7&gl=us (last visited March 27, 2007). "In order to explain the fur trade game depletions, Martin insists that they must be placed in the context of the larger ideological bonds which related the Algonquian to their prey. He then traces their overexploitation to the spiritual notions of hunter-prey reciprocity active in documented fur trade Native ideology. Because Algonquians believed transgression of these bonds by either party to result in disease or illness, Martin continues, they interpreted the postcontact spread of European epidemics as a brutal declaration of war from the animals. The result: Algonquians responded, in anger, with a sort of seek and destroy military policy. Hence the documented game depletions. The storm of debate inspired by Martin's hypothesis has turned up more than enough evidence to effectively confute it. While his explanation may apply to a limited number of cases, disease etiology among Algonquians included many factors; and hunting ethics seem to have been less important than others such as witchcraft."

60. Calvin Martin, "The War Between Indians and Animals," in Shepherd Krech III, ed., *supra*, note 7, at 11, 18.

61. *Ibid.*, at 11, 15; Calvin Martin, *supra*, note 1, at 33, 39. Most of North America's large mammals were wiped out around 13,000 years ago. A new hypothesis, derived from geochemical analyses of sedimentary sites across that continent, suggests that a comet or asteroid exploding above or on the northern ice cap at that time destroyed not just these mammals but their human hunters. Rex Dalton, "Blast in the Past?" 447 *Nature* 256 (May 17, 2007).

62. Thomas Hariot, A Briefe and True Report of the New Found Land of Virginia: of the Commodities and of the Nature and Manners of the Naturall Inhabitants: Discouered bÿ the English Colonÿ There Seated by Sir Richard Greinuile Knight In the ÿeere 1585: Which Remained Vnder the Gouernment of Twelue Monethes, At the Speciall Charge and Direction of the Honourable Sir Walter Raleigh Knight Lord Warden of the Stanneries Who therein Hath Beene Fauoured and Authorised bÿ Her Maiestie and Her Letters Patents / This Fore Booke Is Made in English by Thomas Hariot seruant to the Aboue-Named Sir Walter, a Member of the Colonÿ, and There Imploÿed in Discouering; CVM GRATIA ET PRIVILEGIO CÆS. MATIS SPE-CIALIi. Francoforti ad Moenvm, Typis Loannis Wecheli, Svmtibvs Vero Theodori de Bry anno CIC IC XC. Venales Reperivntvr in Officina Sigismvndi Feirabendiii 25, http://docsouth.unc.edu/nc/hariot/hariot.html (last visited March 6, 2007).

63. N.C. G.S. 11–2 provides that "Judges and other persons who may be empowered to administer oaths, shall (except in the cases in this Chapter excepted) require the party to be sworn to lay his hand upon the Holy Scriptures, in token of his engagement to speak the truth and in further token that, if he should swerve from the truth, he may be justly deprived of all the blessings of that holy book and made liable to that vengeance which he has imprecated on his own head." Sec. 11–3 states that "When the person to be sworn shall be conscientiously scrupulous of taking a book

oath in manner aforesaid, he shall be excused from laying hands upon, or touching the Holy Gospel; and the oath required shall be administered in the following manner, namely: He shall stand with his right hand lifted up towards heaven, in token of his solemn appeal to the Supreme God, and also in token that if he should swerve from the truth he would draw down the vengeance of heaven upon his head, and shall introduce the intended oath with these words, namely: I, A.B., do appeal to God, as a witness of the truth and the avenger of falsehood, as I shall answer the same at the great day of judgment, when the secrets of all hearts shall be known (etc., as the words of the oath may be)." Sec. 4 states that "When a person to be sworn shall have conscientious scruples against taking an oath in the manner prescribed by G.S. 11–2, 11–3, or 11–7, he shall be permitted to be affirmed. In all cases the words of the affirmation shall be the same as the words of the prescribed oath, except that the word 'affirm' shall be substituted for the word 'swear' and the words 'so help me God' shall be deleted."

64. P. Marion Simms, *supra*, note 2, at 47.

65. David Daniell, *The Bible in English: Its History and Influence* 248, 552 (Yale University Press, 2003). See Alister McGrath, *In the Beginning: The Story of the King James Bible and How It Changed a Nation, a Language, and a Culture* 3 (Anchor Books, 2001). "Throughout the sixteenth and seventeenth centuries, the Bible was seen as a social, economic, and political text. . . . The Bible came to be seen as the foundation of every aspect of English culture, linking monarchy and church, time and eternity . . . refugees from England, fleeing religious persecution in the seventeenth century, brought copies with them. It would be their encouragement on the long and dangerous voyage to the Americas, and their guide as they settled in the New World." *Id.*, at 393.

66. David Daniell, *supra*, note 65, at 68.

67. Alister McGrath, *supra*, note 65, at 33.

68. David Daniell, *supra*, note 65, at 248.

69. *Ibid.*, at 120–21; P. Marion Simms, *supra*, note 2, at 90, 92.

70. Christopher Hill, *The English Bible and the Seventeenth-Century Revolution* 34 (Viking Adult, 1993). See David Daniell, *supra*, note 65, at 462.

71. "Introduction," *A History of Reading in the West* 32 (Lynda G. Cochrane, trans., Gugliemo Cavallo and Roger Charter, eds., Cambridge University Press, 1999); David Daniell, *supra*, note 65, at 132, 391–92.

72. David Daniell, *supra*, note 65, at 405.

73. *Ibid.*, at 129.

74. P. Marion Simms, *supra*, note 2, at 75–78, 89–90.

75. Stephen Beauregard Weeks, *Libraries and Literature in North Carolina in the Eighteenth Century* 177 (1896) (a complement and supplement to *The Press of North Carolina in the Eighteenth Century* (Historical Printing Club, 1891). This Bible is discussed in VII *North Carolina University Magazine* 100 (1857–58).

76. http://www.unc.edu/news/archives/jul98/lynch.htm (last viewed September 17, 2007).

77. Rev. Dr. Charles C. Forman, *Four Early Bibles in Pilgrim Hall* (Pilgrim Society Note, Series One, Number Nine, April 1959), reprinted at www.pilgrimhall.org (last

77. Rev. Dr. Charles C. Forman, *Four Early Bibles in Pilgrim Hall* (Pilgrim Society Note, Series One, Number Nine, April 1959), reprinted at www.pilgrimhall.org (last visited June 3, 2007).

78. David Daniell, *supra,* note 65, at 221, 314.

79. *Ibid.,* at 156

80. *Ibid.,* at 147.

81. *Ibid.*

82. Alister McGrath, *supra,* note 65, at 141–48.

83. *Ibid.,* at 149–97.

84. John Nielsen and Royal Skousen, "How Much of the King James Bible Is William Tyndale's?" III *Reformation* 49 (1998).

85. Alister McGrath, *supra,* note 65, at 187.

86. *Ibid.,* at 280–84.

Chapter 3: The Genesis Disaster for Native Americans

1. Russell Thornton, *American Indian Holocaust and Survival: A Population History Since 1492* xv (University of Oklahoma Press, 1987).

2. Henry Hugh Brackenridge, *Indian Atrocities: Narratives of the Perils and Sufferings of Dr. Knight and John Slover Among the Indians, During the Revolutionary War with Short Memoirs of Col Crawford & John Slover and a Letter from H. Brackenridge on the Rights of Indians Etc.* 62, 71–72 (U. P. James, 1867) (1853). "During his years as a judge (1799–1814), Brackenridge continued his untiring efforts to instruct the people. In addition to a steady flow of satires, narratives, and published sermons, he devoted himself to his masterwork, *Modern Chivalry,* a long comic narrative in the tradition of Don Quixote and Tom Jones. Written, he said, as an entertaining lecture on morals and society for 'Tom, Dick, and Harry of the woods,' the novel exposes the folly of a people whose ignorance and greed causes them to elect corrupt and hypocritical leaders. Through this work, published in several volumes between 1792 and 1815, Brackenridge finally achieved his goal of reaching a large portion of the people with his moral precepts. His novel was called 'a textbook for all classes of society,' and his son reported that his name 'became a household word for half a century.'" Emory B. Elliot Jr., "Henry Hugh Brackenridge," in Alexander Leitch, *A Princeton Companion* (Princeton University Press, 1978), http://etcweb.princeton.edu/CampusWWW/Companion/brackenridge_hugh_henry.html (last visited October 24, 2007).

3. Jorge Cañizares-Esguerra, *Puritan Conquistadors: Iberianizing the Atlantic 1550–1700* 16 (Stanford University Press, 2006).

4. Charles M. Segal and David C. Stineback, *Puritans, Indians, and Manifest Destiny* 32 (G. P. Putnam's Sons, 1977).

5. *Ibid.,* at 33.

6. Alfred A. Cave, *The Pequot War* 13–15, 17 (University of Massachusetts Press, 1996).

7. Samuel Sewall, *Phaenomena quaedam apocalyptica ad aspectum novi orbis configurata, or, Some few lines towards a description of the new heavens as it makes to those who stand upon the new earth* 56 (Bartholomew Green & John Allen, 1707).

141 (Benjamin Harris, 1693). See Robert Tynley, "Two learned sermons, the one of the mischieuous subtiltie, and barbarous crueltie, the other of the false doctrines, and refined haeresis of the romish synagogue" (W. Hall, 1609); I. Edward Hayes, "A report of the voyage and successe thereof, attempted in the yeere of our Lord 1583, by Sir Humfrey Gilbert Knight," in Richard Hakluyt, *The Principall Navigations, Voiages and Discoveries of the English Nation* 679, 680 (George Bishop & Ralph Newberie, 1589). It was the same with the Spanish; see generally Jorge Cañizares-Esguerra, *supra,* note 3, at 16.

9. Edward L. Bond, "Source of Knowledge, Source of Power: The Supernatural World of English Virginia 1607–1624," 108(2) *Virginia Magazine of History and Biography* 105 (2000).

10. Many Protestants who flocked to America were Established Anglicans, who sought to re-Establish their faith in the Colonies; they succeeded more the further south they settled. But even in the South they moved among clouds of Dissenters, Puritans, Baptists and Anabaptists, Lutherans, Methodists, German Reformed Church, Quakers, Congregationalists, and Presbyterians, Scots, Scots-Irish, English, Dutch, and French Huguenots.

11. Sydney E. Ahlstrom, *A Religious History of the American People* 90 (Yale University Press, 1972).

12. P. Marion Simms, The Bible in America: Versions That Have Played Their Part in the Making of the Republic 47 (Wilson-Erickson, 1936).

13. Sydney E. Ahlstrom, *supra,* note 11, at 93, 125, 188–93. Of the 260 religious bodies identified by *The Yearbook of American and Canadian Churches and Megachurches* (E. W. Lindner, ed., National Council of Churches of Christ, 2003), about 220 were said to be Protestant.

14. P. Marion Simms, *supra,* note 12, at 49–50.

15. Alfred A. Cave, *supra,* note 6, at 18.

16. Sacvan Bercovitch, "Foreword" to Charles M. Segal and David C. Stineback, *supra,* note 4, at 17.

17. David E. Stannard, *American Holocaust: The Conquest of the New World* 238 (Oxford University Press, 1992).

18. Lawrence A. Hirschfield, *Race in the Making: Cognition, Culture, and the Child's Construction of Human Kinds* 13, 20 (MIT Press, 1996).

19. David Berreby, *Us and Them: Understanding Your Tribal Mind* (Little, Brown, and Co., 2005).

20. In 1999, *USA Today* reported that 50 percent of human companions would "very likely" risk their lives to save their companion animals, with 33 percent more saying they would be "somewhat likely." Cindy Hall and Bob Laird, "Risking It All for Fido," *USA Today,* at 1D (June 24, 1999). In 1982, one veterinarian in war-torn Beirut studied nearly fifty people who lived with their companion animals: 75 percent reported they kept companion animals for companionship, 56 percent refused to leave Beirut, partly because of their companion animals, 53 percent took their animals with them when there were bombing or shelling raids, 78 percent took risks to provide for their companion animals, 71 percent shared their food with them, and 27 percent gave their companion animals more food than they had. Odean Cusack, *Pets and Mental*

Health 69–70 (1988). The American Animal Hospital Association found that 83 percent of human companions would be "likely to risk their lives for their pets." Sarah A. Chadwick, "Pet Owners Reveal Strong Feelings for Animal Companions." 14 *Vet. Econ.* (March 1999) (quoting 1999 AAHA survey). Studies reveal that about 70 percent of human victims of domestic violence remain in an abusive situation rather than abandon their companion animal. Chris Lydgate, "Going to the Dogs," *Willamette Weekly* 16 (July 4, 2000).

21. David Berreby, *supra*, note 19, at 66.

22. Jared Diamond, "Race Without Color," *Discover* (November 1, 1994), http://discovermagazine.com/1994/nov/racewithoutcolor444 (last visited March 28, 2008).

23. David Berreby, *supra*, note 19, at 166 (emphasis added).

24. *Ibid.*, at 165 (emphasis in the original).

25. *Ibid.*, at 186–88.

26. *Ibid.*, at 198–99.

27. Alfred A. Cave, "Canaanites in a Promised Land: The American Indian and the Providential Theory of Empire," 12 *American Indian Quarterly* 284, 284–87 (Fall 1988). See Stephen R. Haynes, *Noah's Curse: The Biblical Justification of American Slavery* 144 (Oxford University Press, 2002).

28. Paul Freedman, *Images of the Medieval Peasant* 88–94 (Stanford University Press, 1999).

29. 1 *The New England Society Orations* 298 (Cephas and Evangeline Warner, eds., Century, 1901).

30. Hermann Hagedorn, *Roosevelt in the Bad Lands* 355 (Houghton & Mifflin Co., 1921).

31. Stephen R. Haynes, *supra*, note 27, at 143.

32. http://www.geocities.com/quinnips/histdocs/17/seal.jpg (last visited June 19, 2008).

33. Virginia DeJohn Anderson, *Creatures of Empire: How Domestic Animals Transformed Early America* 6 (Oxford University Press, 2004); Frieda Knobloch, *The Culture of Wilderness: Agriculture as Colonization in the American West* 2–5 (University of North Carolina Press, 1996).

34. Virginia DeJohn Anderson, *supra*, note 33, at 6, 18; Charles M. Segal and David C. Stineback, *supra*, note 4, at 27–28.

35. Frieda Knobloch, *supra*, note 33, at 4.

36. Keith Thomas, *Man and the Natural World: A History of the Modern Sensibility* 145 (Pantheon Books, 1983).

37. William Cronon, *Changes in the Land: Indians, Colonists, and the Ecology of New England* 129–30 (Hill & Wang, 2003) (1983). Indians struggled to fit the Europeans' strange quadrupeds into their world. The Nahua Indians of sixteenth-century Mexico called horses "deer" and sheep "cotton." Mayans referred to horses as the "tapir of Castile." Virginia's Powatans labeled chickens "small birds," while Rhode Island Narragansetts called pigs "woodchucks." Virginia DeJohn Anderson, *supra*, note 33, at 39.

38. Virginia DeJohn Anderson, *supra*, note 33, at 38, 107–40, 184–208.

39. Charles Hudson, *The Southeastern Indians* 291–94 (University of Tennessee Press, 1976).

40. Iroquoan peoples around the Great Lakes consumed 80 percent of their calories from wild fruits they gathered and vegetables they grew, which included at least fifteen varieties of corn, sixty kinds of beans, and six squashes; the rest of their calories they obtained from the flesh of wild animals Indian men hunted. See http://www.dickshovel.com/neutral.html (last visited January 25, 2007); James Axtell, *Beyond 1492: Encounters in Colonial North America* 236 (Oxford University Press, 1992).

41. Charles C. Mann, *1491: New Revelations of the Americas Before Columbus* 99 (Alfred A. Knopf, 2006).

42. Virginia DeJohn Anderson, *supra*, note 33, at 34.

43. *Ibid.*, at 18.

44. Lyall Watson, *The Whole Hog: Exploring the Extraordinary Potential of Pigs* 117 (Smithsonian Books, 2004).

45. Julian Wiseman, *The Pig: A British History* 2 (2nd ed., Duckworth, 2000).

46. Lyall Watson, *supra*, note 44, at 118; Julian Wiseman, *supra*, note 45, at 5.

47. Virginia DeJohn Anderson, *supra*, note 33, at 84.

48. Robert Hughes, *The Fatal Shore: The Epic of Australia's Founding* 96 (Alfred A. Knopf, 1986).

49. Keith Thomas, *supra*, note 36, at 26; Virginia DeJohn Anderson, *supra*, note 33, at 84; P. K. O'Brien, "Agriculture and the Industrial Revolution," 30 *Economic History Review* 169 (1977).

50. Lyall Watson, *supra*, note 44, at 119, quoting Friedrich Engels, *The Condition of the Working Class in England* (Penguin, 1987), and citing Charles Richson, *The Observance of the Sanitary Laws Divinely Appointed* (1854).

51. William Cronon, *supra*, note 37, at 129; James Axtell, *supra*, note 40, at 239.

52. Virginia DeJohn Anderson, *supra*, note 33, at 89.

53. Captain John Underhill, *Newes from America* 36 (Peter Cole, 1638). Two decades later, the Puritan divine Edward Johnson wrote that the Pequots were not "onley men, but Devils, for surely [Satan] was more than ordinarily present with this Indian army." Edward Johnson, *A History of New England from the English Planting in the Yeere 1628 Until the Yeere 1652, Aka The Wonder-Working Providences of Zion's Saviour in New England* 112 (Nathaniel Brooke, 1654). The Reverend John White, a primary founder of the Massachusetts Bay Colony, called the Indians "bond-slaves of Sathan." John White, *The Planters Plea, or The Grounds of Plantations Examined and the Usual Objections Answered* 39 (William Jones, 1630); see http://www.dorchestera theneum.org/page.php?id=917.

54. Thomas E. Ross, *American Indians in North Carolina: Geographic Interpretations* 33 (Karo Hollow Press, 1999): Ruth Y. Wetmore, *First on the Land: The North Carolina Indians* 68–69 (John F. Blair, 1975).

55. Douglas L. Rights, *The American Indian in North Carolina* 46 (John F. Blair, 1957).

56. Theda Purdue, *Native Carolinians: The Indians of North Carolina* 32 (North Carolina Division of Archives and History, 1985).

57. James Mooney, "Population," in 2 *Handbook of American Indians North of Mexico* 286 (Frederick W. Hodge., ed., Smithsonian Institution, Bureau of American Ethnology *Bulletin* no. 30, U.S. Government Printing Office, 1910). To which anthropologist Russell Thornton inserted "genocide" at about the middle. Russell Thornton, *supra*, note 1, at 43.

58. For example, *Eating Fire, Tasting Blood: An Anthology of the American Indian Holocaust* (Marijo Moore, ed., Thunders Mouth Press, 2006); Russell Thornton, *American Indian Holocaust and Survival* (University of Oklahoma Press, 1990); "American Indian Holocaust," http://www.unitednativeamerica.com/aiholocaust.html (last visited August 26, 2007).

59. Charles M. Segal and David C. Stineback, *supra*, note 4, at 37.

60. John Lawson, *A New Voyage to Carolina* 244 (Hugh Talmage Lefler, ed., University of North Carolina Press, 1967) (1709).

61. Sacvan Bercovitch, "Foreword" to Charles M. Segal and David C. Stineback, *supra*, note 4, at 26.

62. William Cronon, *supra*, note 37, at 62. It would be unusual for a modern American court to rely upon biblical dictates. But Puritan courts were expected to rule in harmony with them. Like their judges, Puritan legislators explicitly linked their enactments, such as the so-called "Capitall Laws," part of Liberty 94 of the 100 liberties contained in the Puritan Massachusetts Bay Colony's 1641 Body of Liberties, to biblical chapter and verse. Carolina lawmakers, too, sometimes linked divine command, morality, and law.

63. Geneva Bible, Genesis 1:28, at 4 (Tolle Lege, 2006) (1599). The twentieth-century Revised Standard Version, which often disagrees with the King James Version, also uses "subdue."

64. Victor P. Hamilton, *The Book of Genesis, Chapters 1–17* 139–40 (William B. Erdman's Publishing Co., 1990).

65. Christopher W. Hannen, *Historical Journal of Massachusetts* (Summer 2001), http://findarticles.com/p/articles/mi_qa3837/is_200107/ai_n8959860, at 1.

66. John Cotton, *God's Promise to His Plantation* (William Jones, 1630), http://digitalcommons.unl.edu/etas/22/ (last visited October 24, 2007). In the nineteenth century, Americans were still trying "to coerce American Indians into subduing and replenishing the earth, as explicitly commanded in the Old Testament." Charles M. Segal and David C. Stineback, *supra*, note 4, at 38, 49.

67. Alfred W. Crosby, *The Columbian Voyages, the Columbian Exchange, and Their Historians: Essays on Global and Comparative History* 24–25 (American Historical Association, 1987).

68. Theda Purdue, *supra*, note 56, at 25.

69. Russell Thornton, *supra*, note 58, at 43–44.

70. Charles C. Mann, *supra*, note 41, at 97–101; Russell Thornton, *The Cherokees: A Population History* 11–12, 15–18 (University of Nebraska Press, 1990); George R. Milner, "Epidemic Disease in the Post-Contact Southeast: A Reappraisal," 5 *Midcontinental Journal of Archaeology* 39, 40 (1980).

71. Russell Thornton, *supra*, note 70, at 18.

72. *Ibid.*, at 21, 29, 30, 33, 34.

73. Theda Purdue, *supra*, note 56, at 25.

74. Thomas Hariot, *The Roanoke Voyages, 1584–1590: Documents to Illustrate the English Voyages to North America Under the Patent Granted to Walter Raleigh in 1584* 378 (David B. Quinn., ed., Hakluyt Society, 1955).

75. John Lawson, *A New Voyage to Carolina* 232 (Hugh Talmage Lefler, ed., University of North Carolina Press, 1967) (1709).

76. Russell Thornton, *supra*, note 1, at 45.

77. James Axtell, The European and the Indian: Essays in the Ethnohistory of Colonial North America 248 (Oxford University Press, 1981).

78. Ruth Y. Wetmore, *supra*, note 54, at 48.

79. Karen I. Blu, *The Lumbee Problem: The Making of an American Indian People* 43 (University of Nebraska Press, 2001). In 1754, Bladen County officials reported to the Colonial governor of North Carolina that they were a "mixt crew"; *id.*, at 38; see *id.*, at 36–43. The Lumbees' 1987 "Petition for Federal Acknowledgment" would claim they had "diverse origins, the core of which is Cheraw, and that they were of Siouan origins with, in all likelihood, additions from other linguistic stocks." 1 *Lumbee Petition for Federal Acknowledgment* 2 (1987); Charles Hudson, *supra*, note 39, 493–94.

80. Hamilton McMillan, *Sir Walter Raleigh's Lost Colony: An Historical Sketch of the Attempts of Sir Walter Raleigh to Establish a Colony in Virginia, with the Traditions of an Indian Tribe in North Carolina* [sic]; *Indicating the Fate of the Colony of Englishmen Left on Roanoke Island in 1587* 14 (Advance Presses, 1888), http://digital.lib.ecu.edu/historyfiction/viewer.aspx?id=mcs (last visited October 25, 2007).

81. Hamilton McMillan, *supra*, note 80, at 17. Even today, "Lumbee religion [is] . . . firmly attached to Christian scripture"; http://www.strikeatthewind.com/lumbees.htm (last visited November 4, 2007). It's only since 1955 that these Indians have been called Lumbees. They had been variously known as the "Cherokee Indians of Robeson County," the "Indians of Robeson County," the "Croatans," and the "Scuffletonians," after the nearby neighborhood of Scuffletown; Charles Hudson, *supra*, note 39, at 291–94; Ruth Y. Wetmore, *supra*, note 54, at 166–67. One romantic and persistent, if undocumented, belief holds they derived from the interbreeding of the Lost Colonists of Roanoke with friendly Indians; Ruth Y. Wetmore, *supra*, note 54, at 164; Karen I. Blu, *supra*, note 79, at 135–36. Today the Lumbees are the largest tribe east of the Mississippi, though they "speak no language other than English, and they retain nothing of an aboriginal culture, and they have not done so in historic times"; Charles Hudson, *supra*, note 39, at 481. See "DP-1: Profile of General Demographic Characteristics: 2000," Census 2000 American Indian and Alaska Native Summary File, United States, Lumbee alone; see also http://www.co.robeson.nc.us/hist.htm (last visited March 17, 2007). They comprise almost 40 percent of the population of present-day Robeson County; http://209.85.165.104/search?q=cache:NXkQv6IwFnYJ:www.doa.state.nc.us/cia/pop1.pdf+indian+population+north+carolina&hl=en&ct=clnk&cd=2&gl=us&client=firefox-a (last visited October 15, 2007).

82. Russell Thornton, *supra*, note 70, at 46.

83. The Indian Removal Act of 1830, http://www.civics-online.org/library/formatted/texts/indian_act.html (last visited November 1, 2007); Russell Thornton, *supra*, note 70, at 57–58, 63–77.

84. Russell Thornton, *supra*, note 70, at 112.

85. Percy M. Ashburn, *The Ranks of Death* 19 (Frank D. Ashburn, ed., Coward McCann, 1947).

86. Alfred A. Cave, *supra*, note 6, at 15–16.

87. Alfred W. Crosby Jr., *The Columbian Exchange: Biological and Cultural Consequences of 1492* 41 (30th anniversary ed., Praeger, 2003).

88. *Ibid.*, at 41; Crosby does not cite to an original source. "Native Intelligence," *Smithsonian* (December 2005), http://www.smithsonianmag.com/history-archaeology/squanto.html?page=8 (last visited October 19, 2007).

89. Percy M. Ashburn, *supra*, note 85, at 22.

90. Calvin Martin, *Keepers of the Game: Indian-Animal Relationships and the Fur Trade* (University of California Press, 1978).

91. Charles M. Hudson Jr., "Why the Southeastern Indians Slaughtered Deer," in *Indians, Animals, and the Fur Trade* 165–71 (Shepherd Krech III., ed., University of Georgia Press, 1981).

92. *Ibid.*, at 170, 171.

93. Theda Purdue, *supra*, note 56, at 16.

94. Charles Hudson, *supra*, note 39, at 436.

95. Theda Purdue, *supra*, note 56, at 28.

96. Shepherd Krech III, *The Ecological Indian: Myth and History* 156, 159–60 (W. W. Norton and Co., 1999); Kathryn F. Holland Braund, *Deerskins and Duffels: The Creek Indian Trade with Anglo-America 1685–1815* (University of Nebraska Press, 1993).

97. Shepherd Krech III, *supra*, note 96, at 161.

Chapter 4: The Genesis Disaster for Black Slaves

1. David Brion Davis, *Inhuman Bondage: The Rise and Fall of Slavery in the New World* 64 (Oxford University Press, 2006).

2. William H. Holcombe, "The Alternative: A Separate Nationality, or the Africanization of the South," 32 *Southern Literary Messenger* 81, 81 (1861).

3. Thomas Sr. gave the house and the land surrounding to Thomas Jr., who gave it to his son William, who devised it to his son James Jr., then to William W. Robeson, who sold it to Mary Elizabeth Robeson Myers and her husband, Patrick Henry Myers, who left it to their daughter Sarah Myers Averitte, who lives there today. "Welcome to Walnut Grove Plantation" (Bladen County Historical Society).

4. National Register of Historical Places, nominating form for Walnut Grove, March 5, 1975.

5. C. C. Clark, "Some Early Homes of Bladen County," *Bladen Journal* (April 19, 1934).

6. *Bladen County Will Book*, vol. 1, at 420. The following year, Peter Robeson excised the two hundred acres of land from daughter Mary's bequest.

7. J. Bryan Grimes, *North Carolina Wills and Inventories Copied from Original Recorded Wills and Inventories in the Office of the Secretary Of State* 91 (Clearfield Co., 1912).

8. William Bartram, *Travels Through North and South Carolina, Georgia, East and West Florida, the Cherokee Country, the Extensive Territories of the Muscogulgees, and the Country of the Chactaws* (University of Virginia Press, 1980) (1791); Edward J. Cashin, *William Bartram and the American Revolution on the Southern Frontier* 124–59 (University of South Carolina Press, 2000).

9. William Bartram, *William Bartram on the Southeastern Indians* 16 (Gregory A. Waselkov and Kathryn E. Holland Braund, eds. and annotators, University of Nebraska Press, 2002).

10. http://freepages.genealogy.rootsweb.ancestry.com/~brownandmeares/slavelist.htm (last visited April 7, 2008).

11. *Ibid.*

12. Marjory Bartlett Sanger, *Billy Bartram and His Green World* 141 (Farrar, Straus & Giroux, 1972).

13. 1763 Tax List of Bladen County, North Carolina (in possession of author). "Bartram William Esq." owned ten slaves.

14. Abstracts of Early Deeds of Bladen County, North Carolina, vol. 1, at 17, no. 129 (abstracted by Wanda Suggs Campbell 1977); *id.*, vol. 1, at 7, no. 51.

15. Subsequently I located the library copy online at http://ftp.rootsweb.ancestry.com/pub/usgenweb/nc/bladen/census/1790wilm.txt (last visited April 4, 2008).

16. http://www.us-census.org/research/enumerator.htm (last visited June 21, 2008).

17. Janet Schaw, *Journal of a Lady of Quality; Being the Narrative of a Journey from Scotland to the West Indies, North Carolina, and Portugal, in the Years 1774 to 1776* 176–77, http://docsouth.unc.edu/nc/schaw/schaw.html (last visited April 9, 2008).

18. Johann David Schoepf, *Travels in the Confederation (1783–1784)* (Alfred J. Morrison, trans. and ed., William J. Campbell, 1911), http://www.ah.dcr.state.nc.us/sections/hp/colonial/Bookshelf/Travels/Default.htm (last visited April 9, 2008).

19. http://www.law.unc.edu/calendar/event.aspx?cid=635 (last visited June 24, 2008).

20. *State v. Mann*, 13 N.C. 263, 267, 268 (1829).

21. Harriet Beecher Stowe, *A Key to Uncle Tom's Cabin: Presenting the Original Facts and Documents Upon Which the Story Is Founded* 78 (John P. Jewett & Co., 1853).

22. *My Folks Don't Want Me to Talk About Slavery* 1, 1 (Belinda Hermence, ed., John F. Blair, 1984).

23. Belinda Hermence, ed., *supra*, note 22, at 51, 52.

24. Moses Roper, "A Narrative of the Adventures and Escape of Moses Roper from American Slavery," in *North Carolina Slave Narratives* 41, 41–56 (William L. Andrews, ed., University of North Carolina Press, 2003).

25. Moses Grandy, "Narrative of the Life of Moses Grandy, Late a Slave in the United States of America," in William L. Andrews, ed., *supra*, note 24, at 159.

26. *Ibid.*, at 179.

27. H. G. Jones, *Scoundrels, Rogues, and Heroes of the Old North State* 143, 143 (History Press, rev. updated ed., 2007).

28. David A. Davis, "Introduction" to "The Experience of Rev. Thomas H. Jones Who Was a Slave for Forty-Three Years," in William L. Andrews, ed., *supra*, note 24, at 189, 197.

29. A friend, as related to him by brother Jones, "The Experience of Rev. Thomas H. Jones Who Was a Slave for Forty-Three Years," in William L. Andrews, ed., *supra*, note 24, at 211, 213.

30. *Ibid.*

31. Harriet Jacobs, *Incidents in the Life of a Slave Girl* 48, 49 (Signet Classics, 2000) (1861).

32. *Ibid.*, at 48, 50.

33. *Ibid.*, at 48, 85, 89.

34. *Ibid.*, at 48, 128–76.

35. http://www.findagrave.com/cgi-bin/fg.cgi?page=gsr&GSsr=41&GScid=628488& (last visited June 27, 2008).

36. Charles F. Irons, *The Origins of Proslavery Christianity: White and Black Evangelicals in Colonial and Antebellum Virginia* ix (University of North Carolina Press, 2008).

37. Theodore Dwight Weld, *The Bible Against Slavery: An Inquiry in the Patriarchal and Mosaic Systems on the Subject of Human Rights* 93 (American Anti-Slavery Society, 1838).

38. Charles F. Irons, *supra*, note 36, at 1, quoting James G. Birney, *American Churches: The Bulwarks of American Slavery* (3rd rev. American ed., Parker Pilsbury, 1885).

39. Thornton Stringfellow, "A Brief Examination of Scripture Testimony on the Institution of Slavery," in *The Ideology of Slavery: Proslavery Thought in the Antebellum South, 1830–1860* 136 (Drew Gilpin Faust, ed., Louisiana State University Press, 1981) (1850) (emphasis in original). See Charles F. Irons, *supra*, note 36, at 25 ("Some seventeenth-century Anglicans did believe that the Curse of Ham in Genesis 9 justified the enslavement of Africans, but most did not need to appeal to this mythology in the light of such a clear scriptural distinction between the servitude of Christians and non-Christians"). Stringfellow did not exhaust even the possibilities contained in Genesis, such as the claim of Pre-Adamism that there were multiple Creations, that blacks descend from Satan, and that the Flood was Divine judgment for the racial mixing that had been going on. Stephen R. Haynes, *Noah's Curse: The Biblical Justifications of American Slavery* 15–18 (Oxford University Press, 2002).

40. Thornton Stringfellow, *supra*, note 39, at 140 (emphasis in original).

41. *Ibid.*, at 140 (emphasis in original).

42. *Zondervan King James Study Bible*, Genesis 9:19, at 17 (Kenneth Barker, ed., 2002). For example, "from these the whole earth was peopled"; *Revised Standard Version* 8 (Thomas Nelson & Sons, 1952).

43. Stephen R. Haynes, *supra*, note 39, at 5–8, 23–40.

44. *Ibid.*, at 12, 66–67.

45. Alexander Crummell, *The Future of Africa: Being Addresses, Sermons, Etc., Etc.* 327, 327–28 (Charles Scribner's & Sons, 1862) (1852). For example, David Brion Davis, *In the Image of God: Religion, Moral Values, and Our Heritage of Slavery* 309 (Yale University Press, 2001) ("Students of American slavery are aware that in the eighteenth and nineteenth centuries the biblical curse of Canaan, the son of Ham, was probably the central justification for racial slavery").

46. Alexander Crummell, *supra*, note 45, at 327, 328.

Chapter 5: Wilbur

1. http://wesley.nnu.edu/biblical_studies/tyndale/gen.txt (last visited September 24, 2007).

2. Lyall Watson, *The Whole Hog: Exploring the Extraordinary Potential of Pigs* 37 (Smithsonian Books, 2004).

3. Scott Brady, "Proper Way to Ear Notch Pigs," http://animalscience.unl.edu/swine/nf93-113.htm (last visited February 4, 2008).

4. Monte B. McCaw et al., "Maximization of Farrowing House Production," *Proceedings of the North Carolina Healthy Hogs Seminar*, http://mark.asci.ncsu.edu/HealthyHogs/book1999/mccaw.htm (last visited February 12, 2008); A. F. Fraser and D. M. Broom, *Farm Animal Behavior and Welfare* 236–37 (CABI Publishing, 1997).

5. http://extension.missouri.edu/explore/qa/swine0001.htm (last visited February 4, 2008).

6. Donald D. Stull and Michael J. Broadway, *Slaughterhouse Blues: The Meat and Poultry Industry in North America* 58 (Thomas/Wadsworth, 2004).

7. http://www.agr.state.nc.us/stats/ncrank.htm (last visited October 31, 2008).

8. *McDonald's Corporation and McDonald's Restaurants Limited v. Helen Marie Steele and David Morris*, sec. 8. The rearing and slaughter of animals, http://www.mcspotlight.org/case/trial/verdict/verdict_jud2c.html (opinion of Mr. Justice Bell, June 19, 1997) (last visited October 31, 2008).

9. *Ibid.*

10. Ian Frazier, "Hogs Wild," *The New Yorker* 71–72 (December 12, 2005).

11. Greger Larson et al., "Ancient DNA, Pig Domestication, and the Spread of the Neolithic into Europe," 104(39) *Proceedings of the National Academy of Sciences* 15226 (September 25, 2007); Greger Larson et al., "Phylogeography of Wild Boar Reveals Multiple Centers of Pig Domestication," 307 *Science* 1618 (March 11, 2005).

12. Lyall Watson, *supra*, note 2, at 97; E. Giufra et al., "The Origin of the Domestic Pig: Independent Domestication and Subsequent Introgression," 154 *Genetics* 1785 (2000); Juliet Clutton-Brock, *A Natural History of Domesticated Animals* 95 (Cambridge University Press, 1999).

13. Juliet Clutton-Brock, *supra*, note 12, at 93.

14. *Ibid.*, at 94.

15. http://www.iucn.org/themes/ssc/sgs/pphsg/APchap5-2.htm (last visited February 20, 2008).

16. Juliet Clutton-Brock, *supra*, note 12, at 95–96.

17. Lyall Watson, *supra*, note 2, at 98–99.

18. *Ibid.*, at 54, 55.

19. *Ibid.*, at 46.

20. *Ibid.*, at 53.

21. John J. Mayer and I. Lehr Brisbin Jr., *Wild Pigs of the United States: Their History, Morphology, and Current Status* 8 (University of Georgia Press, 1991).

22. Virginia DeJohn Anderson, *Creatures of Empire: How Domestic Animals Transformed Early America* 97 (Oxford University Press, 2004).

23. Orville K. Sweet, "Immigrant Pigs to North America," in Rolland "Pig" Paul et al., *The Pork Story: Legend and Legacy* 7 (National Pork Producers Council, 1991); John J. Mayer and I. Lehr Brisbin Jr., *supra*, note 21, at 19–21.

24. Lyall Watson, *supra*, note 2, at 108.

25. John J. Mayer and I. Lehr Brisbin Jr., *supra*, note 21, at 34.

26. *Ibid.*, at 219.

27. Timothy E. Blackwell, "Production Practices and Well-being: Swine," in G. John Benson and Bernard E. Rollin, *The Well-being of Farm Animals: Challenges and Solutions* 241, 247 (Blackwell Publishing, 2004).

28. Monte B. McCaw et al., *supra*, note 4.

29. *Ibid.*

30. Emmett Stevermer et al., "Reproductive Efficiency in Managing the Breeding Herd," Purdue University Cooperative Extension Service, http://www.animalgenome .org/edu/PIH/45.html (last visited March 12, 2008).

31. Monte B. McCaw et al., "Maximization of Farrowing House Production," *supra*, note 4.

32. John McGlone and Wilson Pond, *Pig Production: Biological Principles and Applications* 23 (Del Mar Learning, 2003).

33. *Ibid.*, at 267.

34. *Ibid.*, at 275.

35. *Ibid.*, at 269.

36. The last four productivity measures are of comparatively little importance—average sow parity, prewean mortality, matings/service, and sow mortality. *Ibid.*, at 269, table 17–1.

37. J. W. Holl and O. W. Robison, "Results from Nine Generations of Selection for Increased Litter Size in Swine," 81 *Journal of Animal Science* 624 (2003).

38. John McGlone and Wilson Pond, *supra*, note 32, at 271.

39. "Chinese Genes Can Boost British Pig Productivity," http://www.acmc.co.uk/ latest-news-display.asp?id=107 (last visited October 31, 2008); Norman Dunn, "An Extra Pig per Litter," 22 *Pig Progress* no. 5 30, 30–31 (2006).

40. John McGlone and Wilson Pond, *supra*, note 32, at 83.

41. Eric Ipsen, *International Herald Tribune* (June 26, 1992), http://www.iht.com/ articles/1992/06/26/swin.php (last visited March 18, 2008).

42. *Ibid.*

43. *Ibid.*

44. *Ibid.*

45. Norman Dunn, *supra*, note 39.

46. Lon Wagner, "Smithfield Banks on 'Lean Times': It Will Market a Low Fat Pork," *Virginia Pilot* (September 1, 1994), http://scholar.lib.vt.edu/VA-news/VA -Pilot/issues/1994/vp940901/09010551.htm (last visited March 18, 2008).

47. "Smithfield Fattens Up Lean Swine Line," http://www.meatandpoultryonline .com/article.mvc/Smithfield-Fattens-Up-Lean-Swine-Line-0001?VNETCOOKIE= NO (last visited October 31, 2008).

48. "Smithfield Foods, Inc., Announces the Expansion of Its Genetic Development Program" (February 28, 2000, press release), http://www.smithfieldfoods.com/Investor/Press/press_view.asp?ID=19 (last visited February 19, 2008). See http://www.smithfieldfoods.com/consumer/lean/ (last visited March 18, 2008).

49. XV *Oxford English Dictionary* 585 (2nd ed., 1983).

50. http://www.thepigsite.com/articles/1/health-and-welfare/2137/castration-of-pigs (last visited March 15, 2008) (adapted from Purdue Extension, *The New Pork Industry Handbook*, January 1, 2007).

51. Timothy E. Blackwell, *supra*, note 27, 241, 252.

52. http://www.thepigsite.com/pighealth/article/586/teeth-clipping (last visited February 4, 2008).

53. http://www.thepigsite.com/pighealth/article/555/docking-tail-clipping-piglets (last visited February 4, 2008).

54. http://www.aces.edu/pubs/docs/A/ANR-0902/ (last visited February 4, 2008).

55. Scott Brady, "Proper way to Ear Notch Pigs," *supra*, note 3.

56. Timothy E. Blackwell, *supra*, note 27, at 241, 254.

57. A. F. Fraser and D. M. Broom, *supra*, note 4, at 367.

58. *Ibid.*, at 366–67.

59. Timothy E. Blackwell, *supra*, note 27, at 241, 250–51.

60. *Ibid.*, at 241, 253–54.

61. http://www.nda.agric.za/docs/pigs1/breeding.htm (last visited March 12, 2008).

62. Robert Fitzgerald et al., "Optimizing Cull Sow Value," *National Hog Farmer*, http://nationalhogfarmer.com/mag/farming_optimizing_cull_sow/ (last visited February 12, 2008).

63. David Brion Davis, *Slavery and Human Progress* 13 (Oxford University Press, 1984).

64. Anonymous, *Bullwhip Days: The Slaves Remember* 246 (James Mellon, ed., Weidenfeld & Nicolson, 1988).

65. David Brion Davis, *Inhuman Bondage: The Rise and Fall of Slavery in the New World* 38 (Oxford University Press, 2006).

66. David Brion Davis, "At the Heart of Slavery," *New York Review of Books* 51, 52 (October 17, 1996).

67. Winthrop D. Jordan, *White over Black: American Attitudes Toward the Negro 1550–1812* 60 (Penguin Books, 1971) (1968).

68. *Ibid.*, at 233, 366.

69. Juliet Clutton-Brock, *supra*, note 12, at 32.

70. *Ibid.*, at 9; Francis Galton, "The First Steps Towards the Domestication of Animals," 3 *Transactions of the Ethnological Society of London* 122 (1865).

71. Juliet Clutton-Brock, *supra*, note 12, at 31.

72. Karl Jacoby, "Slavery by Nature? Domestic Animals and Human Slaves," 15(1) *Slavery and Abolition* 89, 92 (April 1994).

73. Lyall Watson, *supra*, note 2, at 37.

74. Stephen Budiansky, *The Covenant of the Wild: Why Animals Chose Domestication* 93 (William Morrow and Co., 1992).

75. Stephen Jay Gould, "A Biological Homage to Mickey Mouse," in *The Panda's Thumb: More Reflections in Natural History* 95–107 (W. W. Norton, 1980); Stephen Jay Gould, *Ontogeny and Phylogeny* 303–409 (Harvard University Press, 1977).

76. Lyall Watson, *supra*, note 2, at 37; Juliet Clutton-Brock, *supra*, note 12, at 33.

77. David Brion Davis, *supra*, note 65, at 51, 52.

78. David Brion Davis, *supra*, note 66, at 51, 52.

Chapter 6: The Smell of Money

1. John McGlone and Wilson Pond, *Pig Production: Biological Principles and Applications* 27 (Del Mar Learning, 2003).

2. Eric Ipsen, "The Next Generation Pig: Living Off the Lean of the Land" *International Herald Tribune* (June 26, 1992), http://www.iht.com/articles/1992/06/26/swin.php (last visited March 18, 2008).

3. Esther M. Bauer, "Cattle May Still Be King, but Here Come the Hogs," *Wall Street Journal* (December 1, 1999), http://ebwriters.com/work24.htm (last visited February 4, 2008).

4. Steve Wing et al., "Environmental Justice in North Carolina's Hog Industry," 108 *Environmental Health Perspectives* 225 (2000), http://www.ehponline.org/members/2000/108p225-231wing/wing-full.html (last visited July 18, 2008); U.S. Census Bureau, "State and County Quickfacts, Bladen County, North Carolina," http://quickfacts.census.gov/qfd/states/37/37017.html (last visited July 18, 2008).

5. Joby Warick and Pat Stith, "New Studies Show That Lagoons Are Leaking," *News Observer* (February 19, 1995) (two to four times); "Hogs and CAFOs," http://www.neuseriver.org/whatweareworkingon/hogsandcafos.html (ten times).

6. http://www.scorecard.org/env-releases/aw/county.tcl?fips_county_code=37017#maps (last visited February 4, 2008).

7. Natural Resources Defense Council, "Facts About Pollution from Livestock Farms," http://www.nrdc.org/water/pollution/ffarms.asp (last visited February 4, 2008).

8. http://www.salon.com/news/feature/1999/09/22/hogs/print.htm (last visited March 3, 2008).

9. http://www.enr.state.nc.us/newsrels/ernie08.htm (last visited March 3, 2008).

10. E-mail from Matthew Scully to Steven M. Wise, August 31, 2007.

11. Matthew Scully, *Dominion: The Power of Man, the Suffering of Animals, and the Call to Mercy* 247–86 (St. Martin's Press, 2002).

12. http://www.murphyfamilyventuresllc.com/swine.htm (last visited February 21, 2008).

13. http://www.smithfieldfoods.com/Brands/See/murphy.asp (last visited February 21, 2008).

14. http://www.murphyfamilyventuresllc.com/swine.htm (last visited February 21, 2008).

15. John McGlone and Wilson Pond, *supra*, note 1, at 292, 288.

16. *Ibid.*, at 34–35.

17. http://quickfacts.census.gov/qfd/states/37/37163.html (last visited February 13, 2008); http://factfinder.census.gov/servlet/SAFFFacts?_event=Search&_lang=en&_sse=on&_state=04000US37&_county=Sampson%20County (last visited February 13, 2008).

18. P. H. Hemsworth et al., "Improving the Attitude and Behavior of Stockpersons Towards Pigs and Consequences on the Behavior and Reproductive Performance of Commercial Pigs," 39 *Applied Animal Behavior Science* 349, 350 (1994).

19. *Ibid.*, at 349, 360–61.

20. Timothy E. Blackwell, "Production Practices and Well-being: Swine," in G. John Benson and Bernard E. Rollin, *The Well-being of Farm Animals: Challenges and Solutions* 241, 262 (Blackwell Publishing, 2004).

21. *Ibid.*

22. Murphy Family Ventures, LLC, Sow Farm, Garland, N.C., footage for prosecutorial consideration (PETA, 2007) (in author's files).

23. Timothy E. Blackwell, *supra*, note 20, at 241, 263–64.

24. Bernard E. Rollin, "The Ethical Imperative to Control Pain and Suffering in Farm Animals," in *The Well-being of Farm Animals: Challenges and Solutions* by G. John Benson and Bernard E. Rollin (Blackwell Publishing, 2004), 3, 8–9.

25. *Ibid.*, at 9.

26. Matthew Scully, *supra*, note 11, at 269.

27. *Ibid.*

28. PETA gave me videos, as well as their "Viewing Guide for 'Sow Farm Investigation Footage for Internal Discussion.'"

29. Matthew Scully, *supra*, note 11, at 265.

30. http://www.smithfieldfoods.com/Enviro/Glossary/animalWelfare.asp#gloss_s (last visited February 7, 2008).

31. Matthew Scully, *supra*, note 11, at 265.

32. *Ibid.* at 266–67.

33. John J. McGlone et al., "The Development of Pain in Young Pigs Associated with Castration and Attempts to Prevent Castration-Induced Behavioral Changes," 74 *Journal of Animal Science* 1441 (1993).

34. Matthew Scully, *supra*, note 11, at 265.

35. Temple Grandin and Catherine Johnson, *Animals in Translation: Using the Mysteries of Autism to Decode Animal Behaviors* 6, 103 (Bloomsbury, 2005).

36. Wayne L. Singleton, Ph.D., "Proper Care and Adjustment of Imported Boars," National Swine Registry, at 7.

37. 2006 Genetic Directory, International Boar Semen, Universal Pig Genes, Inc., at 4, 5.

38. Temple Grandin and Catherine Johnson, *supra*, note 35, at 103–4.

Chapter 7: River of Death

1. Upton Sinclair, *The Jungle: The Uncensored Original Edition* 30 (See Sharp Press, 2003) (1906).

2. William Cronon, *Nature's Metropolis: Chicago and the Great West* 225, 256 (W. W. Norton & Co., 1991).

3. Ralph Waldo Emerson, "Fate," in "The Conduct of Life," in III *The Works of Ralph Waldo Emerson* 4 (Hearst's International Library, 1914) (1860).

4. Letter from John Coetzee to Steven M. Wise, November 10, 2005.

5. For example, M. Iacoboni et al., "Grasping the Intentions of Others with One's Own Mirror Neuron System," *PLoS Biol* 3(3): e79 doi:10.1371/journal.pbio.0030079; 92005); Mirella DiPretto et al., "Understanding Emotions in Others: Mirror Neuron Dysfunction in Children in Autism Spectrum Disorders," 9 *Nature-Neuroscience* 28 (December 4, 2006) (published online); Giacomo Rizzolatti and Laila Craighero, "The Mirror Neuron System," 27 *Annual Review of Neuroscience* 169 (July 2004); Evelyn Kohler et al., "Hearing Sounds, Understanding Actions," 297 *Science* 846, no. 5582 (August 2, 2002).

6. Matthew Scully, *Dominion: The Power of Man, the Suffering of Animals, and the Call to Mercy* 282 (St. Martin's Press, 2002).

7. Letter from Smithfield Vice President Larry A. Johnson to Ms. Teresa Rodriguez, March 9, 2007.

8. Letter from Ellen D. Gause to Mr. Bobby Blowe, Chief, Construction, Grants and Loan Section, Division of Water Quality, March 16, 2007.

9. Letter from Michelle Nowlin, Senior Attorney, and Amy Pickle, Staff Attorney, to Carolyn Bryant, March 15, 2007, at 4; letter from Research Associates of America, Inc., to North Carolina Division of Water Quality, March 27, 2007, at 3; letter from Paul Nelson, President, to Teresa Rodriguez, March 13, 2007; letter from Larry Baldwin to Alan W. Klimek, PE Director, March 15, 2007, at 2.

10. Letter from Collin H. Sullins, Director, Division of Water Quality, North Carolina Department of Environment and Natural Resources, June 28, 2007, to Mr. Larry Johnson, Vice President, Smithfield Packing Company, Inc., Tar Heel, North Carolina.

11. 7 USC sec. 1901, *et seq.*; 9 CFR sec. 301.2 (qq).

12. 7 USC sec. 2132 (g); N.C. Stat. sec. 14–360 (2) and (2a).

13. Gail Eisnitz, *Slaughterhouse: The Shocking Story of Greed, Neglect, and Inhumane Treatment Inside the U.S. Meat Industry* 189–201 (Prometheus Books, 1997).

14. Siegfried Gledion, *Mechanization Takes Command: A Contribution to Anonymous History* 73 (Oxford University Press, 1948).

15. *Ibid.*, at 215; William Cronon, *supra*, note 2, at 229.

16. William Cronon, *supra*, note 2, at 228; Siegfried Gledion, *supra*, note 14, at 217.

17. 2 Charles Frederick Goss, *Cincinnati, the Queen City, 1788–1912* 391 (S. J. Clarke Publishing Co., 1912).

18. Siegfried Gledion, *supra*, note 14, at 227.

19. Upton Sinclair, *supra*, note 1, at 28.

20. William Cronon, *supra*, note 2, at 229.

21. Siegfried Gledion, *supra*, note 14, at 78.

22. William Cronon, *supra*, note 2, at 230, 231–32.

23. *Ibid.*, at 256.

24. E-mail from Keira Ullrich to Steven M. Wise, May 2007.

25. Charlie LeDuff, "At a Slaughterhouse, Some Things Never Die: Who Kills, Who Cuts, Who Bosses Can Depend on Race," *New York Times* (June 16, 2000), http://www.nytimes.com/library/national/race/061600leduff-meat.html (last visited July 18, 2008).

26. www.smithfieldjustice.com (last visited August 13, 2007).

27. http://www.ufcw.org/working_america/case_against_smithfield/case_against_smithfld.cfm (last visited August 13, 2007).

28. Mike Ely and Linda Flores, "No Longer Hidden, No Longer Hiding," *Revolution* #76 (January 9, 2007); Mike Ely and Linda Flores, "Strike at Smithfield: Workers Under a Changing Sky; Part 2: The Struggle Erupts," *Revolution* #77 (January 28, 2007); "Tar Heel, N.C.: Slaughterhouse Workers Faced with a Deadly Job" (last visited August 12, 2007); http://www.sierraclub.org/communidades/ingles/tarheel.asp (April 21, 2006); Robert F. Kennedy Jr., "Smithfield Foods," EcologistOnline (January 12, 2003), http:/www.theecologist.org/archive_detail.asp?content_id=387 (last visited August 12, 2007); 2005 Human Rights Watch Report, "Blood, Sweat, and Fear: Workers Rights in U.S. Meat and Poultry Plant," http://www.hrw.org/reports/2005/usa0105/ (last visited July 16, 2008).

29. *Smithfields Foods, Inc. and UFCW*, case nos. 11-CA-15522 et al. (decision of ALJ John H. West, JD-158–00, December 15, 2000) (442 pages).

30. *Smithfield Food, Inc. v. United Food and Commercial Workers International Union*, 3:2007cv00641 (E. D. Va., October 17, 2007).

31. Adam Liptak, "Corporate View of Mafia Tactics: Protesting, Lobbying, and Citing Upton Sinclair," *New York Times*, at p. A14 (February 5, 2008).

32. *Smithfield Food, Inc. v. United Food and Commercial Workers International Union*, 3:2007cv00641 (E. D. Va., October 17, 2007), Complaint, para. #171, at 55–56.

33. *Ibid.*, para. #220, at 74–75. On October 28, 2008, the parties agreed that the Tar Heel plant workers would vote "in a fair election process" whether they wished to be represented by the union. In return the union agreed to "end its public campaign against Smithfield." "Smithfield, UFCW Settle RICO Suit, Agree to Election Using 'Fair Process,'" *BNA Employment and Labor Law, Daily Labor Report*, no. 208 (October 28, 2008), http://emlawcenter.bna.com/pic2/em.nsf/id/BNAP-7KULHA?OpenDocument. On December 11, 2008, the workers voted to unionize by 2,041 to 1,879. Steven Greenhouse, "Workers at Pork Plant in North Carolina Vote to Unionize After a 15-year Fight," *New York Times*, at p. A10 (December 13, 2008).

34. http://faculty.lagcc.cuny.edu/jselden/norma_rae.htm (last visited August 31, 2007).

35. David Barboza, "Goliath of the Hog World: Fast Rise of Smithfield Foods Makes Regulators Wary," *New York Times*, at p. C1 (April 7, 2000).

36. https://www.meredith.edu/professional/faculty.htm (last visited October 23, 2007).

37. http://www.unc.edu/news/archives/mar00/hof032700.htm (last visited October 23, 2007).

38. Timothy E. Blackwell, "Production Practices and Well-being: Swine," in *The Well-being of Farm Animals: Challenges and Solutions* 241, 262 (G. John Benson and Bernard E. Rollin, eds., Blackwell Publishing, 2004).

39. If factory farms are large enough, they are designated CAFOs, or "Concentrated Animal Feeding Operations," for purposes of water quality protection by the U.S. Environmental Protection Agency under authority of the federal Clean Water Act. An Animal Feeding Operation (AFO) includes any facility that keeps animals confined at least forty-five days in a twelve-month period, and for which no grass or other vegetation is provided in the confinement area during the normal growing cycle. Small CAFOs are not subject to these EPA regulations. Medium CAFOs are subject to EPA regulation if animals or their waste come into contact with groundwater, either directly or indirectly. To summarize, the EPA-established "size thresholds" for CAFOs, by animal farming sector: For pigs of fewer than 55 pounds, a small CAFO holds fewer than 3,000, a medium CAFO holds 3,000 to 9,999, and a large CAFO has 10,000 or more. For pigs over 55 pounds, a small CAFO holds fewer than 750, a medium CAFO between 750 and 2,499, and a large CAFO greater than 2,500. www.epa.gov/npdes/pubs/sector_table.pdf (last visited November 6, 2008).

40. U.S. Department of Agriculture, NAHMS, "Swine '95: Part II: Reference of 1995 Grower/Finisher Health and Management Practices," at 19.

41. Charlie LeDuff, *supra*, note 25.

42. My interviews generally echo what *New York Times* reporter David Barboza found there: "Squealing hogs funnel into an area where they are electrocuted, stabbed in the jugular, then tied, lifted and carried on a winding journey through the plant. They are dunked in scalding water, their hair is removed, they are run through a fiery furnace (to burn off residual hair), then disemboweled and sliced by an army of young, often immigrant, laborers." David Barboza, *supra*, note 35.

43. A. F. Fraser and D. M. Broom, *Farm Animal Behavior and Welfare* 282 (3rd ed., CABI Publishing, 1997).

44. John Webster, *Animal Welfare: Limping Towards Eden* 173 (Blackwell Publishing, 2005).

45. Professor John Webster says this traditional belief is false; there is no good reason not to have the heart stopped by stunning. *Ibid.*, at 172.

46. *Ibid.*, at 173.

47. *Ibid.*

48. Erik Marcus, *Meat Market: Animals, Ethics, and Money* 34 (Brio Press, 2005); Joby Warrick, "They Die Piece by Piece," *Washington Post* (April 10, 2001), at p. A1.

49. Charlie LeDuff, *supra*, note 25.

50. Gail A. Eisnitz, *supra*, note 13, at 265–66.

51. *Ibid.*, at 267. Eisnitz said that Price's claims were corroborated by a very reliable source at the USDA.

52. This was partially corroborated by a July 11, 2008, blog that stated, "Here are a few of the things I will be extremely lucky never ever to see again [in Japan]: Pigs' vagina wound around a wooden stick and grille." http://shannonsalter23.blogspot.com/2008_07_01_archive.html (last visited October 20, 2008).

53. Charlie LeDuff, *supra*, note 25.

54. *Ibid.*

55. Venita Jenkins and April Johnston, "St. Paul's Changing Face: The Influence of Immigrants," *Fayetteville Observer* (July 15, 2007), http://www.fayobserver.com/

article?id=267419 (last visited July 18, 2008). This was after a November 2006 raid by immigration officials, whose arrest of 21 illegal immigrants at the plant caused 1,100 Hispanic workers to leave the plant; Steven Greenhouse, "Immigrant Crackdown Upends a Slaughterhouse's Workforce," *New York Times* (October 12, 2007), at p. A1. In 2000, it was about 60 percent Hispanic; Charlie LeDuff, *supra*, note 25.

56. David Griffith, "Hay Trabajo: Poultry Processing, Rural Industrialization, and the Latinization of Low-Wage Labor," in *Any Way You Cut It: Meat Processing and Small-Town America* 129, 148 (Donald D. Stull et al., University Press of Kansas, 1995).

57. Steven Greenhouse, "Workers at Pork Plant in North Carolina Vote to Unionize After a 15-year Fight," *New York Times*, at p. A10 (December 13, 2008).

58. If the Jarvis Products Corporation of Middletown, Connecticut, signals the future of hog slaughter, there may be fewer line jobs available. The company offers the Jarvis Model 3-HD robotic hog head dropper. It can automatically cut off the head of one pig every three seconds. You can see how it's done at http://www.jarvisproducts .com/Jarvis%20Pork%20JR50RHD.htm.

Chapter 8: The World Pork Expo

1. John McGlone and Wilson Pond, *Pig Production: Biological Principles and Applications* 283 (Del Mar Learning, 2003).

2. John D. Lawrence, "The State of Iowa's Pork Industry," http://www.econ.iastate .edu/outreach/agriculture/livestock/pork/dollars_and_scents/chapter1/introduction.ht ml (last visited October 1, 2008).

3. http://mark.asci.ncsu.edu/NCPorkConf/2006/GeneralSessions/williams.htm (last visited March 3, 2008).

4. John McGlone and Wilson Pond, *supra*, note 1, at 16.

5. Nigel Key and William McBride, *The Changing Economics of U.S. Hog Production* 4 (USDA, December 2007).

6. *Ibid.*, at 9.

7. Rolland "Pig" Paul et al., *The Pork Story: Legend and Legacy* 189, 190 (Lowell Press, 1991).

8. V *Oxford English Dictionary* 576 (2nd ed., 1989).

9. Rolland "Pig" Paul et al., *supra*, note 7, at 189.

10. "Ken Prusa," *The National Hog Farmer* 20, 20 (May 15, 2006).

11. Rod Smith, "Solutions," *Feedstuffs* 1 (June 5, 2006), quoting Steve Murphy, CEO of the National Pork Promotion and Research Board.

12. http://www.theotherwhitemeat.com/aspx/all_about_pork/PorkDetails2.aspx ?id=77 (last visited July 10, 2006).

13. *Ibid.*

14. http://www.theotherwhitemeat.com/aspx/promos/contract.aspx (last visited July 10, 2006).

15. John Ruskin, *Lectures on Art*, 3. "The Relation of Art to Morals," February 23, 1870.

16. There was a Library of Congress special presentation called "Hog Heaven: Celebrating 100 Years of the Harley-Davidson," http://www.loc.gov/rr/scitech/harley100/.

17. http://pemtropics.mit.edu/~jcho/spam/sha.html.

18. http://www.webopedia.com/TERM/s/spam.html (last visited October 17, 2006).

19. Marcel Proust, *The Maxims of Marcel Proust* (Justin O'Brien., ed., trans., Columbia University Press, 1948).

20. Orville K. Sweet, "The National Barrow Show," in *The Pork Story: Legend and Legacy* 21 (Rolland "Pig" Paul et al., Lowell Press, 1991).

21. Alan Krell, *Manet and the Painters of Contemporary Life* 59 (Thames & Hudson, 1996).

22. Timothy J. Clark, *The Painting of Modern Life: Paris in the Art of Manet and His Followers* 79 (Princeton University Press, 1984).

23. *Ibid.*, at 83–98.

24. *State v. O'Keefe*, 263 N.C. 53 (1964).

25. Kathryn Louden, "An Historical Commentary on the National Porkettes," in Rolland "Pig" Paul et al., *supra*, note 7, at 174.

26. *Ibid.*

27. *Ibid.* See http://www.ourwaverly.com/html/main/org_display/orgID/3037172/index.html (last visited December 1, 2006).

28. This title was eliminated in 1987.

29. http://www.post-gazette.com/pg/05157/516626.stm (last visited December 1, 2006).

30. Amy Wahle, "Pork Queen Grew Up on a Hog Farm," *The Tribune* (April 11, 2006), http://www.midiowanews.com/site/tab1.cfm?newsid=16462363&brd=2700&pag=461&dept_id=554314&Rfi=6 (last visited on October 2, 2008).

31. Orville K. Sweet, "Packers as Partners," in Rolland "Pig" Paul et al., *supra*, note 7, at 27.

32. John McGlone and Wilson Pond, *supra*, note 1, at 219.

33. Dr. Dennis DiPietre, "From 'Hands-On' to Automated" (on file with the author).

34. Dr. Steve Powell, Technical Programs Director, Premier Pork Systems LLC, "The Importance of Percentage Carcass Yield."

35. "Question-and-Answer Session with NPC CEO Neil Dierks," *Official Souvenir Program and Show Guide*, at 62.

36. "NPPC Successes," *Official Souvenir Program and Show Guide*, at 47.

37. *Ibid.*

38. John McGlone and Wilson Pond, *supra*, note 1, at 217.

39. Central Confinement Service, Ltd.; John McGlone and Wilson Pond, *supra*, note 1, at 208, 209.

40. John McGlone and Wilson Pond *supra*, note 1, at 209.

41. Florida Constitution, article X, section 21(a).

42. *Journal of Extension*, 33(4) (August 1995), http://www.joe.org/joe/1995august/rb4.html (last visited November 10, 2008); 19.1 percent of producers knew this.

43. John McGlone and Wilson Pond, *supra,* note 1, at 240–41.

44. http://www.newsham.com/en/fmpchart.asp (last visited November 11, 2006).

45. AgAlliance, "Dead Sled Mover" (February 15, 2002).

46. AgAlliance, "Quick Load Dead Sled" (January 3, 2006).

47. AgAlliance, "Carcass Carts!" (February 19, 2002).

Chapter 9: A Pork Industry Visionary

1. Whiteshire Hamroc, LLC, at 27.

2. Babcock Genetics, "Pork Quality and Carcass Consistency: How You Can Get It and Why You Should."

3. Orville K. Sweet, "Symbol: The Picture That's Worth More Than a Thousand Words," in Rolland "Pig" Paul et al., *The Pork Story: Legend and Legacy* 182 (National Pork Producers Council, 1991).

4. *Ibid.,* at 183.

5. *Ibid.,* at 182.

6. Document in possession of author.

7. Babcock Genetics, *supra,* note 2.

8. https://ecomm.fass.org/services/join.asp (last visited November 21, 2006).

9. http://www.fass.org/fasstrack/news_item.asp?news_id=795 (last visited November 21, 2006).

10. http://www.meatscience.org/awards/archive/2005/Citations/2005%20IMCA%20Service%20Award%20Citation%20-%20Bill%20Jones.htm (last visited November 21, 2006).

11. http://www.meatscience.org/pubs/rmcarchv/2006/index.html (last visited November 2, 2006).

12. Minutes of Intercollegiate Meat Coaches Association annual meeting, University of Illinois (June 18, 2005) (emphases in the original), http://aolsearch.aol.com/aol/search?invocationType=recentSearch&query=national+pork+board+symbol (last visited October 5, 2006).

13. C. R. Schwab et al., "The Effects of Long-Term Selection for Reduced Back Fat and Increased Loin Muscle in Meat and Eating Quality Traits in Duroc Swine," *Proceedings of the 29th Annual National Swine Improvement Federation* 37, 41 (Ames, Iowa, December 9–10, 2004).

14. Dr. Douglas W. Newcom et al., "Ultrasonic Evaluation of Intramuscular Fat Content," *Proceedings of the 29th Annual National Swine Improvement Federation* 57, 58 (Ames, Iowa, December 9–10, 2004).

15. John McGlone and Wilson Pond, *Pig Production: Biological Principles and Applications* 83, 86 (Del Mar Learning, 2003).

16. *Ibid.,* at 83.

17. Dwain Guggenbiller, DVM, and Bert Van Gils Jr., "Nutritional Support for the Highly Prolific Sow," *Feed Management* (November–December, 2005).

18. Albion Laboratories, Inc., *MAAC Facts*, vol. 10, no. 2 (June 2004).

19. Dwain Guggenbiller, DVM, and Bert Van Gils Jr., *supra,* note 17.

20. Premier Pork Systems, LLC, "Quality Seedstock—Cost Effective—Satisfaction Guaranteed," at 2.

21. *Ibid.*

22. PIC USA, Inc., "PIC 327L."

23. Prince A.I. Boars—LS-100 Females (Premier).

24. http://www.newsham.com/en/supersire.asp (last visited November 11, 2006).

25. Newsham Genetics, LLC, "SuperMom—Delivering More Pigs to Market Each Year" (2006).

26. http://www.newsham.com/en/supermom.asp (last visited November 11, 2006). See also Newsham Genetics, LLC, *supra*, note 25.

27. Newsham Genetics LLC, "The Newsham Advantage" (2006).

28. *Ibid.*

29. John McGlone and Wilson Pond, *supra*, note 15, at 72.

30. http://www.fshn.hs.iastate.edu/faculty/prusa.php (last visited November 2, 2006).

31. http://www.fshn.hs.iastate.edu/faculty/prusa.php (last visited November 2, 2006); *Proceedings of the 29th Annual National Swine Improvement Federation* 71, 73–76 (Ames, Iowa, December 9–10, 2004); S. M. Lonergan, K. J. Stadler, E. Huff-Lonergan, T. J. Knight, R. N. Goodwin, K. J. Prusa, and K. C. Beitz, *Journal of Animal Science* (then in press); S. M. Lonergan, T. J. Baas, M. Malek, J. C. M. Dekkers, K. Prusa, and M. Rothschild, "Correlation Among Selected Pork Quality Traits," 80 *Journal of Animal Science* 617 (2002); M. Malek, J. Dekkers, H. K. Lee, T. J. Baas, K. Prusa, E. Huff-Lonergan, and M. F. Rothschild, "A Molecular Genome Scan Analysis to Identify Chromosomal Regions Influencing Economic Traits in the Pig, II. Meat and Muscle Composition," 12 *Mammalian Genome* 637 (2001).

32. "Ken Prusa," *National Hog Farmer* 20, 20 (May 15, 2006).

33. Dr. Ken Prusa and Chris Fedler, "A New Definition of Pork Quality: 'Good Taste Is Just the Beginning,'" *Proceedings of the 29th Annual National Swine Improvement Federation* 71, 71 (Ames, Iowa, December 9–10, 2004).

34. http://www.cdfin.iastate.edu/sensory2.htm (last visited December 4, 2007).

35. http://www.hs.iastate.edu/rge/research/statements/Prusa.htm (last visited November 19, 2007).

36. Teddi Barron, "Finding Out What People Like—and Why," *Inside Iowa State* (August 10, 2006), http://www.iastate.edu/Inside/06/0810/prusa.shtml (last visited November 19, 2007); http://agwired.com/category/elanco/ (posted by Cindy, May 17, 2007, at 2:52 PM; last visited November 19, 2007).

37. http://www.iowacorn.org/ethanol/ethanol_12.html (last visited December 4, 2007).

38. http://www.fshn.hs.iastate.edu/faculty/prusa.php (last visited November 2, 2006); *Proceedings of the 29th Annual National Swine Improvement Federation* 71, 73–76 (Ames, Iowa, December 9–10, 2004).

39. http://waysandmeans.house.gov/hearings.asp?formmode=printfriendly&id=6076 (last visited December 6, 2007).

40. See Patent 7,303,878, issued to Max F. Rothschild et al., on December 4, 2007.

41. In 2006, the United States exported 1,262,499 metric tons of pork worldwide; http://waysandmeans.house.gov/hearings.asp?formmode=printfriendly&id=6076 (last visited December 6, 2007).

42. "Iowa State University Food Scientist Is Changing the Way We Look at Pork," *Iowa State University News Service* (August 10, 2006), http://www.iastate.edu~Enscentral/news/06/aug/prusa.shtml (last visited on November 19, 2007).

43. "Food Scientist Is Changing the Way We Look at Pork," *Newswise* (August 10, 2006), http://www.newswise.com/articles/view/522683/ (last visited November 2, 2006).

44. Babcock Genetics, *supra*, note 2.

45. *Ibid.*

46. Tom J. Baas, "Meat Quality Traits and Genetic Selection," *U.S. Purebreds: The World's Source of Genetics* 6 (National Swine Registry and U.S. Livestock Genetics Export).

47. "Iowa State University Food Scientist Is Changing the Way We Look at Pork," *supra*, note 42.

48. "Food Scientist Is Changing the Way We Look at Pork," *supra*, note 43.

49. Temple Grandin, an expert on slaughterhouse design, reports that some studies have found that carbon dioxide irritates the pigs' respiratory system and other studies have found that some pigs react violently to the gas. http://www.grandin.com/humane/carbon.stun.html (last visited December 6, 2007).

50. Teddi Barron, *supra*, note 36; Dr. Ken Prusa and Chris Fedler, "Evaluating Pork Quality," Babcock Genetics.

51. Teddi Barron, *supra*, note 36.

52. Dr. Ken Prusa and Chris Fedler, *supra*, note 50, at 2.

53. *Ibid.*

54. *Ibid.*

55. *Ibid.*

56. *Ibid.*

57. Interview with Dr. Ken Prusa, 2:09–2:21, http://agwired.com/category/elanco/ (last visited December 14, 2007).

58. Dr. Ken Prusa and Chris Fedler, *supra*, note 50.

59. *Ibid.*

60. Dr. Ken Prusa and Chris Fedler, *supra*, note 33, at 71, 74.

61. Dr. Ken Prusa and Chris Fedler, *supra*, note 50, at 2; Dr. Ken Prusa and Chris Fedler, *supra*, note 33, at 71, 73.

62. Tom J. Baas, *supra*, note 46, at 6.

63. *Ibid.*

64. *Ibid.*

65. See Patent 7,303,878, issued to Max F. Rothschild et al., on December 4, 2007.

66. *Ibid.*

67. Amy Lorentzen, "Charges Filed Against Six in Iowa Pig Abuse Case," http://ap.google.com/article/ALeqM5jYCps4elThCbt4fcA1bKFoxNscmwD93VQM T80 (October 22, 2008) (last visited October 22, 2008).

Chapter 10: The Genesis Disaster for Animals

1. Alexis de Tocqueville, *Democracy in America* 308, 303–5 (Everyman's Library, 1994) (1835).
2. Quoted in Neela Banerjee, "A Fluid Religious Life Is Seen in U.S., with Switches Common," *New York Times*, at A.1, A.12 (February 26, 2008).
3. Calvin Martin, "The War Between Indians and Animals," in *Indians, Animals, and the Fur Trade* 11, 18 (Shepherd Krech III, ed., University of Georgia Press, 1981).
4. Edward O. Wilson, *On Human Nature* 169 (Harvard University Press, 1988).
5. 2 Corinthians 6:14 (King James Version).
6. Mark Newman, *Getting Right with God: Southern Baptists and Desegregation 1945–1995* 48 (University of Alabama Press, 2001).
7. Peter L. Berger, *The Sacred Canopy: Elements of a Sociological Theory of Religion* 37 (Doubleday, 1967). This is a broad use of the term which in a more narrow sense concerns the issue of how God's goodness and evil can coexist. http://www.newadvent.org/cathen/14569a.htm (last visited May 12, 2008).
8. Mark Newman, *supra*, note 6, at 48.
9. Peter L. Berger, *supra*, note 7, at 47–50.
10. Zondervan KJV Study Bible 2 (Zondervan, 2002).
11. Nelson's NLJV Study Bible 21 (Earl D. Radmacher, ed., Thomas Nelson, 1997).
12. Zondervan KJV Study Bible, *supra*, note 10, at 18. The Geneva Bible was the first to annotate biblical passages. Seven or eight billion Bibles have been printed in hundreds of languages, and perhaps one hundred million are added each year, as commented upon by a worldwide array of energetic companies; http://www.biblestudy.org/beginner/why-are-there-so-many-bibles-in-the-world.html (last visited September 24, 2007). Since the early 1930s, Zondervan has published Christian evangelical Bibles in the United States. In the early 1970s, it cofounded the Evangelical Christian Publishers Association (ECPA), whose number-one "Statement of Faith" is "the Bible [is] the inspired, the only infallible, authoritative Word of God"; http://www.ecpa.org/about_ecpa.php (last visited September 26. 2007). There are now about 260 ECPA members worldwide. Following Martin Luther, evangelical Protestants almost invariably believe the Bible was written by God in a way clearly understandable to the careful reader; http://en.wikipedia.org/wiki/Evangelical_Christian_Publishers_Association (last visited September 26, 2007). I chose Zondervan's annotated King James Study Bible as a typical, conservative example of modern evangelical Protestant Genesis interpretation. Its editors describe their Bible as "the work of a transdenominational team of conservative Biblical scholars. All confess the authority of the Bible as God's infallible word to humanity. . . . Where editors were aware of significant differences of opinion on key passages or doctrines, they tried to follow an evenhanded approach by indicating those differences."
13. Genesis 1:26–28 (William Tyndale, trans.) (1530), (http://wesley.nnu.edu/biblical_studies/tyndale/gen.txt (last visited September 2007) (emphasis added).
14. Thomas Hobbes, *Leviathan*, part 1, chap. 16, sec. 81, at 112 (Richard Tuck, ed., Cambridge University Press, 1992) (1651).

15. Zondervan KJV Study Bible, *supra*, note 10, at 811. See Geneva Bible 588 (Tolle Lege Press, 2006) (1599): "His dominion shall be also from sea to sea, and from the river unto the ends of the land."

16. Zondervan KJV Study Bible, *supra*, note 10, at 811; Geneva Bible, *supra*, note 15, at 588.

17. Folk theology is "unreflective belief that revels in subjective feelings brought by slogans or legends and that resists examination. Generally speaking it is quite comfortable with inner inconsistency and unquestioning belief in sensational stories and pithy clichés, which are the primary media for its communication. . . . It encourages gullibility, vicarious spirituality and simplistic answers to difficult dilemmas." Stanley J. Grenz and Roger E. Olson, *Who Needs Theology: An Invitation to the Study of God* 28–29 (InterVarsity Press, 1996).

18. For example, Arch Stanton, *Animals in Heaven: Fantasy or Reality?* (Trafford Publishing, 2006); J. R. Hyland, *God's Covenant with Animals: A Biblical Basis for the Humane* (Lantern Books, 2000); Andrew Linzey, *Christianity and the Rights of Animals* (Crossroad, 1987); C. W. Hume, *The Status of Animals in the Christian Religion* (Universities Federation for Animal Welfare, 1957).

19. Keith Thomas, *Man and the Natural World: A History of the Modern Sensibility* 18 (Pantheon Books, 1983).

20. *Ibid.*, at 25.

21. http://www.luminarium.org/sevenlit/carew/saxham.htm (last visited October 9, 2007) (c. 1640).

22. http://www.luminarium.org/sevenlit/jonson/penshurst.htm (last visited October 9, 2007) (1612).

23. William Somerville, "The Chace," XI *The Works of the English Poets* 166 (Alexander Chalmers, ed., J. Johnson, J. Nichols and Son, 1810) (1735).

24. http://www.ccel.org/h/herbert/temple/Providence.html (last visited October 9, 2007) (1633).

25. Keith Thomas, *supra*, note 19, at 146.

26. Geneva Bible, *supra*, note 15, at 11 (emphasis in the original).

27. N.C. Gen. Stat. sec. 14–360 (c) (2) and (2a) (1999).

28. Lynn White Jr. "The Historical Roots of Our Ecological Crisis," 155 *Science* 1203, 1205 (1967).

29. See, for example, "Introduction: Beyond Lynn White, Jr.," http://www.counter balance.net/enviro/intro-body.html last visited May 9, 2008).

30. Garry Wills, *Saint Augustine* xii (Penguin, 1999); Frank Eggleston Robbins, *The Hexaemeral Literature: A Study of the Greek and Latin Commentaries on Genesis* 64 (University of Chicago Press, 1912).

31. Saint Augustine, *The City of God*, Book 1.20, at 26 (Marcus Dod, trans., Modern Library, 1950).

32. Saint Augustine, *De moribus Manichaeorum*, Book 2.17 59, quoted in Richard Soprabji, *Animal Minds and Human Morals: The Origins of the Western Debate* 196 (Cornell University Press, 1993).

33. *Ibid.*

34. Thomas Aquinas, *Summa theologica*, Question 96, Art. 1 in *The Basic Writings of Saint Thomas Aquinas* 918 (Anton C. Pegis, ed., Random House, 1944).

35. Thomas Aquinas, *Summa contra gentiles*, Book 3, Chap. CXII, in 2 *The Basic Writings of Saint Thomas Aquinas* 220 (Anton C. Pegis, ed., Random House, 1944).

36. *Ibid.*, at 220, 221.

37. Thomas Aquinas, *Summa theologica*, *supra*, note 34, Question 75, at 682–94; Thomas Aquinas, *Summa contra gentiles*, *supra*, note 35, Book 3, Chap. CXIII, at 224. See Steven M. Wise, "How Nonhuman Animals Were Trapped in a Nonexistent Universe," 1 *Animal Law* 26–34 (1995).

38. Thomas Aquinas, *Summa theologica*, *supra*, note 34, Question 102, at 918; Thomas Aquinas, *Summa contra gentiles*, *supra*, note 35, Book 3, Chap. CXII, at 222. The "Apostle" is Paul.

39. Thomas Aquinas, "Whether Irrational Animals Also Ought to Be Loved Out of Charity?" in *Summa theologica*, Second Part of the Second Part, Question 25, Article 3, http://www.newadvent.org/summa/3025.htm#3 (last visited October 9, 2007).

40. Zondervan KJV Study Bible, *supra*, note 10, at 762.

41. *Ibid.*, at 1190.

42. Geneva Bible, *supra*, note 15, at 558. "The Lord is my shepherd: I shall not want"; Zondervan KJV Study Bible, *supra*, note 10, at 762.

43. Geneva Bible, *supra*, note 15, at 558.

44. Zondervan KJV Study Bible, *supra*, note 10, at 762.

45. Zondervan KJV Study Bible, *supra*, note 10, at 763. "He leadeth me in the paths of righteousness"; Geneva Bible, *supra*, note 15, at 558.

46. Zondervan KJV Study Bible, *supra*, note 10, at 763.

47. *Ibid.*, at 6.

48. Genesis 9:2–4 (William Tyndale, trans.), http://wesley.nnu.edu/biblical_studies/tyndale/gen.txt (last visited September 24, 2007). The Geneva Bible (and King James Version) translation was close: "Also the fear of you, and the dread of you shall be upon every beast of the earth, and upon every fowl of the heaven, upon all that moveth on the earth, and upon all the fishes of the sea: into your hand are they delivered. Everything that moveth and liveth, shall be meat for you: as the green herb, have I given you all things"; Zondervan KJV Study Bible, *supra*, note 10, at 15; Geneva Bible, *supra*, note 15, at 11.

49. Geneva Bible, *supra*, note 15, at 11.

50. John Calvin, *Commentaries on the First Book of Moses, Called Genesis* (John King, trans., Eerdsman, 1948).

51. Henry Vesey, *The Scope of the Scripture. Containing a brief exposition of the Apostles creed, the tenne commandements, the Lord's Praye, and the sacraments, by short questions and answers. Wherein the ignorant are taught the sauing knowledge of God and of Themselues.* (Printed by W. I[ones] for Samuel Man, and are to be sold at his shop in Pauls churchyard at the signe of the Swan 1621), http://tulips.ntu.edu.tw/record=b2803354*cht (last visited November 11, 2008).

52. John Calvin, *supra*, note 50.

53. Erica Fudge, *Perceiving Animals: Humans and Beasts in Early Modern English Culture* 39 (University of Illinois Press, 2002).

54. http://www.11th-hour.info/Articles/Land_Letter.html (last visited June 5, 2008). These include the disproven facts that Saddam Hussein possessed weapons of mass destruction and that he was in cahoots with Al-Qaeda.

55. http://www.srnonline.com/talk/talk-land.shtml (last visited November 11, 2008).

56. Richard D. Land, "Overview: Beliefs and Behaviors," in *The Earth Is the Lord's: Christians and the Environment* 21 (Richard D. Land and Louis A. Moore, eds., Broadman Press, 1992).

57. *Ibid.*, at 21, quoting Francis Schaeffer, "Pollution and the Death of Man: The Christian View of Ecology," in 5 *The Complete Works of Francis A. Schaeffer: A Christian World View* 143–44 (Crossway, 1982). Evangelical theologian William M. Pinson Jr. agrees that God owns Creation and humans are its stewards, required to administer it properly: "Unfortunately our stewardship record in relation to plant and animal life is poor indeed"; William M. Pinson Jr., "A Denominational Perspective on Biblical Stewardship," in Richard D. Land and Louis A. Moore, eds., *supra*, note 56, at 126, 131. Evangelical pastor Jack N. Graham is more explicit: "We in the evangelical church often are slow to accept our ethical and moral responsibilities. Nowhere is this more evident than on the issue of the environment"; Jack N. Graham, "Accepting Our Responsibility," in Richard D. Land and Louis A. Moore, eds., *supra*, note 56, at 144, 144.

58. John Paul II, *Centesimus annus*, para. #37 (January 5, 1991), http://www.vatican.va/holy_father/john_paul_ii/encyclicals/documents/hf_jp-ii_enc_01051991_centesimus-annus_en.html (last visited May 2, 2008).

59. John Passmore, *Man's Responsibility for Nature* 112 (Charles Scribner's Books, 1974).

60. Matthew Scully, *Dominion: The Power of Man, the Suffering of Animals, and the Call to Mercy* xi (St. Martin's Press, 2002). "Folk dominion" is my term, not Scully's.

61. Adrian House, *Francis of Assisi: A Revolutionary Life* 177 (Hidden Spring, 2001). Aquinas was born the year Francis died.

62. Roger D. Sorrell, *St. Francis and Nature: Tradition and Innovation in Western Christian Attitudes Toward the Environment* 8, 47, 125 (Oxford University Press, 1988); Brother Leo, "The Legend of Perugia," in *Scripta Leonis, Rufini, et Angeli Sociorum S. Francisci* 51 (Rosalind B. Brooke, ed. and trans., Oxford University Press, 1970).

63. Roger D. Sorrell, *supra*, note 62, at 52, 53, 66.

64. Brother Leo, "The Legend of Perugia," in Rosalind B. Brooke, ed. and trans., *supra*, note 62, at 49.

65. *Ibid.*, at 43.

66. Roger D. Sorrell, *supra*, note 62, at 48; "The Fioretti," in *English Omnibus of the Sources for the Life of St. Francis* 16 (Marion H. Habig, ed., Raphael Brown, trans., Franciscan Herald Press, 1973). See St. Francis, "The Canticle of the Creatures," http://www.appleseeds.org/canticle.htm (last visited April 26, 2008); Thomas of Celano, *Saint Francis of Assisi: First and Second Life of Saint Francis with Selections from the Treatise on the Miracles of Saint Francis* 73 (Placid Hermann, trans., Franciscan

Herald Press, 1988) (1229, *First Life*; 1244, *Second Life*); *id.*, at 270 ("He called all animals by the name *brother*").

67. Roger D. Sorrell, *supra*, note 62, at 128, 134.

68. *Ibid.*, at 128.

69. *Ibid.*

70. *Ibid.*; Thomas of Celano, *supra*, note 66, at 71, 272, 273.

71. *Ibid.*, at 55–56, 71, 72; II, 270, 271–72 .

72. Saint Bonaventure, "The Major Life of St. Francis," in Marion H. Habig, ed., Paul J. Oligny, trans., *supra*, note 66, at 8:11.

73. Roger D. Sorrell, *supra*, note 62, at 133.

74. C. K. Chesterton, *Saint Francis of Assisi* 79 (First Image, 2001) (1927).

75. Roger D. Sorrell, *supra*, note 62, at 48; "The Fioretti," in Marion H. Habig, ed., Raphael Brown, trans., *supra*, note 66, at 16. See St. Francis, "The Canticle of the Creatures," *supra*, note 66.

76. Joseph Cardinal Ratzinger, *God and the World: A Conversation with Peter Seewald* 78 (Ignatius Press, 2000).

77. Letter from Monsignor Gabriele Caccia to Steven M. Wise, May 2, 2006 (in author's possession).

78. Matthew Scully, *supra*, note 60, at 17.

79. John Passmore, *supra*, note 59, at 112.

Chapter 11: "A Newfound Passion"

1. "The Great Warming," interview with Richard Cizik, http://www.thegreat warming.com/revrichardcizik.html (last visited May 22, 2008).

2. Philip Martin, "Interracial Marriage Ban," *Morning Edition*, National Public Radio (April 15, 1999), quoting a Southern Baptist Convention spokesperson pointing out that the Southern Baptist Convention had apologized for its racism in a 1995 Resolution; http://www.npr.org/templates/story/story.php?storyId=1050621 (last visited June 22, 2008).

3. Lynn White Jr., "The Historical Roots of Our Ecological Crisis," 155 *Science* 1203, 1206 (1967).

4. Upton Sinclair, *The Jungle: The Uncensored Original Edition* 30 (See Sharp Press, 2003) (1906).

5. U.S. Religious Landscape Survey 5, 12, 14, 91, 98 (Pew Forum on Religion and Public Life, 2008), http://www.adherents.com/rel_USA.html#bodies (last visited April 12, 2008).

6. http://www.thearda.com/mapsReports/reports/counties/37017_2000.asp (last visited May 16, 2008).

7. http://www.bladenbaptists.com/templates/System/default.asp?id=22145 (last visited May 13, 2008).

8. Association of Religious Data Archives, Bladen County, http://www.thearda.com/mapsReports/reports/counties/37017_2000.asp (last visited May 20, 2008).

9. See, for example, Peter Singer, *A Darwinian Left: Politics, Evolution, and Cooperation* (Yale University Press, 2000).

10. Richard D. Land, "Overview: Beliefs and Behaviors," in *The Earth Is the Lord's: Christians and the Environment* 23 (Richard D. Land and Louis A. Moore, eds., Broadman Press, 1992).

11. *Ibid.*, at 23.

12. Type "Creation Care" into the Amazon.com search engine to see dozens of relevant titles, such as *Redeeming Creation: The Biblical Basis for Environmental Stewardship*; *Saving God's Green Earth: Rediscovering the Church's Responsibility for Environmental Stewardship*; *Care for Creation: A Franciscan Spirituality of the Earth*; *For the Beauty of the Earth: A Christian Vision for Creation Care*; *Christians, the Care of Creation, and Global Climate Change*.

13. http://www.zondervan.com/Cultures/en-US/Company/Letter.htm?Query StringSite=Zondervan (last visited June 3, 2008).

14. J. Matthew Sleeth, MD, *Serve God, Save the Planet: A Christian Call to Action* 24 (Zondervan, 2006). See, for example, Tri Robinson, *Saving God's Green Earth: Rediscovering the Church's Responsibility to Environmental Stewardship* (Ampelon, 2006).

15. Amanda Griscom Little, "Cizik Matters," *Grist* (October 5, 2005), http://www.grist.org/news/maindish/2005/10/05/cizik/ (last visited April 17, 2008); http://www.nae.net/index.cfm?FUSEACTION=editor.page&pageID=516&id Category=1 (last visited May 9, 2008).

16. Amanda Griscom Little, *supra*, note 15. Houghton argues that "one of our God-given tasks as humans is to care for creation. That, I think, is a strong imperative right at the beginning of the Bible"; Amanda Haag, "The Man Who Preaches Science," 440 *Nature* 136 (March 9, 2006).

17. Amanda Griscom Little, *supra*, note 15.

18. Amanda Haag, "Church Joins Crusade over Climate Change," *supra*, note 16, at 136, 137.

19. "The Great Warming," interview with Richard Cizik, *supra*, note 1.

20. Evangelical Climate Initiative, announced on February 8, 2006, http://www.christiansandclimate.org/statement (last visited May 1, 2008).

21. http://www.cornwallalliance.org/articles/read/appeal-letter-to-the-national -association-of-evangelicals-on-the-issue-of-global-warming/ (last visited May 1, 2008).

22. http://www.christianitytoday.com/ct/2007/marchweb-only/109–53.0.html (last visited April 17, 2008) (click on hyperlink to the March 1, 2007, letter).

23. http://www.pbs.org/moyers/moyersonamerica/print/commongroundclass _print.html (last visited May 9, 2008).

24. Charles Colson and Nancy Pearcey, *Science and Evolution* (Tyndale House Publishers, 1999); Charles Colson and Harold Fickett, *The Faith: What Christians Believe, Why They Believe It, and Why It Matters* 178 (Zondervan, 2008).

25. http://www.cornwallalliance.org/articles/read/the-cornwall-declaration-on -environmental-stewardship/ (last visited May 9, 2008).

26. Chuck Colson: "Just Do It: Good Stewardship and Global Warming," no. 071102 (November 2, 2007), http://209.85.207.104/search?q=cache:Zm6vLqZ ZOpkJ:www.energyeducation.com/Portals/0/BreakPoint%2520Good%2520 Stewardship%2520and%2520Global%2520Warming%2520110207.pdf+Chuck+

Colson+Just+do+it+Good+stewardship&hl=en&ct=clnk&cd=1&gl=us&client=firefox-a (last visited May 1, 2008).

27. *Ibid.*

28. Neela Banerjee, "Southern Baptists Back a Shift on Climate Change," *New York Times* (March 10, 2008), http://www.nytimes.com/2008/03/10/us/10baptist.html (last visited May 1, 2008).

29. Nancy Tatum Ammerman, *Baptist Battles: Social Change and Religious Conflict in the Southern Baptist Convention* 74 (Rutgers University Press, 1995).

30. http://www.sbc.net/bfm/bfm2000.asp#i (last visited May 11, 2008). The 1963 Baptist Faith and Message Statement used identical language, while the 1925 Baptist Faith and Message Statement stated: "We believe that the Holy Bible was written by men divinely inspired, and is a perfect treasure of heavenly instruction; that it has God for its author, salvation for its end, and truth, without any mixture of error, for its matter"; http://www.sbc.net/bfm/bfmcomparison.asp (last visited May 11, 2008).

31. http://ellisonresearch.com/ERPS%20II/release%209%20versions.htm (last visited May 23, 2008). Among all Protestants, 34 percent embraced the New International Version, 23 percent the King James Version, 14 percent the New Revised Standard Version, 13 percent the New King James Version, and 10 percent the New American Standard Bible; *id.*

32. Robert A. Baker, *The Southern Baptist Convention and Its People 1607–1972* 159 (Broadman Press, 1974). See Mark Newman, *Getting Right with God: Southern Baptists and Desegregation 1945–1995* 1 (University of Alabama Press, 2001); Sydney E. Ahlstrom, *A Religious History of the American People* 664 (Yale University Press, 1972).

33. *The Ideology of Slavery: Proslavery Thought in the Antebellum South, 1830–1860* 136 (Drew Gilpin Faust, ed., Louisiana State University Press, 1981).

34. Sydney E. Ahlstrom, *supra*, note 32, at 660.

35. Ernest Trice Thompson, 2 *Presbyterians in the South 1861–1890* 61–62 (John Knox, 1973).

36. "Resolution on Reconciliation on the 150th Anniversary of the Southern Baptist Convention," http://www.sbc.net/resolutions/amResolution.asp?ID=899 (last visited May 13, 2007).

37. Mark Newman, *supra*, note 32, at 51, 53.

38. Paul Harvey, "God and Negroes and Jesus and Sin and Salvation," in *Religion in the American South: Protestants and Others in History and Culture* 283, 287–89 (Beth Barton Schweiger and Donald G. Matthews, eds., University of North Carolina Press, 2004).

39. Mark Newman, *supra*, note 32, at 65. The term "progressive elite" is taken from Andrew Michael Manis, *Southern Civil Religions in Conflict: Black and White Baptists and Civil Rights, 1947–1957* 26–27 (University of Georgia Press, 1987).

40. Mark Newman, *supra*, note 32, at 71–84, 205–6.

41. *Ibid.*, at 66, 74.

42. *Ibid.*, at 77–78. Nonracist interpretations span a history of more than three centuries; Stephen R. Haynes, *Noah's Curse: The Biblical Justifications of American Slavery* 181–200 (Oxford University Press, 2002).

43. Curtis W. Freeman, "'Never Had I Been So Blind': W. A. Criswell's 'Change' on Racial Segregation," 10 *Journal of Southern Religion* 1, 6 (2007), http://209.85.215.104/search?q=cache:6c8yBomv-1YJ:jsr.fsu.edu/Volume10/Freeman.pdf+an+address+by+W.A.+criswell&hl=en&ct=clnk&cd=1&gl=us&client=firefox-a (last visited May 13, 2008). It's unclear whether Criswell's change in public stance tracked a change in private belief.

44. Mark Newman, *supra*, note 32, at 66–67, 86.

45. Bob Allen, "Southern Baptists Reject Scientific Consensus About Global Warming," June 14, 2007, http://www.ethicsdaily.com/article_detail.cfm?AID=9058 (last visited April 12, 2008). A month on, Pastor Drake endorsed Mike Huckabee for the Republican presidential nomination on a radio station run by his tax-exempt church. When two members of Americans United for Separation of Church and State filed a complaint with the Internal Revenue Service, Pastor Drake issued a statement asking Christians to ask God to target the two "enemies of God"; http://www.christiannewswire.com/news/44143894.html (last visited May 20, 2008).

46. On this point, the language closely tracks "Climate Change: An Evangelical Call to Action," at 3 (Evangelical Climate Initiative, January 2006), http://www.christiansandclimate.org/statement (last visited April 17, 2008): "Over the last several years many of us have engaged in study, reflection, and prayer related to the issue of climate change ('global warming'). For most of us, until recently this has not been treated as a pressing issue or major priority. Indeed, many of us have required considerable convincing before becoming persuaded that climate change is a real problem and that it ought to matter to us as Christians. But now we have seen enough and heard enough to offer the following moral arguments related to the matter of human-induced climate change."

47. "A Southern Baptist Declaration on the Environment and Climate Change," http://www.baptistcreationcare.org/node/1 (last visited April 12, 2008). The section on Christian duty and moral conviction closely tracks "Climate Change: An Evangelical Call to Action," *supra*, note 46, at 3: "While we cannot here review the full range of relevant biblical convictions related to care of the creation, we emphasize the following points: Christians must care about climate change because we love God the Creator and Jesus through whom the creation was made. This is God's world, and any damage that we do to God's world is an offense against God Himself. . . . Christians, noting the fact that most of the climate change problem is human induced, are reminded that when God made humanity he commissioned us to exercise stewardship over the earth and its creatures. Climate change is the latest evidence of our failure to exercise proper stewardship, and constitutes a critical opportunity for us to do better (Gen. 1:26–28)."

48. http://www.touchinglives.org/about/dr-merritts-bio/ (last visited April 13, 2008).

49. http://www.touchinglives.org/about/what-we-believe/ (last visited April 13, 2008).

50. Joe Westbury, "Younger Conservative Leaders Need a Voice in the SBC," *The Christian Index* (April 10, 2008), http://www.christianindex.org/4329.article (last visited June 5, 2008).

51. http://jonathanmerritt.blogspot.com/ (October 20, 2008).

52. http://jonathanmerritt.blogspot.com/2007/07/doubly-disgusted.html (last visited April 13, 2008).

53. See *Nelson Study Bible, New King James Version*, Genesis 9:8–12, at 21 (Thomas Nelson, 1997): "Then God spoke to Noah and to his sons with him, saying: 'And as for Me, behold, I establish My covenant with you and with your descendants after you, and with every living creature that is with you: the birds, the cattle, and every beast of the earth with you, of all that go out of the ark, every beast of the earth. Thus I establish My covenant with you. Never again shall all flesh be cut off by the waters of the flood; never again shall there be a flood to destroy the earth.' And God said, 'This is the sign of the covenant which I make between Me and you, and every living creature that is with you, for perpetual generations.'" A comment notes that "this covenant extends to animals of every sort," *id.* "God . . . enters into promissory arrangements with [animals]"; Victor P. Hamilton, *The Book of Genesis, Chapters 1–17* 316 (William Erdman's Publishing Co., 1990).

54. Matthew 5:13–16, KJV Study Bible, at 1361 (Kenneth L. Barker, gen. ed., Zondervan, 2002). On "salt and light," Wikipedia says that "'salt' may refer to a purifying agent, a sign of God's covenant, a preservative of the purity of the world, a metaphor for wisdom, a metaphor for helping the world grow and prosper, and an order that Christians participate in, and not withdraw from, the world" (last visited May 20, 2008).

55. Kevin L. Howard, interview with Daniel Akin (August 2007), http://www.neednotfret.com/content/view/169/106/ (last visited May 19, 2008).

56. http://www.uu.edu/dockery/ (last visited May 19, 2008).

57. See Cathy Lynn Grossman, "Young Adults Aren't Sticking with Church," *USA Today* (August 6, 2007), http://www.usatoday.com/news/religion/2007-08-06 -church-dropouts_N.htm (last visited April 16, 2008).

58. Laurie Goodstein, *New York Times*, at A20 (November 7, 2008).

59. Joe Westbury, *supra*, note 50.

60. http://www.sbc.net/presidentspage/Frankpage/PressRelease-5-15-2007Page.asp (last visited May 1, 2008).

61. Under the Bush Administration, the opposite has been true; http://www.red herring.com/Home/21049 (last visited April 24, 2008).

62. http://www.abpnews.com/1090.article (last visited April 21, 2008).

63. http://www.cnn.com/2008/US/01/30/undercover.slaughter.video/#cnn STCVideo (last visited April 24, 2008).

64. Benji is a fictitious dog who has been the protagonist in several movies and television shows; http://en.wikipedia.org/wiki/Benji (last visited October 5, 2008).

65. "ERLC President Reacts to 'Southern Baptist Declaration on the Environment and Climate Change'" (March 10, 2008), http://erlc.com/article/erlc-president-reacts -to-southern-baptist-declaration-on-the-environment-an (last visited April 18, 2008).

66. http://www.sbc.net/resolutions/amResolution.asp?ID=967 (last visited May 22, 2008).

67. Genesis 1:12, 1:21, 1:24, 1:25, 6:20, 7:14, KJV Study Bible, *supra*, note 54, at 6, 13, 14.

68. http://www.cornwallalliance.org/press/read/cornwall-alliance-releases-policy
-agenda/ (last visited June 6, 2008).

69. Richard D. Land, "Overview: Beliefs and Behaviors," in Richard D. Land and
Louis A. Moore, eds., *supra*, note 10, at 25, quoting William H. Stevens, *Doctrine of
Creation* (BSB, 1990) (audiocassette).

70. Aldo Leopold, *A Sand County Almanac* 239 (Oxford University Press, 1966)
(1949).

71. *Livestock's Long Shadow: Environmental Issues and Options* xx (UNFAO, 2006).

72. *Ibid.*, xxi (emphasis added).

73. I have the PowerPoint presentation from this talk, which contains this asser-
tion.

74. http://www.adherents.com/adh_dem.html (last visited May 9, 2008).

75. Laurence H. Tribe, "Ten Lessons Our Constitutional Experience Can Teach
Us About the Puzzle of Animal Rights: The Work of Steven M. Wise," 7 *Animal Law*
15 (2001).

76. http://www.biblegateway.com/versions/ (last visited May 14, 2008).

77. Peter J. Thuesen, *In Discordance with the Scriptures: American Protestant Battles
over Translating the Bible* 4 (Oxford University Press, 1999).

78. Laurence H. Tribe, *American Constitutional Law* 30–89 (3rd ed., Foundation
Press, 2000); see *id.*, at 32.

79. Millard J. Erickson, "Biblical Theory of Ecology," in Richard D. Land and
Louis A. Moore, eds., *supra*, note 10, at 36, 42.

80. *Ibid.*, at 36, 48.

81. James Madison or Alexander Hamilton, *The Federalist*, no. 51, 335, 337 (Modern Library, n.d.) (1787–88).

INDEX

Abraham, 35, 54
Adam, 58, 185, 186, 220, 221
    fall of, 24
    sons of, 35
African-Americans
    slaughterhouse work of, 118
    See also Blacks
AgAlliance, Inc., 142
Agricareers, Inc., 135
Agriculture, 31
    animal husbandry and, 84–85
    Indians and, 30
Agritec, 137
Agrovision, 137
Akin, Daniel, 213, 214, 215
Alabama Baptist, on segregation, 203
Albemarle Sound, 4, 7, 21, 234n7
Albion Laboratories, Inc., 151
Albion MAAC (Metal Amino Acid
    Chelates), 151
Alden, John, 21
Algonquians, 8, 18, 236n9, 239n59
American Dairy Science Association, 147
American Embryo Transfer Association,
    147
American Meat Science Association
    (AMSA), 147–148, 149, 150
American Pork Congress, 125
American Registry of Professional
    Animal Scientists, 147
American Revolution, 5–6, 7, 25
American Society of Animal Science, 147

Ames *Tribune,* 132
Amish, 174
Anderson, Virginia DeJohn, 32
Andosterone, 67
Animal husbandry, 32, 59, 82, 84–85,
    146
Animal rights, 223–224
Animal rights activists, 82, 223
Animal rights law, 112
Animals
    attitude toward, 79
    Christians and, 32, 219–220
    domesticated, 30–31, 71–74
    as God's creatures, 188–191
    greenhouse gases and, 222–223
    humans and, 14, 31, 32, 84–85,
        179–180, 182–185, 188,
        189–190, 225, 236n6
    Indians and, 12–13, 30–31
    right to use, 195
    sick/injured/compromised, 84
    slaughter of, 18–19, 39, 239n60
    suffering of, 84, 99–100
    welfare of, 75, 85, 138
Antibestiality statutes, 130
Antibiotics, 85
Anticruelty statutes, 104, 180
Appleton, Amber, 132, 143
Aquifer Protection Section (Division of
    Water Quality), 77, 78
Aristotle, 183
Ashwood (Bartram family home), 47

About the Author

Steven M. Wise, JD, has taught Animal Rights Law at the Harvard, Vermont, Lewis and Clark, St. Thomas and John Marshall law schools. He is President of the nonprofit Center for the Expansion of Fundamental Rights, headquartered in Coral Springs, Florida (www.cefr.org.), which he founded in 1995. His pioneering work in animal rights law focuses on the connections between animal rights and human rights. His books, *Rattling the Cage*, *Drawing the Line*, and *Though the Heavens May Fall*, have been widely praised, with reviews in the *New York Times Book Review*, the *New York Review of Books*, the *London Times*, *Nature*, and the *Times Literary Supplement*. Wise has been profiled nationally by such publications as the *New York Times*, the *Washington Post*, and *Time* magazine. He lives in Coral Springs with his wife, Gail, and their three children, Siena, Christopher, and Mariana.

ML   3/09